FABRIC MAGIC

FABRIC MAGIC

MELANIE PAINE

WINDWARD • FRANCES LINCOLN

CONTENTS

Fabric Magic was conceived,
edited and designed by Frances Lincoln Limited,
Apollo Works, 5 Charlton King's Road, London NW5 2SB

Windward
an imprint owned by W. H. Smith and Son Limited
Registered No. 237311, England
Trading as W.H.S. Distributors,
St. John's House, East Street, Leicester LE1 6NE

ISBN 0 7112 04861

Filmsetting by Vantage Photosetting Co Ltd.
Eastleigh and London
Printed and bound in Hong Kong by
Kwong Fat Offset Printing Co., Ltd.

Editor   Sybil del Strother
Art direction   Bob Gordon
Assistant editor   Gian Douglas-Home
Designer   Anne Wilson
Editorial secretary   Susan George

Picture research   Anne Fraser

Managing editor   Susan Berry

INTRODUCTION

In fabric furnishings, often the understated and the simple are the most stunning: a straightforward black and white stripe bordering a white tablecloth, for instance, the colour pared down to a minimum so that the form is overtly on display. Similarly, unbleached crisp calico – essentially an inexpensive and functional cloth – can look magnificent made into a window curtain with light filtering through its folds and pleats. The natural creasing or ruching of a piece of fabric, whether over an entire window length or a small cushion, produces effects of light and shadow that look wonderful – though totally different – both by day and under artificial light.

All this means that the manipulation of form is for me one of the most exciting aspects of creating soft furnishings. Really quite dramatic effects can be very simply achieved – take the folds of dustsheets hastily slung over furniture, or the outline of a length of raw silk casually snaked over a pole and draped to the floor. The excitement lies in the combination of control and chance – on the one hand you can direct fabric, cut it, fold it according to a pattern, while on the other you can leave it to work quite on its own.

Apart from form, colour is probably the most important element I work with, and of course often it will stand out as the most dramatic feature. But even so, if the form or outline is sloppy and ill-defined, colour can lose all its impact. I believe colour is something you can 'see' or you cannot, but in interiors – more so even than in fashion – it has to work. And using colour is not easy. I know immediately whether a colour or combination of colours is successful or not, but I still tend to prefer working within a particular range – muted tones, lots of blues from darkest navy to subtlest Wedgwood, yellow ochres, mid-greys, terracottas and deep reds.

Heavily patterned fabrics often attract people because they look more exciting than plain ones when seen in a fabric book in a shop, but they are often disappointing when translated into real interiors. Rooms in which the fabrics dominate – whether because of pattern or colour – are usually very hard to live with. The quality of soft furnishings should come from the way they complement their setting, their suitability for their purpose and the excellence of their construction. The touches of dramatic colour or pattern are best left to items that can be moved and repositioned as the mood dictates – cushions or throws perhaps. For the large expanses of fabric – at windows, on beds or on furniture – the subtle woven cream with an interesting self-textured pattern, which looked so insignificant in the shop, comes into its own. The exciting form of the curtain or blind, with its full swags and ruches, is clearly visible and, as the fabric catches the light, the folds stand out in deep relief.

Because I am so interested in the form that soft furnishings take, the detail of their making is extremely important. Many ideas develop from experiment, but a sound knowledge of fabrics is necessary if you want something to work and, more importantly, to last. When you opt to work, as I prefer to do, in predominantly simple fabrics, accurate cutting and measuring are vital. Far better to choose a plain fabric, add a touch of visual interest with a border, and then concentrate your efforts on ensuring that the curtain, or bedcover or tablecloth hangs well, drapes elegantly and fits exactly the area that it was intended to cover. I have included the methods that I have developed professionally which I use because they produce more accurate and elegant results, although I do also include some useful short cuts. But the finish has to be perfect.

Some of the ideas contained in this book need little expertise and the book is primarily about ideas, rather than a mapping out of how to create this or that 'look'. Sources of inspiration range from traditional, lavish decoration to skilful and subtle minimalism. I discuss some fabric effects that can be created without the need for a sewing machine, or indeed a needle and thread, to emphasize my delight in the way fabric can look, just as it is, draped across a pole. But if you take the techniques as a practical starting point, I hope you will be encouraged by this book to experiment with your own ideas, inspired, as I am, by the versatility and magic of fabric.

Author's acknowledgments

Writing and making *Fabric Magic* has been, quite simply, a thrill. I was enormously pleased when asked to write the book, so my special thanks to Frances Lincoln for being its initiator.

For much of the important groundwork, thanks to Anne Fraser and Steve Wooster. Thanks also to Susan Berry for her continual encouragement and enthusiasm (and for not giving up on the 'Blinds' section!). Thanks to art director Bob Gordon for his thoroughness and to Anne Wilson for her hard work. Also to Penny David for her inspiration, to Gian Douglas-Home for her dedication, to Michael Dunne for location photography and to Jacqui Hurst for studio work.

Special thanks must go to Sybil del Strother, editor, for keeping my head above water and throwing me a lifeline, as well as for making the most difficult part of the book the most enjoyable.

The book could not have been written without the considerable assistance of all those at Paine & Co, especially Jill Roberts, who so admirably coped with my many absences. Thanks too to Martin Spenceley for allowing some of his upholstery to be shown in the book, to Caroline Stacey for her quilt and help with samples, and to Jim Spenceley for all the curtain fitting. Thanks should also go to the many customers who waited patiently to see me while editorial demands took up my time.

Finally, thanks to Sam Simpson who, in taking care of my son, has made both this book and the business possible, and to Mark Nicholls, my partner both at home and at work, for keeping things running smoothly.

MELANIE PAINE
JULY 1987

FABRICS

CHOOSING FABRICS
• Texture • pattern • special finishes & fabrics •

TRANSFORMING FABRICS
• Combining fabrics • colouring fabrics •

CHOOSING FABRICS

Fabric fascinates me and collecting it has become a passion. Perhaps the vibrancy of a particular colour catches my eye or the subtlety of a weave, or even the striking simplicity of a new fabric. Whatever the reason, I want to feel how it drapes, to see what cutting, folding and stitching in different ways can create – even before I consider adding original colour or pattern.

Buying fabric

Although simply liking a piece of cloth can be a good enough reason for buying it, instinct should be backed by some knowledge of how fabrics behave. Too many people use the sense of sight alone when choosing a fabric, seeing only the pattern, of red flowers on a white ground, for instance. The colour and design may well determine your initial reaction to a fabric, but then you must think of its texture (how it handles, drapes, folds), of its flexibility and of its interplay with light – whether it is opaque, dense, reflective or absorbent. You need to imagine the fabric in its proposed setting. You may yearn after the beautiful draughtsmanship of, for example, the Toile de Jouy prints (one of the fabrics suggested for Austrian blinds on page 86), but there is no point in buying these fabrics, with their exquisitely detailed and intricate patterns, unless their setting is to be relatively plain and uncluttered.

Sometimes I am so attracted by a piece of fabric that I buy it without any specific project in mind. The setting and what I eventually do with it come later. On such occasions, when I set about making something I am entirely inspired by the colour, texture and feel of the cloth. A dull, heavy calico, for instance, might look splendid made into deeply pleated curtains, caught into full folds with a natural rope tie-band. The same calico made into ruched blinds would quickly look creased and crumpled. I let the fabric dictate the form.

Often, however, I do work from the context of a room and the soft furnishings I have in mind, knowing that I need, say, a smooth, firm-textured fabric for a blind, or a lightweight, billowy fabric for a summer curtain. But I am always prepared to modify a design to take account of some unexpected facet of the selected fabric – adjusting the depths of the folds of a Roman blind, for instance, so that the stripes lie evenly across it.

This dazzling array of stripes embraces a wide range of styles, moods and fabrics – including plain and glazed cottons, canvas, moiré and silk taffeta. Linked by their linear quality, they suggest the glorious abundance of both printed and woven fabrics available today.

The timeless, restful quality of stripes makes them well suited to both modern and traditional interiors. Perhaps at their most perfect in simply furnished rooms, they can, if combined with care, work well together or with quite different patterns, especially if the colour range is deliberately restricted. When striped fabrics move, they come alive and, for this reason, they are at their most attractive when draped full-length at windows.

Experimenting with fabric

Start by taking home three or four small samples of fabric. When you have decided which you like best, buy a metre length, draping it, folding it, letting light fall on it. Or you might gather it, pleat it, dye it, paint a border around it, cut it into strips and resew it. Whatever the result, you will have achieved two vital things: you will know what the fabric can do and you will have seen (and felt) it in the context where you will be using it. Both in daylight and in artificial light it may look very different from the way it struck you under store lighting. Equally, the small print, say, of a fabric sample may look insignificant when you stand away from a larger piece, or the bold pattern you liked so much may overpower the room when you see it in context and can imagine the full effect of the pattern repeat. (Some shops are prepared to lend potential customers large pieces of fabric, making it easier to visualize the final effect.) Should you decide in the end that the fabric is not the right one, you can always use the metre length to make a small cushion, perhaps, or drape it over a larger tablecloth. Or you might consider one of the possibilities on pages 27 – 35.

Some of the ideas explored in this chapter came about by accident, and I cannot emphasize too much the importance of keeping an open mind. Explore as many outlets as possible that display and sell fabrics. The soft furnishings section of your local department store and sample books from well-known textile houses are the obvious places to look, but they are not the only ones. I have come across successful fabrics from many unusual sources: the haberdashery and dress fabric departments, as well as artists' supply shops, all stock a wide range. You can find organzas, stiff and starchy cotton tickings, cambrics, unusual coat linings, canvas, scrim and butter muslin, even sailcloth and kite fabric, and all of these can be used to great effect in different ways.

Market stalls also have an ever-changing selection of fabrics, while sales and second-hand shops offer the chance to buy old pieces. Not only do fabrics from such sources retain their appeal long after this year's textile designer has ceased to be fashionable, they are usually infinitely less costly.

The more imaginative you are with fabric, the better it will serve you. Whether it is a plain unbleached sailcloth, a deep-dyed sumptuous silk or a subtle combination of the two, stitched and pleated in an intriguing way, your fabric, if thought about creatively, will reward you with splendidly original soft furnishings. The starting point is to choose the fabric with care and to make sure that, quite literally, it feels right for the job.

The very nature of the weave makes some fabrics stiffer or softer than others, and fabric, of course, folds more naturally along the grain than on the diagonal. Because of this, in the chapters that follow, I have recommended fabric types that I think work best for the soft furnishings under discussion. But rules are made to be broken, and I hope you will have as much fun experimenting with fabric as I do.

The hallway on the right has been given a very deliberate Renaissance feel, intensified by the unusual and imaginative use of fabric.

The space is defined by the striped, awning-like fabric draped along the ceiling, which leads the eye down to the intricately painted wall panelling. The full, opulent curve of the red silk curtain adds a further degree of importance and warmth to the area.

TEXTURE

The characteristics that distinguish different fabrics – appearance, feel, pliability and wearing qualities – depend upon combinations of the following: the fibre and the way it is spun, the weaving techniques and the finishing processes. The raw fibre is the starting point.

Raw materials may be natural (cotton, linen, silk, wool) or man-made (chemically constructed polyester, viscose and so on). Only a number of animal and vegetable fibres are suitable, either structurally or economically, for producing yarns; but although the range of natural fibres is limited, the diversity of fabrics produced with these fibres is almost infinite. Different fibres can be blended or mixed to make a cloth with additional properties – extra strength, lower cost, or improved texture and weight. Many of the synthetics imitate the qualities of natural fibres but do not share their properties. I say a little about synthetics on page 24, but first I want to describe the natural fibres in some detail, because I prefer them and because they provide touchstones for comparing other types of fabric.

Cotton

The fibres come from the seed case of a plant grown in hot, moist climates, most notably the southern United States and India. They are short and have a 'fuzzy' nap (unlike the dirt-resisting smoothness of silk and linen), twisting into strong and durable lightweight yarns that wash and wear relatively well. Cotton can be dyed successfully at all stages – in the raw, when spun and when woven – and the smooth weaves are particularly receptive to printed pattern.

Cotton is relatively economical to produce and is one of the most versatile fibres, offering the widest range of weights and textures as well as pattern. It is not luxurious, but it is tough, resilient and practical, so its uses are widespread.

Different grades of cotton will produce varying qualities of fabric – an Indian cotton used to make calico is of poorer quality than a more lustrous, silky, poplin-like Sea Island cotton. On the other hand, the type of weave and the various finishing processes can improve quality: in ticking the twill weave and special finishing turn fairly low-grade cotton into strong and durable fabric. But even the inexpensive low grades, conventionally used for linings or backings, can look wonderfully sculptural if used in lavish amounts – the stiffer the raw fabric the better.

Linen

The bark or bast of the flax plant produces long fibres that are naturally smooth and strong, and that spin into lustrous, dirt-resistant and hard-wearing thread. Linen is less widely grown than cotton and undergoes a more elaborate set of processes from raw fibre to finished cloth; it is therefore more expensive and is often blended with other fibres – with cotton, for instance, to make the more supple fabric known as linen union.

Texture lends individuality and emphasis to a fabric and plays as important a role as colour in a decorative scheme. Apart from three made of silk and linen, the rolls in this picture are all of cotton and show the diversity of textural effect that can be achieved with just one fibre. The bolts are either cream or off-white and yet the multiple ways in which they have been interwoven have created a remarkably varied tonal range, in which subtle contrasts are emphasized by texture.

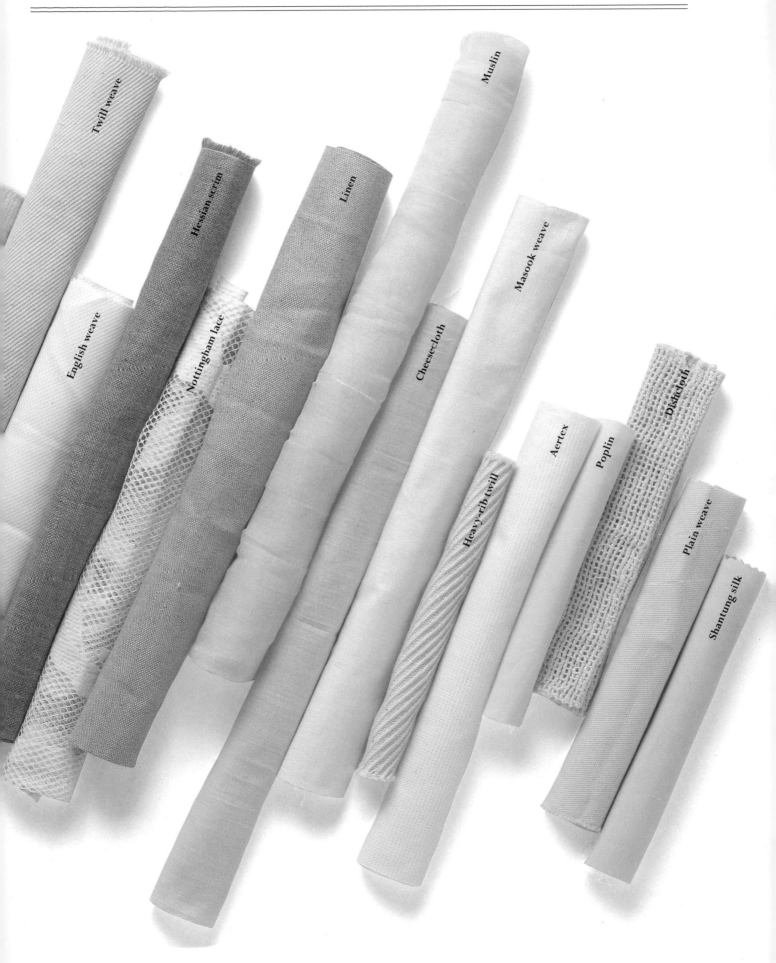

Twill weave

Muslin

English weave

Hessian scrim

Linen

Masook weave

Nottingham lace

Cheesecloth

Dishcloth

Aertex

Poplin

Heavy-rib twill

Plain weave

Shantung silk

The fibre is characterized by its strong, smooth texture, which is generally stiffer than cotton and less flexible. It creases easily and lacks suppleness, but is ideal for firm tailored coverings. Because its weight makes such heavy folds, it is also suited to interlined, full-draping curtains bunching on the floor.

Silk
The raw fibre is the long filament (some 750–1100m/800–1200yd in length) secreted by the silkworm in forming its cocoon. Each filament is unwound and reeled together with three to eight others to form a single, flawlessly smooth thread. (Shorter lengths from cocoons are spun together in the same way as other natural fibres to make rougher spun silk.) Silk is the finest, smoothest and strongest natural fibre, and its lustre gives fabrics a luxurious texture, with a liquid suppleness that drapes beautifully.

Silk is long-lasting if it is handled and treated carefully. It accepts dye well, and is often mixed with wool or linen for extra durability. However, silk is delicate and needs to be used considerately – it is best not to stretch it taut at the seams of a cushion cover, for instance, or force it into the disciplined folds of a Roman blind.

The most expensive Thai silks tend to be the most beautiful, but even the less expensive types can make exquisite borders, for instance, or look splendid as a twisted 'snake' above a pair of curtains. Many outlets specialize in cheap, lightweight Indian or Chinese silk.

Wool
Each breed of sheep produces different types and grades of wool, but all of it shares the quality of warmth that derives from the protein structure of the fibres and from the crimp that holds air between them. These are designated either for 'carding' (producing a fluffy yarn in which the fibres criss-cross each other) or for 'combing' (producing a smooth yarn in which the fibres lie parallel).

Wool always feels warm and comforting, and its elasticity makes it capable of draping in supple folds and gentle contours. For soft furnishings it is mostly blended with other fibres, such as linen or silk. Blending and special manufacturing processes counteract the tendency of wool to shrink, as well as producing stronger fabrics that are smoother to the touch.

Types of weave
Fibre comes in different qualities and can be spun into threads of various degrees of strength, thickness and so on. Spinning alters, but never totally masks, its natural propensities, which are further modified as the threads are combined to form cloth.

Weaving is the interlacing of two sets of threads that cross each other at right angles. The way lengthwise/vertical threads (warp) intersect with crosswise/horizontal threads (weft) is a theme capable of infinite variation, and it is the patterns thus created (sometimes pronounced, sometimes barely discernible) that give fabric its

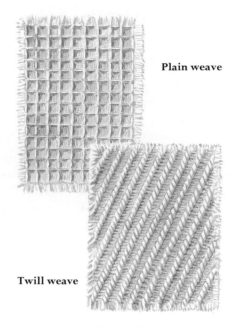

Plain weave

Twill weave

In plain weave, the weft (horizontal) threads travel under and over the warp (vertical) threads, creating a fabric that is identical on both sides. It is the simplest weave, used in muslin, calico, hessian and gingham.

In twill weave, the staggered interlacing of two warp and weft threads creates a slightly different diagonal pattern on each side of the cloth. There are many variations of twill (including herringbone and chevron); a hard-wearing weave, it is used for fabrics like denim, drill, ticking, tartan and serge.

textural properties of smooth or rough, stiff or supple. (The root of the words 'texture' and 'textile' comes from the Latin for weaving.) Patterns and textures also depend on the use of different colours and weights of threads. A heavy thread creates a ribbed texture – like poplin, for instance.

Basic weaves include plain weave and twill weave (see opposite), with satin weave as a broken variation of twill. There are also fancy weaves, like those used to make damasks and brocades, and pile weaves, where additional threads are woven in with the warp and weft, used for corduroys and velvets. Velvet drapes and hangs exceptionally well, but it demands special care and attention when being handled.

Each strip of fabric in the picture on the left has a distinctive form and character. The top three samples show how different fibres (in this case linen, jute and Indian slub cotton) can change the appearance of a plain weave. Twill weave, as used on the middle two samples, looks very different on silk and on heavy cotton. On the bottom two samples, the texture of cotton is transformed by the choice of weave – herringbone produces a stiff, hessian-like fabric, whereas waffle creates a softer, more pliable cloth.

PATTERN

The first mass-produced patterns in Europe appeared in the eighteenth century, mainly copies or elaborations of Eastern designs. Today, most widely available printed patterns are still adaptations of traditional designs. The appearance of bolder motifs intended to be enjoyed as individual designs rather than merely as part of a pattern repeat is relatively recent, and the choice remains limited by what manufacturers choose to offer.

If you simply accept a manufacturer's product without question, your interior may well end up looking very impersonal. Take the coordinated looks popular at the moment: put one pattern on all the surfaces of a room and the effect is often flat and dreary rather than harmonious. This is because the effect of pattern depends on its interplay with the other colours and objects in the room, with the quantity and types of pattern usually contributing more to the overall look and feel than any individual design.

The essence of all pattern is the presence of some degree of contrast, defining a motif or figure that is repeated regularly over the surface. The scale of the pattern motif and the amount of contrast determine how well the pattern 'reads' at a distance, so that pronounced contrast in a large motif makes a bold pattern, while the more subdued contrasts of blending colours result in subtle pattern. In extreme cases this is no more evident than the light-and-shade relief from a pronounced weave, and indeed all-over patterning is often referred to as 'texturing' in contrast with the unbroken surfaces of plain fabrics.

Woven pattern

When warp and weft threads of different colours are grouped in specific configurations, woven pattern, subtly present in every woven fabric, becomes explicit. Geometrical checks and stripes are the most basic; jacquard looms make more complicated figurative motifs possible. Where bands of two different colours intersect (as in gingham), the minute chequerboard of plain-woven warp and weft in different colours forms a half-tone, just as tiny dots of newsprint 'read' as a particular shade of grey. Several colours can be incorporated quite easily, often building up over the width of the cloth to produce very detailed designs.

Because the colour is diffused through the yarn itself rather than simply applied to the surface of the finished fabric, woven patterns have a potential depth and richness that stem from texture, as well as simply the quality of colour. They tend to be more muted than

The woven fabrics on the right all have a depth and textural feel that is richer than anything found on printed cloth. Colour and texture combine to give the fabrics an immediate tactile appeal, with their reverse sides often quite as interesting as the front.

Although on the whole hard-wearing and suitable for upholstery, the woven fabrics gathered here span a wide range of strengths and weaves: they include a striped moiré finish, lace, Thai silk and Indian slub cotton.

printed patterns, with the distinction between the pattern and the ground colour less defined so that colours seem to merge. Robust and hard-wearing, woven fabric makes excellent upholstery or heavy-duty drapes. The time and trouble taken to prepare and dye the yarn for handweaving make craft products such as Ikat – where strands of yarn may be individually dyed in several different colours – both beautiful and expensive.

Woven patterns are easy to identify, because the colours show on the underside of the cloth, which reveals the reverse of the design (unlike printed cloth, where the dye often seeps through in blurred form). The reverse of woven cloth is often as interesting as the intended design on the right side, and in some cases more so.

The clarity and definition of a woven pattern depends to some extent on the texture and fibre character (as well as the thickness of the yarn used). Compare the crisp definition between colours woven in a smooth fibre like cotton with the more blurred effect of woollen herringbone and tweed checks.

Printed pattern

Most fabrics today are either printed with some form of abstract design or decorated with floral motifs. The larger and bolder the pattern, the more attention it draws to itself and the greater the overall scale needs to be. Large geometric or floral prints look best where there is a large expanse of flat fabric, particularly when the pattern is on a plain ground. They need space around them for their full effect to be appreciated, and so look best on a bed or a large curtain. Very small patterns can look lost on a large surface, because from any distance their character becomes blurred optically into an all-over 'texturing' of surface, creating only a very subtle effect. For small patterns to make their own impact, they usually need to be kept for small objects. Remember that when fabric is ruched or folded patterns are only partly visible, so make sure your pattern works well with your design.

Choosing the right fabric involves predicting what will happen to the pattern when it is in position, as well as what will happen to a shape when the pattern is used to cover it. Strong motifs that read clearly over distance need to be arranged symmetrically over flat and regular surfaces, for example. Some swirling floral patterns disguise form and contours, while some geometrical patterns look unbalanced on forms that do not match their own proportions. Some patterned fabrics look better tightly stretched, others will happily drape. Where the form is striking, plain fabrics or subtle patterning allow it to speak for itself.

Sinuous complicated floral designs suggest opulence and are therefore in character with forms that use fabric extravagantly – elaborate bed hangings or formal swags and tails. Designs displaying single large floral motifs are displayed to best effect in floor-length curtains. Strong patterns can be toned down by the use of contrasting plain borders (see page 28), which help to define the shape of the furnishings.

The four samples of identical natural cotton above have been interwoven in a variety of ways to produce an intriguing variation in pattern and surface texture.

The grand four-poster on the left has been dressed with wonderfully strident, dominant fabric. It needs to be the principal feature in a spacious and otherwise unpatterned interior.

The woven West African fabrics have a powerful visual impact; the intricacy of their two-tone design is emphasized by the strength of the contrasting colours. Each width of fabric has been made out of several smaller strips of cloth, which have been woven on narrow looms and dyed in natural indigo blue and silvery white.

Types of printed cloth

With direct printing, coloured pattern is applied to the surface of the woven fabric. The ground that receives the printed colour needs to be as smooth and textureless as possible to depict motifs with fine details, and so is very often a plain or satin weave. Printed patterns can be pictorial, with curves, areas of pure colour and subtle gradations not dependent on the chequerboard basis of weave patterns. In the more complex methods colour is deployed as if painted. Some printed fabrics are extremely sophisticated in their detail, others imitate the naivety of craft products or the simplicity achieved by old-fashioned methods.

There is an unprecedented range of colours and designs available today on printed cloth. Not only are the chemical interactions between fabrics and dyes very well understood, there is also a choice of manufacturing processes. Most commercially available cloth is printed by machine, although expensive block-printed designs can be bought. Block printing remains essentially a hand process, very labour-intensive and expensive, practised as a 'craft' by individuals or small firms. Its chief merit is individuality. Block-printed fabric can be the perfect solution for an unusual site – for a single curtain on a stairway, perhaps, where the asymmetry of the drape would complement the individuality of the fabric. Since every object produced is a one-off, block printing offers rich potential inspiration for experiments with fabric.

Most printed furnishing fabrics nowadays are made industrially by some mechanized version of the screen-printing process. This technique is derived from the Japanese art of stencilling delicate patterns on to fine silk or muslin. Each screen is a rectangular wooden or metal frame of standard size covered with tightly stretched gauze – originally silk, now usually nylon or terylene. A separate screen is made for each colour element in the design and for each area of pattern repeat: areas of the mesh where colour is not required are treated with material that will prevent the dye from penetrating.

Screen printing can be done by hand as well as by machine. Hand printing involves forcing thick-textured dyestuff through the exposed mesh by means of a rubber scraper, as each screen in succession is laid over the stretched-out fabric. When the first screen has printed the first section of pattern, it is moved along to the position of the next repeat and the same colour applied, and so on along the fabric. When this first colour is dry, the screen for the next colour is brought into play. As a hand process and a craft, screen printing, like block printing, offers individuality and the charm of slight irregularities in the presentation of the design, together with extremely fine detail.

This diverse collection of figurative, geometric and abstract prints displays the vast range of pattern to be found in printed fabrics. The bold motifs in the centre need a large surface area to have their full effect, whereas the smaller prints on the outskirts look best as cushion covers or defining borders.

SPECIAL FINISHES & FABRICS

I have described how either the colour and design of the weave, or a superficial printed design, create pattern and texture. In addition, many chemical processes can be applied to otherwise finished fabric. These special finishes, when applied to either the natural fibre or the woven cloth, alter some of its original characteristics.

Compare, for instance, an unglazed printed cotton with a glazed one. The unglazed fabric has a solid, flat and opaque colour quality, its matt surface absorbing light and not bouncing much back. Should you change your unglazed cotton curtains for glazed ones, especially in light, plain colours like mushroom grey and pale yellow or blue, you will at once notice how the glaze affects the light-reflecting quality of the cloth: its shiny surface gives the cloth a silvery, luxurious sheen, while the colour appears richer. The curtains will crease more easily than before – a possible disadvantage. This is because the glazing treatment, which subjects the lengths of cloth to friction, heat and pressure, also alters the character of the fabric: it becomes less flexible, stiffer, papery if the glaze is heavy, and less versatile in its usage. Should you want the effect of glazed cotton without the expense, there is an alternative: waxed cambric.

Delicate or durable?

Some synthetic fabrics are more durable than their natural equivalents. Synthetic sheers, for instance, wash more easily and need less careful ironing than their natural counterparts, muslin, cheesecloth and lace. However, it is a fact that most fibres and fabrics with special finishes need more care and attention than natural fibres. They work best in unusual situations or on objects with a decorative, not practical, function. In general their uses are more restricted. For example, glazed cotton is not suitable for a roller blind, because stiffening the fabric removes most of the glaze. PVC (polyvinyl chloride) would not make a Roman blind, as the fabric would stick to itself and the blind would not work.

I mention the few special finishes and fabrics that seem to me to have a definite use not better served by any natural fibres.

Moiré finish

Finishes that make a surface pattern create subtle changes in the way light is reflected. One such finish, moiré, is a watermark effect applied to fabric in a technical process involving intense heat and pressure. Originally always silk taffeta, these days moiré is usually a cotton and viscose mixture. The transformed fabric is grander and has more depth than the original, but it also becomes more delicate. Any contact with water removes the watermark and causes staining, and even dry cleaning will eventually cause the watermark to fade.

There are many different qualities of moiré. I only really like the stiffer fabrics with matt and subtle watermarks, which come in many plain dark shades. The smoothness of a moiré finish makes it ideal for an eiderdown or bedspread, or a tablecloth bunching on the floor.

Above is an assortment of special fabrics and finishes.

The white, blue and yellow PVC strips, clearly displaying their waterproof qualities, would make excellent cushion covers – just the thing to brighten up a plain bathroom. The cream waxed cambric, traditionally used only for the inside of quilts and cushions, is robust enough to make superb ruched blinds and provides an inexpensive alternative to glazed cotton. The glazed patterned cotton samples look their best as borders on unglazed fabric. The green rip-stop nylon, with its unique feel somewhere between tissue paper and parachute silk, can be used in unexpected ways.

PVC

Many people have wipeable PVC tablecloths. White PVC, tacked in lengths from ceiling to floor and slightly gathered, would also create unusual screens, like fluted pillars. If you are working with PVC on a sewing machine you will need to spray a special lubricant directly on to the machine foot and needle.

Rip-stop nylon

The fabric used for making kites, rip-stop nylon, is a favourite of mine. It is available by the metre in many colours, and some stockists sell a full range of weights from flimsy to heavy duty. It could simply be used for a straightforward shower curtain, but it makes up well enough to be used more unexpectedly – into interesting festoon blinds, for instance (see below).

The white festoon blind, below, is a striking example of the versatility of rip-stop nylon. The folds are stiff and sculptural, managing to avoid the excessively ruched and floppy look that silk sometimes has. Should you want to make such a blind even more interesting, you could use coloured cords, whose bright hues would be gently diffused through the white nylon.

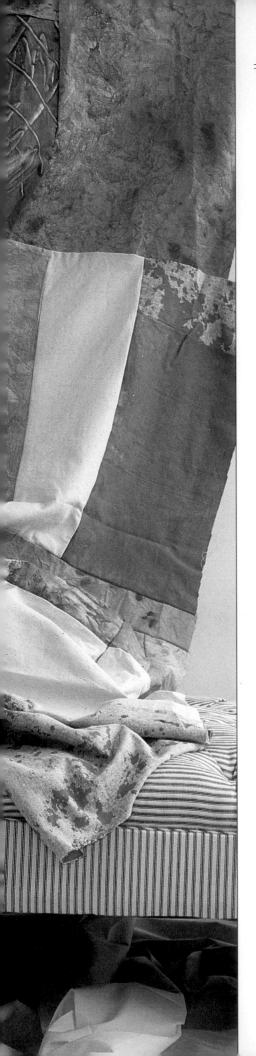

TRANSFORMING FABRICS

There are occasions when you set out to find a fabric, knowing exactly what colour, texture and feel you want. But few fabrics match your needs precisely and there are times when you want something original and unusual. As an alternative to settling for something conventional, why not apply ingenuity and invention to existing fabrics, and make them personal and different?

Imagination, enthusiasm and a small amount of practical knowledge are all you need for 'building' your own fabrics. It pays to be adventurous with both colour and texture. I like to add borders for definition, to exploit differences between existing fabrics by combining them in unexpected ways, to apply my own special finishes to suitable fabrics.

The more you know about the fabrics you are using, the more successful your improvisations and experiments are likely to be. You will find that the raw or minimally treated natural fabrics (see pages 14–17) are not only the most receptive, but are also the most economical. But only by handling the fabric samples and trying various methods will you discover that, for instance, a particular colour diffuses light beautifully, or that a fabric dull on its own becomes exciting in conjunction with a contrasting one – black Bolton twill takes on a different character when joined to bright yellow glazed cotton, for instance. You may like the wrong side of your fabric better than the right, or notice that the rag you have been using to mop up dripped dye has assumed unexpected colour effects all of its own. Make notes as you experiment, particularly with dye or paint (see pages 36–44), so that you can reproduce an effect you like at a later date.

If you want to make something that is functional as well as original, do not ignore the fundamental characteristics of the different fabrics. However delicately you colour or crinkle your piece of unexciting white fabric (and I do not mean that all white fabric by definition is unexciting), it remains muslin or calico or silk, with the draping and folding characteristics and the durability of the basic material only slightly modified.

Adapt your technique to the project you have in mind. If you are decorating a finished article, design borders and pattern repeats so they work well over the given dimensions. If you are making a complicated structure like a cord-hung blind (see page 72), your decorative effects should not interfere with the mechanism.

The hanging displayed here could also be used as a throw or bedcover. Small pieces of calico have been cut and dyed, and their angular shapes joined into the final irregular pattern. Showy and vibrant in colour and effect, the very textured hanging is a versatile and personal creation.

COMBINING FABRICS

Why combine fabrics? There are many possible reasons. Try giving crisp definition to the shape of a blind, say, by adding a single stripe in the form of a contrasting border. For the effect of two or three muted colours diffusing the light, use several layers, enjoying the contrast of translucent fabrics with opaque ones. Create new textures by joining fabrics of different weight in such a way that ridges stand out and cast shadows, or create new patterns by combining contrasting strips of similar weight.

Originality is often a question of turning convention on its head. Linings are usually unseen, but why not make them interesting and visible? Normally you hide the reverse side of a fabric; why not expose and enjoy it? Instead of being careful not to let seams show, exploit their ridged pattern. Rather than matching the weight and texture of materials to avoid stretch and distortion, allow the differences to create fascinating effects of contrast and movement. But remember to experiment with fairly small samples, testing the effects as you go to make sure that the result will work for the item you plan to construct.

The character of a fabric is bound to alter if other fabrics are combined with it, or even if stitch lines run across its surface. Don't ignore the practical aspects, such as wear and tear. Superimposing fabrics or seaming them together will add weight and increase stiffness: the created fabric may feel more substantial and behave differently, but it is unlikely to be any more robust than its weakest element.

Often you will be experimenting to find a way of getting the fabric right for a particular project or window. This means that you can work to approximately the finished size, without wasting materials or time. You can sometimes make up the fabric and design the item simultaneously, avoiding difficulties as you go, for instance ensuring that any thick seaming does not interfere with zips or blind cording.

Borders

Contrast between main fabric and border can be bold and dramatic or subtle and understated: plain against pattern, two different patterns, simple colour contrast, or contrasting textures. This last includes not only additional elements such as cords and braids, but the purely textural contrast of firm lines of piping worked in matching fabric – an emphatic yet subtle way of outlining shape without introducing new elements.

You need to decide how eye-catching your border is to be. Is it a functional delineating border, a simple edging or a substantial decorative element? Whatever you decide, the border must seem to be an integral part of the finished look. Like a frame, it defines a separate area and, in the same way as a frame, its dimensions can enhance and improve proportions.

Whether inset or used as an edging, a border will define and emphasize the shape of the fabric it outlines. The addition of a border

I chose the fabrics on the right purely for their visual appeal: in every case some extra quality has been added to the main fabric by the one used to border it. In fact, they are all practical combinations and would look splendid made up – into Roman blinds, bedspreads, curtains or even circular tablecloths.

1 Mottled cotton is given style by a double inset border in plain glazed cotton.
2 Using the reverse side of the main fabric creates a striking border on striped cotton canvas.
3 An inset border of loosely woven printed cotton gives a distinctive character to plain silk noil.
4 A standard double border in patterned and glazed cotton alters the form and outline of mottled cotton (also used in the top sample).
5 The silk noil used in the third sample is given a definite jazzy feel by a striped border in yellow and blue glazed cotton.
6 Blue mattress ticking looks distinguished with a border in grey mottled cotton.

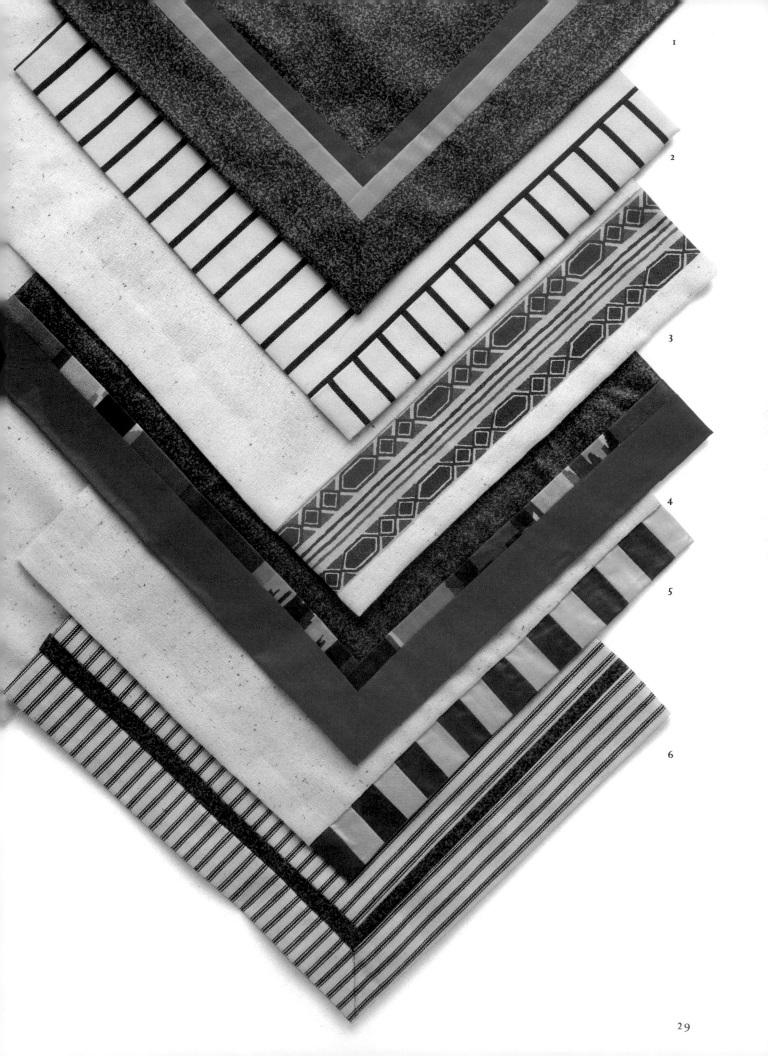

1

2

3

4

5

6

to an existing item is not easy but sometimes transforms an otherwise unexciting blind or bedspread, say, if it is done with skill. However, borders are best not considered simply as finishing touches; it pays off to plan a project with the border in mind, so that it is included in the original fabric calculations and forms an intrinsic part of the design from an aesthetic viewpoint. Even introducing a narrow line of piping entails decisions about what pattern colour to pick up or whether to use matching fabric. It is important to take even the simplest border seriously.

Like frontiers, borders separate potentially conflicting areas. A jigsaw of different patterns (colour-coordinated stripes, spots and tartans, for example) will work well together and be neither dazzling nor overwhelming, if the edges of each pattern area are bordered by the same firm contrasting lines. Plain fabric borders, picking up one of the colours in a heavily patterned fabric at a dressed window, will draw attention to the shape of the cloth draping across the window space and to the full line of the leading edges of the curtains, without introducing any distracting elements.

Deep and dramatic borders running across the base of a blind, for instance, can add architectural 'weight' and offset a narrow shape. A single border set along one side only of a cushion or blind in a contrasting colour makes a bold statement – asymmetry always catches the eye.

Borders are a strong justification for keeping a collection of scraps of fabric, but they can be made from other elements: eye-catching braids or tassels, cords, even beads and baubles can, used appropriately, enrich a simple fabric. Stencilling (see page 42) or just painting around the edge of a fabric (see page 38) is an effective and straightforward method of adding decoration.

Borders can be flat or raised. Flat borders are particularly suited to articles that are themselves essentially flat, such as bedcovers, tablecloths or Roman blinds, where straight lines and true angles emphasize a simple geometry of shape. The weighted, heavy look of raised borders is perhaps only appropriate when the desired effect is opulent and theatrical.

Planning borders

Whatever borders you make, be accurate when planning: have in front of you the finished measurements of the item you are making. Sketch the effects that you want and note the measurements, then double-check to make sure that you have taken into account all seam allowances, double thicknesses for any frills and hems, and enough fabric to overlap lengthwise for mitred corners, for example. If you make adjustments to your plans to allow for the width of your fabric (to maintain proportions or to balance stripes), recheck your figures yet again.

Look at your sketch in position to see how the border will work with any other elements in the same field of vision: for instance, you might find it pleasing to make it the same width as the window sill, or to echo it elsewhere in the room's soft furnishings.

Above, a double border neatly contains the complex fabric design of a glazed cotton drape, with colours carefully selected to pick up the two strongest colours in the pattern, navy and yellow ochre. The tie-band, pulled tight, is made from the same sateen lining fabric as the yellow ochre border.

The addition of a three-coloured border to the otherwise unassuming curtains on the left has served to make a pair of ordinary windows look thoroughly dramatic. Unusually, as well as running down leading and base edges of the curtains, the border runs the width of the deep pencil pleat heading, adding welcome height to a low room. (It is not difficult to use a border in this way, as long as calculations are exact: the border fabrics are added to the flat curtain and the heading is then applied in the usual way.)

The effect of the fabric border is reinforced by a painted border running along the bottom of the wall. Together the two borders add complexity and sophistication to a room that would otherwise have an almost cottage feel.

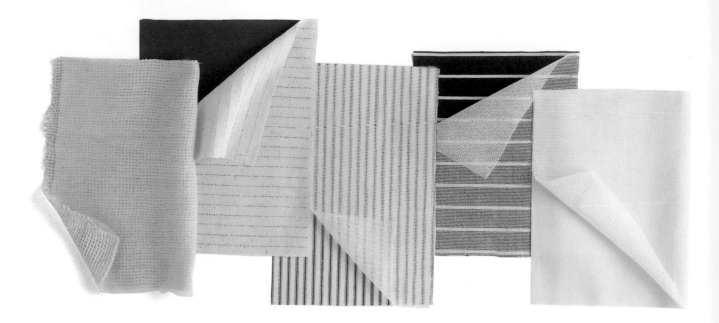

Layering fabric

I find it interesting to exploit the contrast between different densities of fabric. One way of doing this is to choose two very different weave structures and to use them together. This technique works especially well if the layered fabrics are hung at windows, where the light heightens the effect.

Fabrics for the 'top' layer need to be translucent, either closely woven, but extremely fine, or medium-weight fibre in a very open weave: a regularly structured mesh (as in net) or a fine plain weave (such as muslin), and either white or a natural unbleached colour. The more solid 'lining' fabric needs colour or pattern strong and definite enough to show through, albeit with a soft, filtered effect. If you lay the loose weave of a fine undyed butter muslin over a smooth-textured, richly coloured cotton chintz, you will see how the muslin diffuses the strong colour beneath it. The effect of each fabric is subtly altered by the presence of the other.

In practical terms, both fabrics are made up as one, but different techniques are necessary for finishing edges: using the 'lining' fabric to create borders is a good solution. When layering fabrics of different widths, calculate the amounts carefully (see page 200) and try to position seamlines in both fabrics at the same point. If you double up two finer fabrics for the effect of a contrast lining, remember that you probably now have the equivalent of one medium-weight fabric. The combination of layers naturally creates a thicker and more substantial cloth, which will form soft rounded folds rather than crisp pleats.

Simplicity of line in the finished item is important, to allow the new textural properties to speak for themselves: layered fabrics are unsuitable for anything as structured as Roman blinds. Some of the firmer 'top' layers, such as nets, might be substantial enough for cushions or even bedcovers, but muslin would be too fragile for anything needing to take any degree of wear.

The appearance of a fabric changes quite dramatically when covered with a layer of lighter, translucent fabric – solid colours are subtly diffused, weaker ones strengthened. Dishcloth covered with muslin gains in delicacy and form; solid blue filters through perforated silk in faint, dotted stripes; black and white ticking or butcher's apron cotton covered with organza become muted and less linear; solid yellow is pleasantly diffused and lightened by a second layer of muslin.

Joining fabrics

At its most basic, joining different-coloured strips of the same fabric makes an original striped pattern, but it need not stop there. The stripes can be designed to enhance the form of the finished item — tonal gradations moving up or down a Roman blind, for example, or around the lower edge of a bedcover. Since stripes are linear and directional, they suit rectangular items best. Building stripes of already patterned fabric into new texture and pattern configurations can turn over-familiar, bought patterns into ones that are excitingly different and fresh.

Apart from the purely visual aspect of patterning, keep an open mind for exploitable side-effects: the seaming on the reverse side of the fabric can become an interesting feature, while the lines of stitching create secondary stripes. I discovered one particularly attractive effect by accident when seaming lengths of rip-stop nylon (see page 25). As I moved the sewn fabric around, pulling the sides and folding them, the 'walls' took on a movement of their own. Kite

When joining fabrics, experimenting is essential. Only in this way will you stumble across the revelation that two unlikely fabrics look superb together. Perhaps you will discover an unexpected combination of colour and texture, or create an unusually concave design by choosing to use the reverse side of the fabric.

Above, the yellow glazed cotton on the bottom left has been joined to a mottled grey one. Next to it, a plain black cotton has been lifted by being joined to a two-tone, light grey silk. At the top, a dark green cotton sets off the multi-coloured check of a grey-green weave. In the centre, a delicate muslin has been given strength by being attached to an unbleached calico.

Although you may just want to experiment with decorative samples, joined fabrics can be very practical. The last-mentioned sample of panelled muslin and calico can be seen on the left as an original and elegant half-sash curtain — a fine alternative to a net. The heading and hemming have been kept very simple so as not to interfere with the ribbed effect.

fabric is ideal since it does not fray; otherwise French seams or an overlocking stitch are necessary to finish the raw edges.

Another side-effect of joining strips is that the whole fabric acquires new textural characteristics, because the stitching creates ridges, like ribs, dividing the flat areas of fabric. I prefer not to eliminate this effect by pressing the seams flat, but to let the stripes swell and billow. On the wrong side, the stripes are concave and set back beneath the seams. Sometimes you might prefer this to the rounded contours on the right side.

Creating new fabrics by joining strips is a good way of using up scraps and leftover pieces. Since a certain amount of fabric is 'lost' in the seaming, you would not want to cut up expensive fabric deliberately. But this technique is a good way of using up long narrow strips too good to waste – perhaps pieces of old fabric in good condition (see page 35) or fabric left over after cutting and joining widths to make a blind.

Overlapping fabric edges

This is another interesting effect I came across by accident while joining strips of fabric for a small cushion cover. Holding the sample up to the light to check the straightness of the lines, I noticed an attractive secondary striping where the seam allowances lay. I then set about creating this effect deliberately by overlapping the edge of one fabric on another, gradually building up a series of 'stripes' of alternate lines of one and more layers of fabric.

At its most simple, ridging can be a series of tucks or stitched pleats made in a single piece of fabric; alternatively, strips of the same or of different fabrics may be sewn together. (Either way, the technique makes a good disguise for seaming scraps of fabric.) Stitching lines can be concealed or emphasized with additional top-stitching to make a feature.

The best fabrics to use are lightweight cottons with a smooth surface, such as calico, glazed cotton and poplin: heavier fabrics and weaves with a raised surface tend to be too thick for neat folds and difficult to sew, while very fine fabrics may not withstand repeated stitching. A slightly translucent cloth used in conjunction with another more substantial fabric could diffuse colour and pattern (see page 32). Fabrics patterned with stripes or squares not only look striking sewn into ridges, but are easy to work with as they provide their own parallel lines.

Since the technique creates decorative stripes, it is especially suitable for rectangular shapes such as blinds, curtains, bedcovers and cushions. All-over sewn ridges build simple fabric up into a three-dimensional texture of regular or random corrugations. The longitudinal stiffening that results gives a distinct ribbed effect, which can be used vertically or horizontally as appropriate. At a window, the striped, shadowy effect of a slightly translucent fabric shows to best advantage. In curtains, parallel lines of ridging, stitched full-depth, offer a structured alternative to the more usual loose fullness falling from the pleated heading.

The pleats and ridges in the fabrics above have been achieved by overlapping the edges of pieces of cloth and stitching them together. I enjoy this technique because it creates form with fabric. Pleats can be widely spaced to give an impressive panelled effect as in the sample on the right, or you can go for a gentler, ridged effect as in the adjoining piece, where shadow adds further visual interest.

Both samples have been given extra textural interest by the use of white stitching on a red, glazed ground fabric.

Using old fabrics

Whether they are 1930s or 1950s printed cottons or linens, glazed chintz with an unusual design or antique lace, old fabrics very often have faded colouring and soft texture. Their presence in soft furnishings is the equivalent of patina in furniture: they add subtleties of depth and character, and an interesting mellowness.

Whole widths of old fabric show to best advantage in surroundings that are not ultra-modern, combining well with natural materials, like stone, brick and polished wood. Small pieces of old fabric inserted into larger amounts of new fabric, on the other hand, look right in any setting.

Even relatively small amounts of an old fabric with a little motif design, inset as narrow borders, will turn a very plain modern fabric into something original. However, it is important that modern fabric should provide a sympathetic context: beware of dyes that are too strident; creamy colours and natural fibres provide the most effective low-key accompaniment. Large amounts of fabric can be joined in strips, which will disguise faults and improve weaknesses in old or worn fabric. Small amounts can be attractive used as edgings, though they need to be inset or positioned where handling will not cause extra wear.

Decorating fabric with stitching

One of the simplest ways of changing a fabric is to decorate it with lines of machine stitching, building up a simple linear pattern with coloured thread. Running the stitch lines close together begins to alter the fabric in a more textural way: areas where the stitching is dense will be stiffer, while areas where there is little or no stitching will remain contrastingly more supple. Imagine using a length of heavily stitched fabric in curtains that sit on rather than hang above the ground, forming large bunched mounds.

Begin by sewing parallel lines up and down the fabric. Then vary the distance between the lines, adjust the tension and length of the stitches, and play around with proportion. Since the technique is relatively laborious, it is wise to have a fairly accurate idea of how much fabric you will need to make the finished article, otherwise much of your time may be wasted on stitching surplus fabric. It is not necessary to tie off the loose thread ends; if not impractical, they can be left to form an interesting multicoloured fringe.

Experiment with different kinds of fabric. Since the stitching is essentially creating the pattern, the best results arise from plain, unpatterned cloth. Flimsy fabrics such as muslin or thin plastic look entirely different with coloured stitching running across the surface and, when hung (without lining) at windows, the areas of dense stitching contrast effectively with the delicate fabric. Thicker fabrics take on some of the textural patterning of brocades and become more substantial and moulded. The effect is almost as if you were drawing on fabric, using the thread as your ink. Stitching in this way is a freer extension of the more traditional and time-consuming crafts such as crewel-work.

Much loved old fabrics are often too fragile to be used alone, and are best joined or inlaid into newer, firmer fabric. Old silk gains in durability as a double inset border on a tablecloth or pelmet of cream poplin. The blue and white print of an old summer dress is gently diffused by strips of strong, cream cotton, which help to reinforce the old fabric.

COLOURING FABRICS

There is something very exciting about spreading a clean white fabric out in front of you and making your own marks across its surface – whether scribbled hieroglyphics, solid bands of colour or thin delicate lines. There are also the apparently random all-over spatterings, daubings and scribblings. You may produce something usable first time, but I say 'apparently' random because the most successful creations usually only happen after time has been spent testing the thickness of the medium and the stroke by which it is applied to the fabric. Control and confidence come with practice; as you become accomplished, you may well develop a distinctive personal style.

Experimenting with colour

As you experiment, you make unexpected discoveries. Once, when staining fabric with dye, I was delighted at the shadowy images that seeped through to the layers beneath, preferring them to the intended effect. You also find that, as you develop the pattern, ideas emerge about how best to use it in an end product. You may just cut your sample swatch into strips for an original border (see page 28) or for joining to other strips (see page 33). You may colour and pattern your own fabric and use it as you would a ready-made. Or you may plan to enhance the form of a specific item: for example, you can stencil a well-proportioned border in position, or increase the density of spattering or the intensity of colour to give 'weight' towards the base of, say, a Roman blind. If you become very skilled, you may even want to work systematically on each cut-out section of a complicated bedcover.

Only trial and error will show what effects you can achieve with a particular medium on a particular fabric. On a practical level, you need to observe what happens at every stage. Many colouring processes change the texture of the fabric. Some effects are virtually permanent, but many are delicate and may fade in daylight or alter if the fabric is washed. Dry cleaning is virtually essential for all hand-coloured fabrics, which can be heat-sealed with a very hot iron. Use fast dyes, follow manufacturers' instructions and take into account how much wear your fabric will have to endure. Most of the techniques I describe are so inexpensive that you may find it acceptable to opt for short-lived glory rather than an heirloom.

On the aesthetic level, only by experimenting will you be able to connect your design with what you can achieve. It is a question of taste as well as of ability, just as it is when choosing colours and

The odd combination of fabric styles on the right owes its success to scrupulous planning followed by deliberately casual execution. The painted urn in 17th-century mural style had its outlines drawn first in pencil to get the correct perspective;

thinned emulsion paint was then daubed on, the wobbly lines intended to complement the soft, floppy fabric.

The mural is framed by a pair of 1920s curtains, whose crisp black and white stripes neatly contain the fresco-like image.

patterns in ready-made fabrics. Some methods produce subtle, blurred outlines, with overlapping colours blending deep into the fabric itself, others result in crisply defined motifs, emphasized by layers of paint lying on the surface of the fabric.

Begin with something modest, in scale and in cost. Ingenuity and effort are more important than costly materials. Make the most of cheap cottons and tickings – even Chinese silk is not expensive. Natural fibres are the most receptive to all forms of dye and paint, but, as long as you use appropriate dyes, synthetics give good and practical results. Rip-stop nylon (see page 25) offers a wealth of inspiration – think of the marvellous decorations seen on kites.

There are many different dyestuffs and the range of colours is unlimited. Ready-made synthetic dyes offer the most predictable results. For hot and cold water dyes, consult the maker's instructions to ensure that the fabric you have in mind is suitable. If you are considering natural dyestuffs, a specialist book will tell you which mordants you will need to fix particular colours on particular fibres. Such a book will also give you full instructions about timing, suitable vessels and so on.

Make at least a small sample with the fabric and colour medium that you intend to use for the end product. Apart from the basic fact that different fabrics react differently to dyestuffs, unseen differences in quality or finish between what appears to be the same basic calico, for example, could give rise to uneven results. Keep notes of amounts and procedures in case you want to achieve the same effect again later on: you may end up with a different result if, for instance, you omit the initial washing of a fabric.

Try to have an open mind as the most inspiring results often stem from a mistake or even an accident. For instance, most people make great efforts to prevent a dyed fabric crinkling as it dries, but you may find that it produces just the look you want (see page 43).

A full account of even the most basic processes and materials for colouring fabrics at home would fill several books. For detailed information consult the reading list on page 212 or ask for advice at artists' supply shops. Here I simply suggest some ideas that will provide a starting point.

Painting on fabric

Special-purpose paints and pens for fabrics are now easily found, but acrylics, gouache, poster colours, dye solutions and even car paints are worth experimenting with.

Of all the methods discussed, applying paint freehand on to the surface of the fabric most resembles straightforward drawing or painting. Depending on the scale of the brush and the thickness of the medium, your strokes may be bold or delicate. Smooth-textured weaves can take the whole range, from fine lines to areas of solid colour, and they offer the possibility of strong graphic designs as well as sketchy representational images; a coarser-grained fabric needs a robust paint mixture applied with a chunky brush, and the patterning needs to be correspondingly more vigorous.

The deep rich colours of this African fabric result from a special form of resist technique used by the Nigerian Yoruba tribe. They use cassava instead of wallpaper paste and boil it up into a liquid paste. This is then painted on to the fabric with a feather dipped in blue indigo dye to give a subtle two-tone effect.

The choice of a gently ruched, interlined style of blind, with tasselled rope down the centre, is ideally suited to the long, rectangular window and to the fullness of this weighty, substantial fabric. The deep blue in the fabric picks up the blue and white painted birds on the tiles, while the subtle pattern mirrors the carving on the kitchen cupboard.

1

2

3

Patting and daubing

Lovely textural effects are obtained by patting colour on to smooth-textured fabric with a sponge or screwed-up rag soaked in paint or dye solution. (Though expensive, natural sponge is more effective than foam.) You can thin the paint with water or wallpaper paste. Daubing liquid dye stains the fabric; daubing more solid paint creates interesting marbled texturing, as some paint soaks into the fibres while the rest remains on the surface of the fabric. Dipping the paint-soaked rag into water will make the colours run and bleed into attractive gouache-like blurs.

It is possible to exercise great control over detail: build up layers of tone over specific areas, using one or more colours, or concentrate the patterning on particular parts of the fabric. Calico, poplin and — especially — silk are receptive to this treatment. Small items such as cushions and tablecloths offer the opportunity for controlled and intricate lines and areas of colour detail.

Spattering

One of my favourite techniques is spattering. Brushes that spatter paint well have stiff bristles with straight ends, and are preferably long-handled. For small items old toothbrushes are ideal. It is useful to have several clean, dry brushes ready so that you can pick up a fresh one as each becomes clogged. Spattering is done by passing a knife, or a finger, over the paint-soaked bristles. It is a messy business, so keep plenty of rags nearby.

The aim is to flick all the ends of the bristles over the surface of the fabric, trying to spray the paint so that it covers the fabric in a fine even mist. Depending on the fabric and the consistency of the paint, the colour will sit on the surface or be absorbed into the weave. Calico, cotton and smooth-surfaced fabrics are the most suitable, because they allow the colours to build up on the surface. It is important for the paint to be liquid enough to make a good thin

It took a long time before I felt able to plan designs in the confident knowledge that the results would look as I wanted them to — although the intermediate stages are fun too.

1 I painted deliberately blurry lines on to this natural Shantung silk, using specially diluted pink acrylic paint. For the more distinct lines, I used undiluted black acrylic paint.

2 The striped pattern on this perforated silk noil was inspired by the structure of the fabric weave. Using watered-down acrylic and powder paints, I painted the blue and black lines on with a brush, and then applied the brown blobs with the tips of my fingers.

3 To achieve this crisp chequered design, a thick layer of decorators' paste was left to dry on calico, and the entire fabric then dipped into a blue cold-water dye. Once dry, I spread the fabric on the ground and scoured across it with a comb, before using orangey-brown paint to colour in the lines.

4

5

spattering consistency: it may be watered down, but a quick-drying sort is useful. Water-based poster paint, gouache and acrylic are ideal, although the spattered cloth needs to be heat-sealed with an iron if these paints are not to come off when the fabric is washed.

A haze of droplets can be built up on the ground fabric in one colour or more, and different thicknesses and types of paint can add real texture to the fabric's surface. Small-scale samples can be cut up to contribute small amounts in joined fabrics, or whole areas can be covered relatively fast. Spattering is therefore suitable for a large item, such as a curtain, bedcover or tablecloth. The effect need not be that of random all-over misting: the density of the spattering and the incidence of different colours can be planned so that there is a directional change of tone or a more systematic swirling. Stencils or shields can be used to mask off 'negative' areas, which remain plain and unspattered.

Spattering is unpredictable: the paint may be applied too thickly, or with too much water so that the colours run into one another. If the brush is overloaded, the paint will fall off in drops and run on to the fabric or spread into larger areas. The odd blob or blot may be part of the charm, of course, but do allow some practice time on scraps of fabric before beginning the real thing.

Spraying, with aerosol cans of car paint or other types of paint in a diffuser, is a more conventional cousin of the toothbrush spattering technique. The effect is an aura of misting around a denser patch of colour. The paint tends to sit on the surface of the fabric and the sheen of car paints creates textural interest, especially in metallic gold, silver or bronze. Metallic paint against either simple white muslin or sombre dyed calico is particularly dramatic and unusual. Because sprays are generally fast and efficient, you have to be sure of a deft stroke when using them freehand; they really come into their own when you use them together with stencils, when the effects are less bland.

4 Covering calico with a thick coat of paste and pinky dye, rubbing it off and then pouring water over the whole sample, produced this watery bleached effect. The horizontal lines resulted from leaving the fabric to dry on the radiator.

5 The freckled effect on this tussah twill silk was achieved by flicking on watered-down dye and paint with a toothbrush. The border was painted on in terracotta and then spotted with black.

Stencilling

An inexpensive and versatile method, stencilling is a marvellous way of adding painted decoration to plain, smooth-textured fabrics. It provides a great deal of enjoyment for the stenciller, and produces results that can be uniquely adapted to the character of the surroundings. Stencilling also makes splendid borders.

You can stencil on to undyed fabric, which I personally think is often most effective, particularly if the paint is interestingly applied. If you work on a dyed surface, choose your stencil colours carefully to avoid losing them on too deep a ground. When the smooth sheen of solidly painted areas stands out in textural contrast with the matt, light-absorbent fabric background, you are doing more with stencilling than just making colour patterns.

As well as stencilling with spray, you can apply paint with a sponge, pat it on with a rag or use something that looks like a shaving brush. The most important requirement is that the paint should dry fairly quickly and not be so thin that it floods beneath the edge of the stencil: poster colours and acrylics, heat-sealed when the design is completed, give good results. In many traditional stencils the paint is fine and the colours delicate. The less paint you apply at one time, the more you can build up the texture on your design, working from the sides to the middle and filling the shapes with colour.

Lavish drapes of inexpensive muslin, stencilled in gold, give a rich luxurious feel to this plain cream bathroom. The focal point of the design is the concentration of pattern, in the valance at the top and at the base of each curtain, providing a natural border and giving weight and substance to the flimsy fabric.

A one-off stencil can be cut from thin cardboard or thick polythene. Artists' supply shops are the source for special stencil board or sheets of acetate from which to cut stencils that will withstand repeated use. You can also buy motifs ready-made. Otherwise, seek inspiration from pattern source books that will complement the setting – be it Art Nouveau, Art Deco or Arts and Crafts. When the architecture offers no ready-made cues to translate on to fabric, invent them. The character of the design as well as the colour creates mood: stylized floral motifs in primary colours on white for allusions to folk art; Greek key borders in black on white for a classical simplicity; Byzantine elaborations (especially done in gold) for a mysterious and exotic atmosphere.

Swirling leafy floral designs can twist the length of the fabric, creating an eye-catching border. Crisp geometric shapes can enrich a plain muslin curtain or adorn the base of a calico Roman blind. The more disciplined the design, however, the more accurate and symmetrical it needs to be: geometrical motifs need to be positioned evenly over a shape as simple as a flat blind where any imbalance will show clearly, whereas gathering and ruching can conceal a multitude of flaws.

Multicoloured stencils (one sheet for each colour) and all-over designs, where motifs interlock to form continuous pattern, also call for careful managing to keep the register correct. You are really building up your own printed cloth, so take care not to let the colours run into each other and keep the outlines well-defined. Doing detailed sketches to scale before you start will help. But complexity is not necessarily laborious: when it takes only seconds to spray-paint a really elaborate filigree motif, stencil printing can be thrillingly easy.

Resist techniques

Simply dyeing fabric is straightforward enough, and for me that is just the starting point. What really interests me are the associated texturing effects. In a resist technique hot wax is painted, drawn or printed on to the fabric in areas of pattern that retain the ground colour when the fabric is subsequently immersed in cold-water dye. Although batik in itself does not literally mould or texture the surface of the fabric (the wax is subsequently removed), the contrasts in the depth of colour, and the fine webbing of lines where the dye has seeped through cracks in the wax, result in a more figurative texturing: batiks have a dynamic, vibrant quality of patterning, far from the flat quality of fabrics that have simply been immersed in dye. Once again, some of the most attractive results are those that would conventionally be considered unsuccessful or wrong. The 'wash and crinkle' techniques belong in this category. There are two versions.

In one method the fabric, which should be fairly light, perhaps muslin or calico, is washed, dyed and then screwed up tightly to be dried. The resulting creases in the cloth are permanent, and often the colour is unevenly distributed. Paste or starch can be added to

In this selection of dyed and painted fabrics I was experimenting with pattern obtained by scouring or by versions of wax resist.

The rolled-up sample on the right was painted and then part scraped off with a comb or other hard edge. In both the pieces to its left, I made patterns on undyed calico with hot wax and then covered the samples with a blue-black mixture of acrylic paint. Finally, when the paint was dry, I placed a scrap piece of fabric on top of the calico and used a hot iron on it; this slowly melted the wax, which was absorbed into the intermediate fabric.

The soft cream cotton at the bottom is the result of the simplest wax resist technique. I just rubbed crayons and candles across the surface of the fabric in solid areas and lines and then applied a coat of royal blue paint to achieve the pleasantly cloudy look.

the dye solution to make the fabric more crinkly and sculpted. (Of course, you do not *need* dye for this texturing effect: take a lightweight natural cloth, wash it and twist it as if you were wringing out water, and leave it to dry rolled up.) This versatile method is one of my favourites. It creates a springy twisted tension when the fabric is eventually opened out, contributing interest and movement to hanging swathes of fabric, around a bed or at a window.

The second version of wash and crinkle is to weight the fabric with a substance that will both make it stiffer and allow scope for colour play. My favourite medium is wallpaper paste: it is inexpensive and, because it can absorb water again after it has dried, it offers the possibility of repeating the process in successive stages. The end result in terms of texture is to increase the bulk of the fabric. If plenty of paste is left to dry in the fabric, it becomes stiff and hard. The more paste is removed or the more the dry fabric is handled, the softer the fabric becomes. Calico is the ideal candidate for this technique.

Start by spreading a length of fabric out flat. Cover it with paste and leave it to dry. Immerse the dried pasted fabric in a cold-dye bath. The paste absorbs the dye and becomes gloriously slimy. Remove the fabric from the dye and spread it out again. If you simply leave it to dry crinkled, you get an overall crushed texturing. Alternatively, you can create pattern by removing some of the blancmange-like mixture of dye and paste on the surface of the fabric before it dries. You can do this either by scouring the surface with a hard dry rag for a cloudy blotchy all-over effect, or by scraping lines on the surface with a stick, comb or paintbrush handle, drawing fairly regular and systematic markings as pattern repeats or making all-over scrawls. You then leave it to dry.

At this stage you can repeat the procedure with a different dye. The more you mix dyes the more you risk ending up with a discouragingly muddy pattern, so it is essential with this process that you cut up your experimental sample at each stage and keep a piece for reference, together with a note of how it was achieved. It is easy to get carried away and go too far.

Small pieces of fabric given this treatment make attractive cushions, but I find that the exciting scrunchy texture works best on the grand scale, in curtains that fall to make bunched mounds of fabric on the floor, or ruched blinds with simple swags that hold their form crisply.

Tie and dye
'Tie and dye' conjures up tired pictures of sunbursts on T-shirts, but I have seen the most beautiful effects created by tying waxed string around pleated fabrics which are then immersed in dye. The cloth that has been covered by the string retains its original colour, and the fabric dries in irregular lengthwise pleats crossed by jagged stripes of colour. Streaks of ground colour also remain in the folds where the dye has not reached. You can either enjoy the concertina effect of the fabric made into a curtain, or press out the folds and use the pattern flat.

WINDOWS

CHOOSING A STYLE
• The simple window • sheers • the dressed
window • draping • adaptable arrangements •
• window styles • measuring the window •

BLINDS
• Roman blinds • roller blinds •
• Austrian blinds • frills •
• festoon blinds •

CURTAINS
• Linings • poles & track • headings & hooks •
• making up curtains • making up sheers •
• tie-bands • pelmets & valances • loose drapes •
• swags & tails •

CHOOSING A STYLE

Of all the aspects of interior decoration, I enjoy dressing windows the most. Because the fabric is seen hanging over a large area, it gets shown off to its best advantage — whether falling in sharp pleats, defined folds or gentle curves. The light behind the fabric also plays an essential role in many of the different effects you can produce. Layers of fabric together can complement each other, especially when darker, stronger colours are seen blurred through pale translucent ones. There are wonderful shimmery muslins and silks that diffuse light and work well next to more opaque dense-textured fabrics. If you find nothing ready-made to your liking, you can adapt some of the ideas on pages 27–44, perhaps joining strips of different fabrics to make new lengths, or just adding a crisp border — to create your own very personal look. The choices are vast, as long as you abide by the following rules.

The combination of fabrics that you use to decorate your windows should suit the style and proportions of the room. Although an elegant town house with high ceilings and tall windows might benefit from lavish decoration with full, richly textured floor-length curtains and elegant swags and tails, a modern flat would probably look better with plain blinds or crisply tailored curtains.

It is only in relatively recent times that window dressing has been carried out for decorative reasons. Before then, the main function of curtains or blinds had been to prevent draughts and exclude sunlight. Wooden shutters were available for the same purpose. Even in the early nineteenth century it was still not unusual to find some windows in a house left plain and bare, although by then more prominent windows elsewhere in the same house might be receiving lavish attention.

It was during the nineteenth century that fabric arrangements first exploited the variety of different textures, weights, patterns and colours. Windows were made tall and often quite narrow, ideal for complex curtain arrangements, with a variety of blinds, sheers, curtains and drapery. Several fabrics were often hung at a window together and decorative pelmets and drapery became fashionable to the point of extravagance. Elaborate braids were sewn onto the leading edges of curtains and sometimes round the base, tasselled tie-bands became popular, and elegant fringing decorated the base of pelmets. Today, as I hope to show, there is more scope for design and individuality than ever.

This chapter is divided into sections: for blinds and how to make them see pages 69–95; for curtains and how to make them turn to pages 97–140.

The windows are the focal point of this room, summing up its cool, soft elegance. The glowing textures of glass, stone, terracotta and bleached pine are perfectly offset by the creamy cotton of the curtains. These fall in fluted columns to the floor, balanced by a fluidly draped classical swag and pair of tails.

THE SIMPLE WINDOW

A bare window, simply framing the view beyond it, invites the eye to focus on the form and style of both the room and the window itself. In the same way, so does a minimal window dressing – a flat blind, an unlined curtain or just a drape of plain, undyed fabric. A simple swag of fabric draping over a pole to the floor makes a quiet but definite statement, for example, or a single drape casually tied to one side of a French window. I often prefer such simplicity to more elaborately contrived window arrangements, as long as overall the look remains balanced.

Because it emphasizes the form, a single hanging at the windows suits a room where the lines are clean and unfussy. A cluttered room with bare windows merely looks unfinished. Simple window arrangements belong in interiors with, perhaps, uncarpeted floors, little pattern or decoration and minimal furniture, but with a large expanse of windows; they also suit unpretentious rooms with small windows, like country cottages. Whatever the type of room, simple decoration will generate a feeling of light and space.

In principle, if I am deliberately 'dressing down' a window, I avoid strong colours or patterns and keep the fabric plain. Unpatterned roller blinds, perhaps in a lightweight calico, are the most unobtrusive answer, virtually disappearing when pulled up, but Roman blinds are equally plain; a simple contrasting border (see page 28) adds just enough colour and textural interest without becoming fussy. I also like to concentrate on texture. A woven cloth keeps the minimal look intact while adding interest – perhaps a ridged twill weave, a finely ridged cotton drill or a rough hessian or linen. The eye is then drawn to the natural folds and undulations of the cloth, to the line of the fabric as it drapes and falls.

The colours most generally suitable for a simple look are pale or muted – whites, greys, Wedgwood blue or olive green. A fabric made up of colours that blend into one at a distance strikes the right note. Of course, you do not have to keep the colours pale. It can look stunning to use a plain strong colour in an otherwise pale room, perhaps a dark red blind with navy blue piping.

Although curtains give the impression of being more dressy than flat blinds, they do not have to be elaborate. Without being obtrusive, the shiny surface and speckled light patterns caused by a perforated silk drape would attract the eye. A plain fabric like white ticking, used unlined, would look simple and elegant, minimally enhanced perhaps by the addition of an inset border in a strong, dark colour.

Decoration has been kept to the minimum in this self-consciously casual interior. Drapes of crumpled white cotton hang straight but artfully at the windows to bunch at the base, emphasizing the interplay of light with form and texture. Barely gathered, simple lengths of fabric with rings clipped onto them, they bring out the other natural and light-reflective surfaces – the off-white walls, polished floor and white linen bedcover – while simultaneously enhancing the dark colours of the wooden beams and metal furniture.

SHEERS

All sheers are fine and light, translucent or semi-translucent; they filter light without completely obliterating the view. Almost always white or cream, a few have colour in the pattern. The choice of textures, fibres and patterns is extensive – in the category of sheer fabrics or 'nets' come Tergalin, voile, silks, muslin and lace. The natural fibres are delicate; one advantage of the many man-made fibres now available is that they withstand washing and do not need ironing.

Sheer fabrics such as gauze and muslin have been used as sunscreens for hundreds of years. They were pretty and decorative even in the early seventeenth century, a time when curtains otherwise were mostly utilitarian. Thin fabrics were popular, because the main purpose of curtains was to soften angular outlines and to keep out unwanted light; not until well into the eighteenth century did warmth and insulation become priorities. When, in the nineteenth century, heavy draperies flourished and window dressing became truly elaborate, sheers were still much in demand. Instead of being used on their own, however, their status was often reduced to that of 'sub-curtain' – one of many layers in a complex curtain arrangement.

Using sheers

Sheers offer many decorative possibilities, whether used as a simple window dressing in their own right or as part of a multi-layered design. Draped lavishly across a window they filter the morning sunlight, softening the outline of the window and creating a gentle, romantic mood. Screening the glass, taut and stretched, their uncluttered, cool elegance can be a key ingredient of an austere, minimalist interior. In contrast, a slot head (see page 119) run into a piece of muslin and gathered on a basic brass pole or rail has a casual, cottagey look to it – pretty and practical.

Because sheers are so fine, you can pull them into narrow pleats, ruche them into full Austrian blinds or crinkle them into icy swirls to swag across a pole. They will adapt easily to whatever mood you wish to create. In formal arrangements, sheers can be one of many layers of drapes, their light-filtering qualities emphasized by their proximity to textured brocades or luxurious velvets. Fine silks look exquisite with sunlight behind them – but beware of using dyed silks, as their colours quickly fade if they are frequently exposed to bright sunlight.

Pieces of lace or burn-out voiles can be curtains or blinds in their own right, unadorned in the summer months, perhaps, while benefiting from the addition of dress curtains in the winter. If you want to create a nostalgic, period feel, try hanging a piece of old lace on its own at a small window. Look for lace in antique shops, stalls specializing in lace and other textiles, or even jumble sales. Specialist manufacturers and suppliers are listed on page 208. For instructions on making up sheers, see page 123.

A permanent arrangement of soft, translucent sheers sweeps across the regular lines of these French windows. Lavish amounts of fabric are used sometimes in single, sometimes in double, layers so that while light enters it is diffused in varying degrees of softness.

A single drape of striped voile, echoing the pattern of the wallpaper, is tied back simply with a knotted cord. Overhanging this, a fine textured voile forms a delicate swag before falling in a straight line the full length of the window. The edging of decorative braid mirrors the ethereal quality of the fabrics, adding form and substance but not weight.

The arrangement's appealing asymmetry has the practical advantage of allowing the window to be easily opened.

THE DRESSED WINDOW

Large rooms with high ceilings are well suited to sumptuous window treatments – the grander the setting, the more elaborate these can be. The lavish effects so popular in the nineteenth century, produced by layers of fabric, curtains and blinds hung together and crowned with swags and tails, are now firmly back in fashion.

For a grand style, let the fabric make the impact. Go for brocades, dazzling paisley weaves, heavy silks or checked silk taffeta in dark or rich colours – reds, ochres, indigo or turquoise. Colour and texture are more crucial to the look than the actual number of layers.

For warmth and cosiness, use woollen cloth, tartan or tweeds. If you just want a warm effect, introduce lighter fabrics in strong vibrant colours – rich reds, pinks, oranges and yellows. In a large room with white walls you could achieve a startling balance between austerity and lushness by dressing the windows in heavy, luscious taffetas, brocades or silks – but all in white.

You do not need expensive fabric for extravagant window arrangements. By using lots of cheap, undyed calico, or silky poplin dyed a rich colour, you can create an opulent sculptural look, particularly with a clever use of borders in a more expensive fabric, perhaps even an antique one. Swags and tails, snakes and drapes of a simple fabric, looped around a pole and cascading down to the floor, successfully draw attention to a window without being overfussy. For an unusual look combine several different textures or weaves, perhaps in rough, undyed fabrics.

Draped with rough silk in luxurious quantities, the window on the right is topped by two very gathered and substantial swags. Full and deep, they each catch over the brass rosettes at the centre and the sides of the windows before falling into long, fluted tails.

The ends of the tails have been shaped to show off the fringed braid that has also been used to define the solid, heavy drapes. The subtle and wonderful colours of the braid tone in deliberately with the heavy silk cord tie-bands and the tasselled cord around the neck of the bust.

The two-storey window on the left has been made truly impressive by a grand arrangement of interlined drapes, triple swags and parallel tails. An overlying swag hangs in weighty prominence – its two neighbours partly hidden from view by the unusually wide tails, whose fluted form is defined by a flat fringe of cream braid. The loose drapes fall the length of the window architrave before being caught back just above the dado rail.

DRAPING

It is not enough simply to hang a curtain at the window and leave it. If the arrangement is to have any impact − by showing off the fabric, displaying a border more clearly or emphasizing the form of the window − the curtains need to be shaped. At the least, this means making sure that the folds in your curtain hang evenly from the heading to the floor, but you can also go for a more elaborate form of 'dressing in', as designers call it.

Curtains that will be pulled back and dressed in such a way that the leading edge trails often benefit from either particularly decorative tie-bands (see page 124) or a contrast lining (see page 63), as the underside of the curtain will be on view. If you are using tie-bands, you could consider draping your curtains from the centre of the track or pole and catching them at the base of a full swag. Tie-bands are usually most effective when placed about two-thirds of the way down a floor-length curtain, but their position depends on whether there is also a blind, or possibly a sill, both of which influence the proportions.

Ruched blinds (see pages 86−95) also need some dressing in once the blind is in position. Shape the swags so that they fall evenly and make sure that the base of the blind is level. You can make adjustments by undoing and repositioning the cord on the lower ring.

To perfect a look, give some thought to the final touches. A pole with unusual finials (see page 103) or a pair of padded silk tie-bands (see page 127), held by a brass rosette, enhances the simplest arrangement. Pelmets or valances (see page 128) give a more interesting and perhaps formal finish to the top of curtains, at the same time as concealing the track mechanism. Pelmets help to balance out the proportions of a room or a window: you can use them to give additional height or to enhance particularly tall windows, so that the curtains hang from the cornice.

Single drapes

Before the middle of the seventeenth century it was usual to have only a single curtain hanging at each window. As curtains ceased to be purely utilitarian, pairs of drapes came into fashion: they emphasized the decorative function of the fabric, as well as satisfying a human pleasure in symmetry.

But sometimes a pair of curtains is impractical, for instance if a cupboard abuts the window frame or if the window is too near a perpendicular wall to allow a full curtain to hang comfortably. If you want simplicity without the structured look of blinds, a single drape can still be the answer. On stairs, where windows are often

The elegant use of lavish snakes and tails is in keeping with the impressive architecture of this room and the view beyond. A grey and white print on a pale yellow ground − chosen to tone in with the sofa and walls − has been draped from the centre to achieve symmetry, and then snaked over a wall-to-wall pole so that the grey contrast lining in glazed cotton stands out clearly against the denser areas of patterned fabric.

Making an impact

All these windows, tucked away in corners or on stairs, could justifiably have been left bare. But, in different ways, each has been turned into a focal point.

The window on the landing, left, has been dressed traditionally, using old embroidered fabric, solid and heavy. The soft pelmet at the top has been caught up with pins, and the effect is one of timeless permanence.

The small window, right, has been decorated with a hemmed piece of Indian cotton cheesecloth simply draped over a pole. It is casually hung, with the tails artlessly balanced, but this is enough to make a feature of the view beyond.

The single drape of creamy cotton, below right, is an attractive solution to the problem of an awkwardly positioned stair window. Set higher than the window and thus altering its proportions for the better, the curtain, backed by a longer sheer, is caught back and fringed with appliquéd Picot braid.

inaccessible or too small to take a pair of curtains, a single curtain can just be draped to one side. French windows also benefit from being decorated in this way: the free side leaves you access to the door.

Single drapes look less cluttered than pairs of curtains, and the asymmetry is intriguing. The effect is not casual, however, and a single drape needs careful arranging or it will look as if it wants its pair. Tied back with a straightforward rope or cord tie-band, the drape can cover as much or as little of the window as you like, depending on where you position the tie-band. The higher up the curtain you put it, the more of the window will be visible. With single drapes an informal pelmet looks better than a formal one, in the shape of loose drapes – 'swags' of fabric over a pole.

Loose drapes

To create a particularly effective yet informal decorative effect, try making loose drapes, for which the fabric does not need to be carefully cut into patterns (unlike formal swags and tails – see below). You just take a length of fabric and drape it into loose 'swags' over and around a pole, which is fitted directly above the window. 'Tails' of fabric hang down at each end of the pole.

There is an immense variety of possible effects and combinations. First you must work out exactly how much fabric you need for a particular effect (see page 134). Then you are free to experiment: try wrapping the fabric once around each end of the pole, so that one full swag runs along the pole's length. Twist the fabric over the pole at the centre to make two swags. Wrap the fabric round and round to form several swags.

Once you have become skilled at handling the fabric and draping it, you can plan more complex effects. Create an asymmetrical look for instance, or use a contrast lining (see page 63) for the main fabric or even add a second length of fabric, matching or contrasting, and intertwine it with the first for a lavish double-layered effect.

Swags and tails

Formal swag draperies are elaborate constructions, ranging from the single full swag to complicated intersections of draped fabric. They are generally lined and often interlined, to give maximum fullness, before being individually hung from a timber board so that they drape in front of the curtain heading. Because they need to be fairly deep to drape impressively, they look best at tall windows in rooms with high ceilings. On shallow windows they can look top-heavy.

Swags and tails are not easy to make because it takes skill to cut them out accurately. However, instructions for making a basic swag and simple tails are given on pages 136–40.

The off-white, soft cotton drape at the window of this north-facing study lends warmth and vitality to an otherwise cool interior. Its textured self-stripe complements the room's smooth surfaces.

The drape flows in classic style across the pole and down to the floor on either side, but the choice of the creamy cotton, with its gentle folds and bunches, makes the look utterly modern.

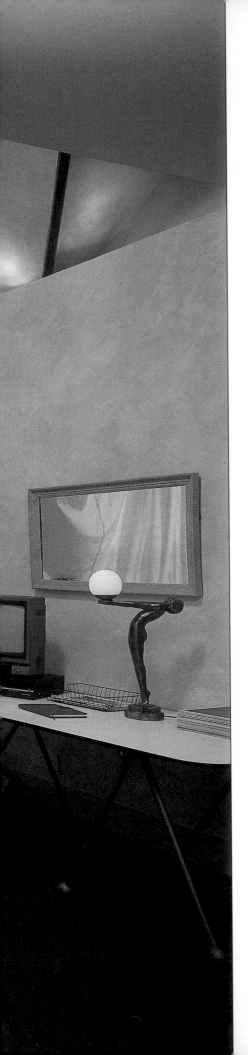

A theatrical solution

This high-ceilinged conversion features two windows of average size and a small circular one. To have fitted ordinary blinds or curtains to the lower windows would merely have diminished the overall scale, ignoring the room's grand proportions, while the circular window would have had no impact at all.

Instead, widths of calico have been joined with French seams to create extraordinarily lavish and dramatic drapes. Closely gathered at the top and stapled to battens on the ceiling, they have been caught and pinned midway down, so that the fabric falls in sumptuous crescent-shaped folds the full length of the twenty-foot wall. They thus provide a breathtaking backdrop to the room.

When the drapes are drawn back, as shown below, the circular and lower windows are made the key elements of a three-sided display.

ADAPTABLE ARRANGEMENTS

Why not think in terms of different looks for different seasons? It was not uncommon for owners of grand houses in the past to adjust their decor in this way – perhaps exchanging the tapestry wall-hangings and velvet curtains of winter for all-silk 'summer furniture'.

These days such an approach is rare. But a large room with minimal window dressing and a stripped wooden floor can be very cold in winter. For maximum insulation and to make such a room feel as cosy as possible, the best window treatment during the winter months would probably be a pair of lined and interlined curtains, covering the entire window space and perhaps bunched on the floor for extra draught protection; a pelmet arrangement would help to cut out draughts from the top of the window.

In the summer, however, these curtains would look too hot and heavy. You might not even draw them, in which case the fabric left to drape at a window untouched for a whole summer would collect dust and possibly fade. All you need is a blind or a simple curtain, perhaps unlined, to give a bit of privacy without the feeling of being closed in. You could choose an inexpensive, lightweight fabric easily made into a simple sunshield and hang it on the same track or pole. Take down the winter curtains, launder them, then fold and wrap them in a plastic bag. Even the most familiar old curtains look fresh and exciting when put up for the first time after months of rest.

It may be, of course, that you have the opposite problem. Perhaps in a bedroom in summer you are disturbed by the early-morning light, which your winter arrangement is inadequate to block out. In this case you need to think in terms of adding either darker curtains or perhaps a blind with a blackout lining (see page 100). Whatever the need, an adaptable solution is original, appropriate and not usually difficult to put into practice. It just demands a fresh approach.

Consider, for instance, adding dress curtains in the winter months to a window with functional blinds. Intended for effect rather than continual use, the dress curtains will introduce a more formal note to the decor. Or, in a large room with high ceilings, you might rearrange the furniture in the winter to enclose a small area for daily use. The simplest approach, perhaps, is to be imaginative about linings. Unlike the main fabric these are often chosen quickly and without much thought, but, used creatively, linings can make your entire window arrangement more versatile.

Detachable linings

Linings for curtains can be detachable, hanging from a separate heading tape (see page 106), so that you have the flexibility of simply removing them, for washing or for the summer. If your main curtain fabric has a wonderful translucent quality, for instance, exploit it in the summer months by removing the detachable lining and letting the light shine through.

You can use detachable linings to great effect in children's bedrooms too. As the days get longer and lighter, conventionally

This interior looks very different in its summer and winter modes. On the right, a summery look is created with bare walls, a pale carpet and chairs positioned so that they face towards the conservatory and incoming sun. The curtain is reversible: its striped ticking 'lining', caught back and tied to the pole, is far more noticeable than the unpatterned main fabric.

For the winter look, the curtain lining is partly concealed by the main fabric, an Indian cotton in warm terracotta. A dark carpet and a paisley throw tone in with the lengths of fabric on the walls. (For more about the wall fabric in this room, see p.180.)

lined curtains often fail to block out enough light, so that children cannot get to sleep or wake at dawn. If the lining is detachable, you can simply exchange it for a detachable blackout lining during the summer (see page 100), provided the main curtain fabric is suitable.

Once you are using detachable linings, linings and fabrics become equal partners. It becomes logical to contemplate having two separate curtains – or a reversible one (see opposite). An extension of the contrast lining (see below), one side can be on view for a time, or a particular season, and then the curtain turned around when you feel like a change.

Coloured and contrast linings

Although pale-coloured cotton sateen has traditionally been the choice for lining fabric, the lining can be just as important a style choice as the main fabric. Dark or richly coloured linings will effectively brighten up your windows and enhance their appearance from the outside. Several manufacturers offer fade-resistant coloured linings which, if chosen carefully, also add extra depth of colour to the main furnishing fabrics.

You can achieve subtle colour combinations by carefully toning both lining and fabric, so that the effect of the coloured lining is seen

The dressed ruched pelmet on the left is intended to be enjoyed from both sides, making it a perfect candidate for a contrast lining. Here the contrast lining on the interior side has been taken up to form a very deep border at the front.

The sunny yellow and airy blue, in the same lightweight silk, are pleasing together, the puffy fabric producing a billowy, almost sail-like effect. The curvy form of the pelmet echoes the curved shapes of the seating.

through the main fabric. A bright sunflower yellow lining would add a touch of gold to the colour of your curtain fabric. A plain Austrian blind lined with striped fabric would look intriguing with sunlight shining through it.

Exploit the properties of different fabrics to create exciting window furnishings. If the main fabric of a curtain or blind is cream muslin, combine it with a deep-coloured lining; or line a fine, rather translucent striped fabric, such as shirting, with a well defined checked cloth.

When contemplating contrast or coloured linings, make sure the window furnishings work as well from the outside of the house. Does the colour complement or clash with the exterior paintwork, for example? In effect, you are considering two curtains at once, in the context of two different surrounds — but the results are worth the extra effort.

Patterned fabric used to line plain curtains will make the window look more attractive from the outside. If you take a contrast or patterned lining round the leading edge of a plain curtain, it will create an interesting border.

WINDOW STYLES

Domestic architecture is rich in window styles. Often one house has several types of window, each presenting a different challenge. When you are deciding how to dress a window, you need to consider both the practical and the aesthetic aspects.

The style of window is only one of several factors. Is the window tall or small, wide or narrow, sash or casement opening, recessed or flush with the wall? How much wall space is there around it? Does it abut an adjoining wall? Is there a radiator beneath it? By narrowing down the choices, answering these questions will automatically exclude certain fixings and should make your ultimate decision easier. Fortunately the range of poles, tracks, brackets and other fittings (see pages 102–4) is so wide today that most needs can be met.

Proportions and style

Keep the window arrangement in style with the period of the house and with both the proportions and the decorations of the room. If in doubt as to what is appropriate, go for understatement rather than excessive embellishment. The dimensions and position of your window, as well as its style, will dictate what you can do with it.

With tall windows, for example, the arrangement can be elegant and generous: at the least, curtains should be floor length, falling in well-formed folds, and you might consider a pelmet. With smaller windows, you need to be more careful: too much crammed into a small space does not work. Much will depend on the feel of the room – heavy lines of horizontal swags do not look right at modern windows. There may be instances where, visually at least, you want to add height to small windows. Fixing a pelmet above the window, if there is room, achieves this by adding extra length to the curtains.

Practical considerations

The window must be easy to open and let in as much light as you want. You also need to think about the type of fittings the window frame, or the space around it, can take. In every case make sure the blinds or curtains do not permanently drape any part of the window you have to open.

Windows are either fitted flush with the surrounding wall or recessed within it. If curtains are hung within the recess they tend to cut out too much light on a smallish window and are usually best hung against the wall, as long as there is enough space for them. The space above the windows can be used to accommodate the fixings of a blind, if too much light is lost when the blind is fitted in a recess.

Window shapes vary considerably – single or double, or in the shape of a bay, either square or angled, or a rounded bow. Double windows can be treated as two or one, depending on their dimensions; for example, you could fit two adjacent roller or Roman blinds, or a single wide blind, fitting into the soffit of the window. Tracks and even poles can be bought to fit a bay window (see page 104), although you can fix the pole or track on the ceiling straight

An unusually shaped window can easily be left to speak for itself. If dressed at all, the arrangement should bring out any special features.

This arched window has been dressed with a pair of navy silk curtains, gently restrained with matching tie-bands decorated with pointed ends and frivolous tassels. To draw attention to the arch, shallow swags of the same silk flow from the centre. Sheers are used to make the textures and light effects more interesting – they provide privacy but, like the silk curtains, do not obscure the window's shape.

across the bay, so that the shape of the bay is obliterated when the curtains are drawn. (Ceiling fixing is often awkward, since the ceiling must be strong enough to withstand any screwing and drilling, and to take the weight of the curtains.)

The position of the window is important. If the window abuts an adjoining wall, or even a piece of furniture, the hanging space for curtains at one side is restricted; blinds might be the best solution, or perhaps a single drape, tied back at one side. If there is just space for a pair of curtains to hang, any pole would have to end at the adjoining wall, with the finial at one end only. Special recess fittings are available for windows that abut walls. Particular difficulties also arise when a window is fitted with internal shutters, where blinds only are probably the neatest solution, or when there is a window seat, where any curtains can only be sill length.

If there is a radiator beneath the window, it is a good idea not to block it with heavy curtains. The best solution here is to fit blinds, with or without dress curtains that will not be drawn. Floor-length curtains are an option if they are only going to be used in the summer (perhaps lightweight, unlined cotton). Sill-length curtains can extend to just above the radiator, depending on the distance between the window and the radiator. I would prefer to get round the problem another way and frame the window more positively — say by hanging a long swag over a pole.

French windows need to open, so that solutions involving, say, deep swags covering the top part of the glass are totally unsuitable. At the same time, their size and scale often make a simple pair of curtains look inadequate.

Here, a lot of heavy cotton has been used to grand effect. A pair of curtains drops solidly to the ground, bunching on the floor, the shape of the tie-bands emphasizing the fullness of the fabric. Above the window two lengths of cotton have been wound round and round a pole in tight snakes of fabric. The result frames the French windows powerfully, without looking in any way intrusive or oppressive.

MEASURING THE WINDOW

Before you start making any blind or curtains, you must accurately measure the window, to arrive at the finished drop and width of what you are making. Take measurements with a steel ruler or tape and ask somebody to help if the window is wide or the drop long.

Take all width measurements at both top and bottom of the window to check that it is in fact square. If the window is badly out of true, avoid plain blinds, which fit the window space precisely.

Measuring up for blinds

Ideally blinds should be recess-fixed beneath the soffit of the window. If this is not possible, the blind must be face-fixed with angle brackets to the window frame or wall. Roman, Austrian and festoon blinds are all first attached to a timber support (see page 73). A roller blind is fitted to a roller.

For a recess-fixed roller blind, the brackets should be fitted about 3cm/1¼in from the top of the recess to allow room for the roller, and the measurement B, right, should be the length of the roller blind kit including the metal caps and pins (you need to deduct 3cm/1¼in from this measurement for the finished width of the fabric). For all blinds fitted to a timber support, fixed to the soffit of the window recess, deduct 5cm/2in from B, so that the blinds do not touch the sides of the window.

For a face-fixed blind, the angle brackets for the timber support or roller must first be positioned. As a general rule, if there is plenty of space all round, fix the brackets about 12cm/5in above the window and the same distance out to the side.

Measuring up for curtains

You first need to decide on what type of heading you are having (see pages 110–22), whether the curtains are to hang from a track or a pole (see pages 102–5). Ideally, fix the pole or track about 15cm/6in from the top of the window, and allow the same distance from the side of the window to the end of the track or to the last ring on the pole beyond the bracket. If space is tight, fit the top of the track level with the top of the architrave; a pole should be a little higher.

The finished drop depends on the length of the curtains. Try to have carpet in position before measuring for full-length curtains. If you want the curtains to clear the floor, deduct 1.5cm/½in from measurement B, right. If you want them to bunch on the floor, add 5–20cm/2–8in to B according to taste.

For sill-length curtains, deduct 12mm/½in from measurement A, right, if the sill protrudes, so that the curtains hang clear of the sill itself; otherwise add 5–10cm/2–4in to A, as the curtains will look better if they hang below the sill. Ideally they should extend beyond the sill by the same amount as the heading projects above the soffit. Some fabrics 'stretch' after hanging for a while. These need an extra 2–3cm/¾–1¼in deducting from the finished drop.

To work out how many fabric widths you need, see page 200.

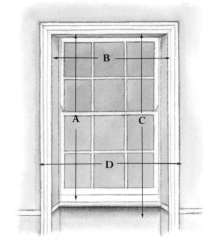

For the finished drop of a recess-fixed blind, measure from the top of the roller or timber support to the window sill, A. The finished width is the width of the recess, B. For the finished drop of a face-fixed blind, measure from the top of the roller or support to 5cm/2in below the window sill, C. The finished width is either the exact width of the flush frame, D, or D plus a little extra on each side to exclude light.

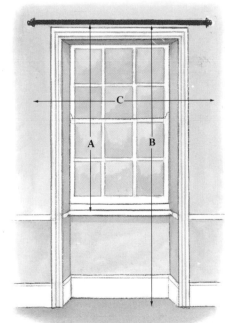

For the finished drop of full-length curtains, measure from the top of the track or bottom of the pole to the floor, B. For sill-length curtains, measure from the top of the track or bottom of the pole to the sill, A. For the finished width, measure the length of the track or pole plus, in the case of track, any overlaps or returns, C.

BLINDS

The earliest forms of blind were purely functional. Made of a translucent fabric, like Italian gauze or half-silk, they protected the valuable drapes and furnishings of the grander houses of the time from the ravages of strong sunlight. The precise history and development of blinds is difficult to date, but by the seventeenth century two distinct forms of blind had appeared – one took the shape of a window curtain that pulled up on a simple cording system to form a loose swag at the top of the window, while the other comprised a plain rectangle of fabric mounted on wooden battens, and inserted into the window recess.

By the eighteenth century, blinds had developed into a more sophisticated form and began to be used as decorative window dressings in their own right, as ruched and swagged blinds, known as curtains *à l'italienne*, the forerunners of today's Austrian blind, and its cousin, the festoon. The more functional form of blind had acquired a spring-operated roller to become little different from the roller blind as we know it today. The origins of the Roman blind – rectangular like the roller but corded like a ruched blind – are unknown, although references were made in newspapers of the eighteenth century to 'Roman drapes'.

Such is the range of styles of blind available today that you can find one to complement every sort of architecture and to gratify any taste in fabric, from the off-white linen of an elegant Roman blind to the voluptuous silky folds of an extravagantly ruched Austrian or festoon blind.

In terms of style, blinds can be divided into two principal groups: plain and ruched.

Plain blinds

Plain blinds, which, when lowered, cover the window with a neat rectangle of fabric, have the virtue that they roll or fold away into a relatively inconspicuous strip of fabric and so let in the maximum amount of light. Roller and Roman blinds are discreet enough to provide the 'functional' layer in a window dressed in more sumptuous style but, equally, they can make a strong statement of their own, incorporating attractive borders or exciting textures and patterns. Roller blinds are the simplest to make and offer interesting creative possibilities in terms of stencilled or painted designs (see pages 36–44), as indeed they have from their earliest days – Madame de Pompadour's boudoir in Bellevue sported a roller blind of 'Italian taffeta, painted with flowers and garlands'.

Original and exhilarating in effect, a simple yet ornate style of heading combines with bold yellow roller blinds, left, to create a decorative masterpiece. The striped fabric has been skilfully draped so that the middle swag complements the twisted snake-like curves of the golden heading, while the loose drapes hanging down at either side lead the eye through to the straight lines of the rectangular blind.

Of the two types, Roman blinds appeal to me more, because they allow greater flexibility in the choice of fabric and I like the linear quality of their crisp folds. They can, unlike roller blinds, be lined easily and therefore offer better insulation.

Undoubtedly, the chief virtue of both types of plain blind is their elegant simplicity. They allow windows to be dressed but not obviously decorated, and they show off good window shapes to perfection, suiting both streamlined modern interiors and classical styles of architecture. Since they take much less fabric than ruched blinds, they are cheaper to make. Their effect depends on their hanging straight, so cutting and make up have to be precise.

Ruched blinds

The main feature of ruched blinds is the opulent effect created by the rich deep swags of fabric. Made from fabric at least twice the width of the window, they are gathered onto a curtain heading tape and then corded to form the swags. The two main types of ruched blinds, Austrians and festoons, are very similar and often confused. I have elected to use the definition adopted by soft furnishing designers and retailers, namely that a festoon blind is ruched from top to base whereas the Austrian is ruched at the base alone.

Designed to fit perfectly into the window recess, the neat rectangular form of these Roman blinds is emphasized by a border in contrasting white. Set down from the top and lying along the base flap, the border shows up as a permanent feature even when, as here, the blind is fully raised. The clear lines of the multiple, crisp folds and carefully mitred corners are in keeping with the surroundings, while the two-tone design mirrors the striking floor of bleached and natural oak.

Generous swags and clearly defined ruches make a prominent feature of the Austrian blind in the picture on the left, although the pale, unobtrusive colour of the fabric blends in well alongside the subdued tones of the rest of the interior. The fabric is closely gathered on a pole at the top to form a slot heading, which provides an interesting, attractive alternative to the standard pencil pleat heading.

Precisely because these blinds have such a decorative form, I find it works best to use a slightly understated fabric for them, which emphasizes the sculptural quality of the swags, rather than drawing attention to their more 'flouncy' characteristics. The most inexpensive fabric, such as unbleached calico or striped ticking, can often be the most effective.

Whatever style of blind you choose, it is crucial that the fabric suits the structural requirements of the design. In the introduction to each type of blind, I have given examples of some of the fabric textures and weights that I think work well, but you also need to consider how the blind will fit with the other soft furnishings and the architecture of the room, in particular the shape of the windows.

Blinds almost invariably look best when their length exceeds their width. Very wide blinds are also difficult to manoeuvre, so if you want to cover a large expanse of window you might do better to use more than one blind, particularly where the windows divide naturally. Don't forget that ruched blinds, even when fully raised, will obscure a certain amount of the window, so if light is at a premium you might find a plain blind a better option.

As a general point on care, I suggest that blinds are always dry-cleaned. The fit is so essential to the look, particularly of the rectangular sort, that shrinkage would be disastrous. Ruched blinds are fitted onto Velcro which makes them easy to take down for cleaning; the stiff surface of a roller blind can be sponged *in situ* to clean it, but Roman blinds, because of their more complex construction, will have to be dismantled.

Construction

Blinds are not particularly difficult to make but to get a professional result you must pay attention to detail. It is important that the blind fits the window space exactly and so accurate measuring up (see page 67) is essential. If the blind is to hang properly, the grain of the fabric must be straight and true, and the cutting precise and square (see page 111).

In construction terms, blinds fall into two groups: roller blinds, which roll up as the name implies, and Roman, Austrian and festoon blinds – all of which pull up by means of a series of cords and rings attached to the back of the blind and are suspended from a stout rectangular timber support, fixed either to the window frame or the soffit or the wall above. As the fixing details for the latter group are almost identical, I have dealt with them here. The relevant making-up instructions can be found on the appropriate pages.

To ensure that no bare wood shows when the blind is complete, the support should be covered with fabric. In the case of a Roman blind, where the actual blind fabric is rolled around the support, I simply cover the ends of the timber with fabric (see page 79). But for the ruched blinds, the support is wrapped in its own fabric, like a parcel (see right).

The simple two-colour print on this Austrian blind blends in well with the cream and dark wood bathroom scheme. The piped double frill along the base of the blind adds charm and definition to the gentle ruches, which help to soften the harsh lines of the square window frame.

Normally a 5×2.5cm/2×1in timber support is needed for a lined blind made of medium-weight fabric, although a 2.5×2.5cm/1×1in timber might be better if the recess is very shallow and the fabric lightweight.

The support is normally cut to the finished width (less 12mm/$\frac{1}{2}$in) of the blind. If the recess has sloping sides, or if several blinds abut each other around a bay window, the ends may need to be mitred (see page 203).

With recess-fixed blinds, the support is normally fixed direct to the soffit or the recess of the window, but if the recess is shallow and the blind has to be face-fixed, then angle brackets are used to fix the support to the appropriate surface.

MAKING THE SUPPORT

1 If the blind is to be recess-fixed, drill two holes, 15cm/6in in from each end of the wide face of the support, making sure their position does not interfere with the cording line screw eyes (see relevant instructions).

2 For both face-fixed and recess-fixed blinds, cut a strip of blind fabric large enough to cover the support and lay the timber, drilled side up, in the centre of the fabric.

3 Fold the fabric neatly over the support to form a parcel, and tack or staple it into position (fig. a).

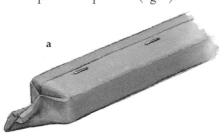

a

4 If the blind has a Velcro heading, fix the reciprocal Velcro down one long narrow edge of the support (fig. b) and around the short ends if necessary (see relevant instructions).

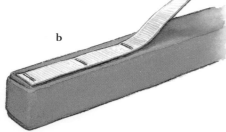

b

5 With a bradawl, mark the position of the cording screw eyes (lined up with the rows of cording rings on the blind) and secure the screw eyes in place (fig. c), making sure they are not so tight that the fabric pulls.

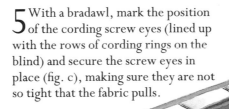

c

FIXING THE BLIND

Cord and complete the blind as appropriate (see relevant instructions).

If the blind is recess-fixed, pierce the fabric cover of the support holes with a bradawl and insert the screws into the holes so that a 12mm/$\frac{1}{2}$in tip protrudes. Mark the fixing position on the recess or soffit, and drill the fixing holes. Screw the support into position (fig. d).

If the blind is face-fixed, with angle brackets, mark the fixing position of the first bracket. Drill the fixing holes and screw the bracket into place (fig. e). Rest the blind on it and check that it is straight with a spirit level. Mark the position of the other bracket (you will need someone to help at this point), drill the fixing holes and screw the bracket into place. Position the blind support on top of the bracket and screw into place.

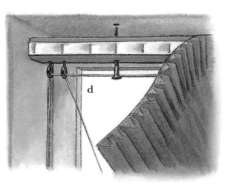

d

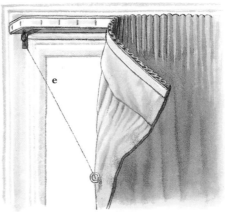

e

ROMAN BLINDS

The most striking feature of a Roman blind is its combination of elegance and simplicity. Pulled up, the blind forms a series of crisp, horizontal folds, one under the other; let down, it is a flat piece of fabric that neatly fits the window space. To keep the folds horizontal, the fabric is normally supported by timber rods contained in pockets attached to the back of the blind. Cord for raising and lowering the blind is threaded through rings or eyelets fixed to the rod pockets.

The unfussy lines of a Roman blind suit the character of most windows, although leaded lights and intricate window pane patterns would detract from the blind's neatly sculpted form. For their architectural qualities to be fully appreciated, Roman blinds need space around them. They look best in rooms with plenty of light and with large uninterrupted areas of plain colour. A clutter of furniture, busy patterns or a hotchpotch of furnishing styles would only draw attention away from the blind.

Fabrics

The rigidity of the rod pockets gives a very disciplined look to the blind, which is enhanced by plain or lightly textured fabric. For the greatest impact, use fabrics that emphasize or exploit the blind's linear quality. Simple patterns like checks or stripes, particularly where no more than two or three colours are incorporated, are particularly effective. Vertical stripes, self-coloured or contrasting, look good on a Roman blind and will lengthen its appearance, emphasizing the height of the window. Horizontal stripes also look striking, if made to fit in with the panels of the folds. They have the effect of 'widening' the blind on a narrow window. Fussy patterns — floral or highly decorative fabrics with large repeating patterns — are unsuitable.

Ideally the fabric should be strong enough to make firm folds. Translucent fabrics, like poplin or Chinese silk, make splendid sunscreens when used unlined, but they are less durable than 'hard' fabrics like strong cottons, calicos or ticking.

Although Roman blinds can be made up to 250cm/100in wide, a blind wider than this is unsuitable as it becomes unwieldy and the rods tend to sway when the blind is pulled up. If the width of the fabric you choose is narrower than the desired finished width of the blind, you can join two widths together (see page 111), or use a border to extend the fabric to fit the window space.

Special effects

A Roman blind takes relatively little fabric — only marginally more than the finished width and drop of the blind — so creating your own fabric, by sewing strips of fabric together for example, is not a particularly time-consuming task. It also lends individuality to your room. Different textures or fabrics could be stitched together in vertical or horizontal panels, or a line of stripes could be set

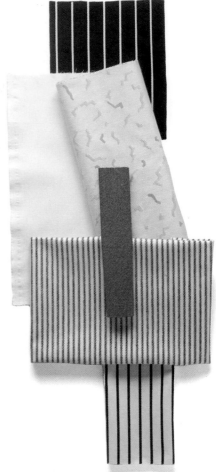

The firm weave of the fabrics laid out above make them particularly suitable for a Roman blind. The wide stripes of the butcher's apron cotton and those of the cotton canvas at the bottom look striking running horizontally or vertically. On the far left, a creamy calico can be attractively bordered by the unusual weave pattern on its right or by the overlying blue cotton canvas, while the black and white mattress ticking benefits from a dark defining border (see p. 76).

The unlined Roman blinds on the right have been precisely designed to fit their recesses exactly, falling straight with front rods absolutely parallel. Their unusual length makes them reminiscent of screens, while their strong colour (made more so by the lack of any diffusing lining) casts a blue wash over the entire room.

asymmetrically into an inexpensive plain fabric, like unbleached calico, to give it dramatic interest.

Alternatively, the horizontal bands of the blind could be emphasized by attaching the rod pockets to the front of the blind instead of the back, and using a strong contrasting colour for them.

Borders

The full design potential of borders comes into its own in delineating the handsome shape of a Roman blind. Borders can be set into the main fabric or used simply to edge it, either in contrasting or in toning colours and textures. Defining the outline of the blind in this way not only emphasizes its proportions, it also allows you to integrate the blind into the colour scheme for the rest of the room. You could pick up a colour, or even the exact fabric, used elsewhere; on plain cottons or calicos, you could stencil or paint a border that picks up a similar one used, for example, on the floorboards or that echoes a painting style used on the walls.

Other simple but effective border treatments are using the reverse side of the main fabric for the border, or running the stripes of the main fabric in the other direction for the border.

The addition of a narrow inset border of glazed black cotton to the blind on the left quite dramatically transforms a plain and inexpensive black and white ticking. The careful positioning of the border in relation to the main fabric is designed to achieve maximum visual impact, providing the only touch of decoration in an otherwise functional interior. To accommodate the flat window frame, the blind has been face-fixed on painted angle brackets fixed above the support.

A deep orange glazed cotton border inset into Roman blinds of unbleached calico, left, has a very dramatic impact, substantially enriching the plain matt fabric. The neat edges and carefully mitred corners of this style of blind are very much in keeping with the clean lines and subdued character of the rest of the interior. Each blind has been designed to fit its individual frame and the outlines of the sharply contrasting borders serve to emphasize the distinctive character and form of the sash windows.

Construction

A Roman blind looks best fixed into the soffit of the window, so that it fits exactly into the recess. When down, the blind then fills the window space neatly, with the architrave of the window making a frame. If the recess is not deep enough, you can fix the blind to the architrave or the wall, using angle brackets (see page 73).

The very simplicity of the blind demands special care in its construction. First, measure the window carefully to check that it is square as, if it is not, the blind will not hang straight. If the window is noticeably out of true, a ruched blind would be a better option, as the window's shortcomings will be masked rather than revealed. It is equally important for the blind fabric itself to be cut square: the cutting instructions on page 201 should be followed implicitly.

There are many different ways of making a Roman blind but I prefer to reinforce the pockets of the blind with timber rods. You do see Roman blinds without this stiffening, but they tend to pull in towards the centre, leaving an unwelcome margin of light at each side. If you want a 'floppy' Roman blind, you can sew tapes, with the cording rings attached, in vertical rows to the back of the blind, but I do not recommend it as the vertical lines of stitching on the front of the blind tend to mar its appearance.

For fixing the fabric to its timber support, I recommend the method described on page 79.

MAKING ROMAN BLINDS

The instructions below are for constructing a lined and rodded Roman blind with four folds and three vertical lines of cording. The general principles of construction can be applied whatever size of blind you opt for. The depth of the folds is a matter of taste but the cording rows on the blind should be positioned about 30cm/12in apart for the blind to fold up neatly. A lined blind gives more support and protects the fabric from fading, as well as providing better insulation, but if the blind is to act as a sunscreen, for example, then an unlined blind would be the best option (see page 80).

Although the rod pockets usually serve only as a practical device to give support to the blind, you can make a special feature of them on the front of the blind, in which case you should follow the instructions given on page 82.

The materials and instructions for fixing the blind to the wall or window are given on page 73.

(see page 80). ... given on page 82. ... given on page 73.

MATERIALS
- Fabric and lining
- 1cm/$\frac{3}{8}$in diameter timber dowels for each rod pocket
- 5cm × 2.5cm/2 × 1in timber support
- Brass rings (3 for each pocket)
- Masking tape
- Staple gun or hammer and tin tacks
- Fine polyester cord
- Drop weight and cleat
- Screw eyes

ESTIMATING THE FABRIC

Decide whether the blind is to hang within the window recess or outside it and measure the width and depth accordingly (see p. 67) to give the finished width and drop of the blind. For the total width and depth of fabric required, add 10cm/4in to the finished width (to allow for two side hems) and 30cm/12in to the finished drop (to allow for a base hem plus sufficient surplus fabric to roll around the timber support). Add a little extra fabric to cover the ends of the support. For the lining fabric, add 4cm/1$\frac{1}{2}$in to the finished width of the blind and for each rod pocket add 12cm/4$\frac{1}{2}$in to the finished length.

CUTTING

Cut out the blind and lining fabric to the total width and depth measurements, and cut out a rod pocket (12cm/4$\frac{1}{2}$in deep × the full width of the lining) for each fold of the blind. It is essential that the fabric is cut square to the selvedge (see p. 111) to ensure that the blind hangs correctly.

POSITIONING THE ROD POCKETS

Decide on the number of folds (four in this case). Subtract from the *finished* drop of the blind (exclude the surplus at the top and base of the blind) an allowance of 10cm/4in (this prevents the pockets catching on the supporting screw eyes and allows folds to lie evenly). From the remaining depth, subtract 6mm/$\frac{1}{4}$in for each fold of the blind (2.5cm/1in for four folds). Divide the remaining depth by twice the number of folds (2 × 4 in this case), plus one, to give the distance (d) from the base of the blind to the first rod pocket. Each subsequent rod pocket is positioned at twice this distance (2d), plus a 6mm/$\frac{1}{4}$in allowance (right).

If you mark the calculations on paper (right), you can check that they fit accurately into the finished drop of the blind.

For a blind with an outside edge border that is to be on show at the base, subtract the border depth from the finished depth of the blind and proceed in exactly the same way as above. Therefore (d) equals the distance from the top of the border to the first rod pocket. The border will then extend below the first fold when the blind is pulled up.

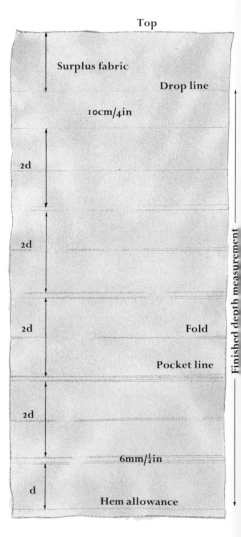

Top

Surplus fabric

Drop line

10cm/4in

2d

2d

2d

Fold

Pocket line

2d

6mm/$\frac{1}{4}$in

d

Hem allowance

Finished depth measurement

CONSTRUCTING THE BLIND

1 Lay the blind fabric, wrong side up, on a flat surface. Press under a 5cm/2in single hem on the base and sides of the blind. Mitre the corners (see p. 203). Secure hems using herringbone stitch.

2 Centre the lining, right side up, on the wrong side of the blind and press under a single hem on the base and sides to leave 12mm/½in of the blind fabric exposed. Slipstitch the lining hem to the blind (fig. a).

a

3 Mark the positions of the rod pockets and the finished drop line in pencil on the lining of the blind, making sure they are parallel with the base of the blind.

4 Make the rod pockets by pressing each one in half lengthwise. With the raw edges together, turn over a double hem 12mm/½in deep on the long side, and machine stitch as shown (fig.b). Similarly, press under and machine stitch the same size double hem on the short side. Continue stitching down the lower edge of the long side (fig.c).

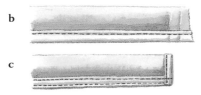

b

c

5 Working from the base of the blind to the top, pin the long folded edge of each rod pocket along the pencilled rod pocket line on the blind, with the stitched edge of the pocket towards the base of the blind and the short, stitched end of the pocket aligned with the edge of the lining. Machine stitch the rod pockets to the blind very close to the folded edge of the pocket (fig.d).

6 Cut the dowelling into rods, each 12mm/½in less than the length of the rod pocket. Insert a rod through the open end of each pocket (fig.d), fold under the surplus lining and slipstitch the pocket edges together.

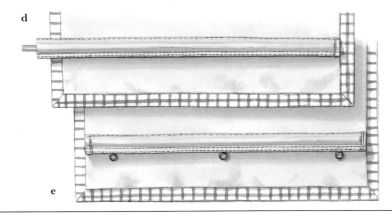

d

e

7 Position the cording rings 8cm/ 3¼in from each side of the blind and at equal intervals (about 30cm/12in) across the blind width. Handstitch securely to the edge of the pocket (fig.e).

ADDING THE SUPPORT

1 Prepare the timber support (see p. 73) and cover the ends neatly with the blind fabric.

2 The timber support must be correctly positioned on the finished drop line of the blind, or the blind may not fit the window space exactly. Stand at the top of the blind and position the narrow side of the support against the drop line on the back of the blind (fig. f). Roll the support twice towards you. Stick the fabric to the support with masking tape and roll the support back carefully to the finished drop line.

3 Once correctly positioned secure the fabric with a row of tacks or staples and remove the tape. Trim off any surplus. If incorrectly positioned remove the tape and try again.

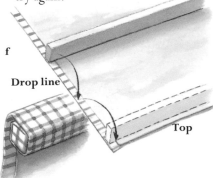

f

Drop line

Top

CORDING

Insert three screw eyes in the underside of the timber support in line with each column of rings on the pockets, with an additional screw eye 2.5cm/1in from the side on which the cords will hang. Tie a length of cord to the bottom ring of each column and thread it up through all the rings above, through the screw eye above, and across through each eye, including the extra one, towards the side where the cords will hang. Thread all the cords through the drop weight and cut them level before tying a firm knot.

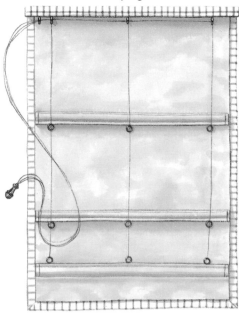

MAKING AN UNLINED ROMAN BLIND

The method for making an unlined Roman blind differs from that of a lined blind in two major respects. Firstly, and obviously, there is no lining and as a result of this the rod pockets are formed from the folds in the main fabric of the blind. Lightweight, even semi-translucent fabrics can be used successfully for an unlined blind, although stiffer canvases and cotton drills also work well. Secondly, because there is no lining, the formula for positioning the rod pockets is different, as these are created from the main fabric. The materials are the same as for a lined blind, excluding the lining, of course, and including a suitably sized lath for the base hem (for lightweight fabrics). The method of construction is similar to a lined blind, apart from the points given below.

Startlingly original in style, the rod pockets and vertical side hems have been used to create web-like internal ribbing for the imaginative Roman blind on the right. The blind lies flat and is probably not designed to be raised any higher than shown, since the choice of translucent fabric allows sufficient light to penetrate. The lower panels, which must fill the window when down, are here cleverly drawn up, by means of a central cord, to create a delightful fanned effect.

ESTIMATING THE FABRIC

The length of fabric required equals the finished drop of the blind plus the hem (4cm/1½in) and top (20cm/8in) allowances plus 5cm/2in for each rod pocket. You will also need to allow a little extra width (about 8cm/3¼in) of fabric to allow for two side hems.

POSITIONING THE ROD POCKETS

Decide on the number of folded pockets (four in this case) and subtract from the finished drop of the blind (exclude the surplus at the top and the hem allowance) an allowance of 5cm/ 2in to prevent the pockets from catching on the supporting screw eyes, and to allow them to lie evenly. From the remaining depth, subtract 5cm/2in for each pocket of the blind (20cm/8in for four pockets). Divide the remaining depth by twice the number of pockets (4 × 2 = 8) plus one, to give the distance (d) from the base of the blind to the stitching line of the first rod pocket. The first rod pocket (p) is then folded 2.5cm/1in above this line. Each subsequent fold for each pocket is positioned at twice the distance (2d), plus 5cm/2in, from this point.

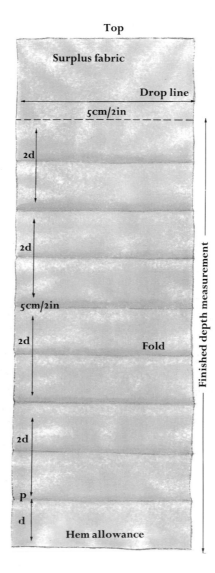

Top
Surplus fabric
Drop line
5cm/2in
2d
2d
5cm/2in
2d
Fold
Finished depth measurement
2d
P
d
Hem allowance

CONSTRUCTING THE BLIND

1 Cut out the blind fabric to the correct width and depth measurements and press and stitch a 2cm/¾in double hem down each side of the blind and at the base.

2 Mark the pocket folds in pencil on the wrong side of the blind, check the distance between the fold lines with a ruler and then fold the blind, right sides together, to form 2.5cm/ 1in deep pockets (i.e. 5cm/2in of fabric, folded in half). Press them in position. Using the folded edges as a guide, machine stitch across the blind 2.5cm/1in in from the fold line to form each rod pocket.

3 If required, insert a lath in the base hem and slipstitch the open ends to secure them.

4 Complete and cord and hang as for a lined Roman blind (see p.79).

MAKING ROMAN BLINDS WITH FRONT POCKETS

In this variation, the rod pockets, normally hidden from view on the back of the blind, are positioned on the front of it. Made from a contrasting fabric, the pockets become an important design feature of the blind. The pocket width is a matter of choice but a good average is about 4cm/1½in. Dowels or flat laths, depending on the width of pocket chosen, are inserted into the pockets to reinforce them. The pockets will, in fact, be on show only when the blind is down; when it is pulled up, they are obscured by the folds.

The choice of white cotton blinds is in keeping with this cool, understated interior, but the use of contrasting rod pockets adds interesting structure and form.

The distinctive grey lines pick up the colour on the surrounding walls, while the lined main fabric allows interesting shadow and light effects.

CONSTRUCTING THE BLIND

Follow the general instructions for a lined Roman blind, up to the point where the lining has been applied (Constructing the blind, step 2, p. 79). Then turn the blind to the right side and mark the pocket positions (left). Pin the lines first, check them for accuracy, and then pencil them in lightly.

1 Cut the pockets out of the contrasting fabric, to twice the required finished depth of the pocket by the finished width of the blind, plus 2cm/¾in hem allowances all round.

2 Fold the pockets in half lengthwise, right sides and long raw edges together, and machine stitch 2cm/¾in in from the edges to form a tube. Trim the allowances and turn the tube inside out (see p. 204) to form the pocket. Press. The stitched line forms the base of the pocket.

3 Working from the base of the blind upwards, pin the stitched base of each pocket on the pencilled pocket line, as shown, and machine stitch to the blind as close to the edge of the pocket as possible (fig. a). Press the pocket over the stitched line, towards the base of the blind, and insert the dowels (fig. b). Slipstitch both ends of the tube to close them.

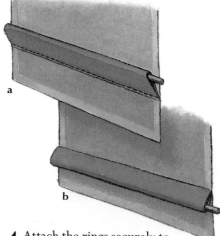

4 Attach the rings securely to the back of the blind, using the stitching line as a guide and sewing through to the pockets.

5 Cord and hang as for a lined Roman blind (see p. 79).

ROLLER BLINDS

These plain blinds draw down from a roller (incorporating a spring mechanism), usually fitted at the top of the window. When lowered, the blind fills the window space with a flat rectangle of fabric; pulled up, it forms a tight cylinder. Roller blinds have the advantage that they obscure little, if any, daylight and, if the window opens inwards, they will fit neatly into the space above. Because the fabric is not on display when the blind is rolled up, the effect is rather austere and some people prefer to use roller blinds as the 'functional' layer of a more decorative window arrangement.

Fabrics

In the earlier part of this century, roller blinds were commonly made from pale brown linen holland. After a brief decline in popularity following the last war, they are back in common use, and many stores now sell fabric created specifically for roller blinds. The fabric, often wider than an ordinary furnishing width, is specially stiffened, with a spongeable surface that makes it particularly appropriate for kitchens and bathrooms. If you prefer, you can use an ordinary furnishing fabric like plain cotton or sail-cloth that you yourself then stiffen. To add an individual touch, you could make your own painted or printed fabric (see pages 36−44).

If the fabric has an all-over pattern, position the repeats so that they fall evenly over the blind. If there is a particularly bold motif or a centred pattern, it should lie symmetrically across the finished blind. As with Roman blinds, accurate measurements and precise cutting are essential if the blind is to hang well.

All of the fabrics displayed above are firmly woven but they still need stiffening before they can be used as roller blinds. The multi-coloured and purple striped samples suit a narrow blind if allowed to run vertically, whereas the wider diagonal stripe and dull purply-blue-grey one need a wider surface area. The minute dog-tooth check and brightly coloured grid of the bottom two samples both benefit from a defining border. Both sides of the black on deep royal blue cotton print are shown − either can be the main blind fabric.

(Overleaf) plain white roller blinds provide the perfect complement to the lush carpeted floor and shiny reflective surfaces of this luxurious bathroom.

This awkwardly shaped window has been covered in a simple, original and effective way. An ordinary roller blind has been fixed to the ceiling so that it hangs at an angle to the window, and the fabric caught halfway down by a pole so that it fits neatly into the lower half of the frame.

MAKING A ROLLER BLIND

I am assuming that you are making the blind from a kit (see right). Roller blinds are simple to make but the fabric must be cut square (see page 201) and the roller cut to the correct length (see below). The instructions here are for a blind made from a pre-stiffened fabric, but if you decide to use ordinary furnishing fabric, you will have to allow extra fabric for the side hems to prevent the edges from fraying. Turn down a 9mm/⅜in hem on the sides of the blind and zigzag stitch over the raw edges. The fabric should then be stiffened with a proprietary fabric stiffener – there are several types available but the easiest to use are the spray-on ones. (It is worth testing the stiffener on a small piece of fabric first to see how the latter responds – glazed fabrics, for example, may lose their sheen).

MATERIALS
- Stiffened blind fabric
- Roller blind kit to the correct length for your window, or longer to be cut to size.
- Masking tape
- Hammer and tin tacks

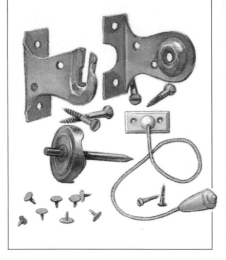

ESTIMATING THE FABRIC

Measure the window carefully (see p. 67). The width of the fabric will be the same as the finished width of the blind (plus 2cm/¾in if making side hems). Measure the drop and add 30cm/12in to the length to allow for a 3cm/1¼in base hem – this will depend on batten size – and to cover the roller completely when the blind is pulled right down.

CUTTING

Lay the fabric on a large flat surface, check the grain is running straight and cut the fabric accurately to the measurements, using a T-square.

CONSTRUCTING THE BLIND

1 Turn up a hem at the base of the fabric wide enough to cover the batten, plus 12mm/½in (fig. a), and zigzag stitch in place.

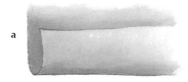

a

2 Cut the roller to the correct size (the finished desired width of the blind).

3 If the roller does not have a guideline, pencil one in to ensure that the fabric hangs level. Tape the top of the blind fabric along the line. Then nail the fabric to the roller at frequent intervals with small tin tacks (fig. b). Remove the tape.

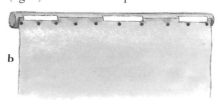

b

4 Cut the batten for the base 12mm/½in shorter than the finished width of the blind. Slot it into the hem (fig. c) and screw the cord holder attachment through the fabric to the batten (fig. d). Slipstitch the ends.

c

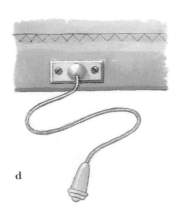

d

FIXING THE BLIND

1 Screw the brackets into the window frame or wall (depending on where the blind is being fixed, see p. 73) ensuring that the blind is positioned centrally on the window. Insert the pin in the end cap of the roller (fig. e), so that the wrong side of the blind faces the window, and the appropriate pin and socket match up.

e

2 Insert the roller into the brackets and pull the blind down and then let it roll back up as far as it will go. Remove it carefully from the brackets, taking care not to release the ratchet. Rewind the blind by hand and then replace it. Check that the blind has sufficient tension by pulling it down again and letting it return to its fully rolled-up position.

AUSTRIAN BLINDS

An Austrian blind differs from a festoon in being permanently ruched only at the base and the soft line of ruched fabric is sometimes emphasized by a frill, which can also extend around the sides of the blind. As the blind is drawn up (on a cording system similar to that of a Roman blind), the fabric ruches further to make deeply scalloped swags across its entire width. The fullness in the width of an Austrian blind – the fabric is normally a generous two to two and a half times the width of the finished blind – is gathered at the top by pencil pleat curtain heading tape.

Austrian blinds look their best in interiors with fairly generous, classical proportions, particularly if the room is graced with elegant architraves and attractive mouldings. On the whole, the blind looks best if the swags on the finished blind are about 30cm/12in wide (75cm/30in on the ungathered fabric) but you may want to adapt the size of the swags to match the divisions in the glazing of the window.

Fabric

Austrian blinds can be made from virtually any fabric, provided it suits the character of the room. The opulent effect of the blind derives as much from the quantity of fabric used as it does from the quality, and even market stall bargains of poplin shirting or plain white ticking can be stunningly successful. When gathered up, the starched ticking, because of its stiffness and weight, has an interesting sculptural quality. With these stiffer fabrics, less inclined by their nature to 'swag', the fullness in the width can be reduced to twice the finished blind width.

Unlined, in fine translucent fabrics like voile, light cotton or even humble cheesecloth, Austrian blinds make excellent sunscreens, diffusing light while offering privacy in daytime.

Precisely because the form of the blind is so decorative, it pays to keep the fabric simple but strong: a plain deep-dyed silk, lined with a contrasting colour that is also used to edge the frill or maybe bright, bold stripes or a textured fabric, such as a plain twill.

As an alternative to a frill on an Austrian blind, you could add a fringe to the base, but be careful not to make the already ornate form of the blind over-fussy. Frills look best with plain or lightly textured fabrics or as a plain edging to those with a simple geometric printed or woven pattern.

Construction

Do not be tempted to skimp on the quantity of fabric or the blind will have a 'mean' appearance. Keep to the rule of two and a half times the finished blind width for lightweight fabrics and twice the width for more heavyweight fabrics.

Although some people suggest attaching the blind heading to a curtain track, I find that it produces a disappointingly baggy effect; securing the head of the blind to a wooden support (see page 73) produces a much better, more professional result.

All these fabrics are ideal for Austrian blinds because they are soft yet crisp, and they form defined folds without sagging. The dark red printed cotton, top right, is suitable for a traditional drawing room. The grey Ikat on its left is an inexpensive Indian cotton with decorative variety in the weave. Below that is a very fluid cream silk noil. The cotton printed in pink with finely engraved figures is based on an 18th-century Toile de Jouy. Finally, the luxurious fabric known as 'pocket' cloth has an almost three-dimensional geometric pattern.

The fringed Austrian blind in the bathroom on the right, in a creamy-yellow textured cotton, adds a touch of frivolity to the otherwise simple lines and clean colours of the room. The bottom of the cording has been set higher up than the usual 5cm/2in (perhaps as much as 15–20cm/6–8in) to create a delightful double-ruched effect.

FRILLS

Frills need not be the fussy edgings that the word tends to invoke, nor do they require extravagant lengths of fabric. Made in a firm fabric such as calico or cambric, a frill has a delightful ridged effect. More firmly edged double or bordered frills both offer the dramatic potential of a clearly defined border rather than an indecisive 'soft' edging.

Frills must be made up separately and then applied to the fabric edge of the main item, such as a blind. Generally twice the fullness of the main item is sufficient, but with very fine fabrics such as muslin or some silks which gather easily and more tightly, three times the fullness might look better. The depth of the frill is a personal choice, but for gathered frills on the base of blinds 7 − 10cm/3 − 4in is usually adequate. Obviously, for smaller or larger items the measurements can be adjusted. Don't forget to allow the usual seam allowances when cutting the frills.

Right, a plain white cotton frill contrasts with a blue glazed cotton. To its left, the main fabric lines and edges a frill of the same blue cotton. Below that, red piping separates the main fabric so that it forms its own border. At the bottom, a double frill enriches a red glazed cotton.

BORDER FRILLS

These double frills are made up from two different fabrics, the main fabric of the item and the border or lining fabric. The border on the base of the front of the frill continues to the back of the frill and acts as a lining for it.

1 For the main fabric cut a strip to the required width (see left) by the finished depth of the frill less depth of border visible from the front plus 4cm/1½in hem allowance. For the border fabric cut to the required width by the finished depth of the frill plus depth of border visible from the front and 4cm/1½in hem allowance.

2 Place the right sides together and stitch along base edge. Turn to right side and press frill with raw edges together, thus forming the border round the lower edge.

3 Finish ends and gather up the frill in the same way as for a plain frill (see opposite).

LINED FRILLS

These frills are simply made up of two pieces of fabric of the same depth that are joined together at the base to form a crisply edged lined frill, one side main fabric and the other lining fabric. If a dark colour is used to back a lighter one, the lining will glow through the front fabric when hanging against the light and produce a pleasing effect when, for example, it is incorporated at the base of an Austrian blind.

1 Cut a strip of main fabric to the required width by the depth of the frill plus 4cm/1½in plus 2cm/¾in seam allowances on each short side. Place lining to fabric with right sides together; stitch one long edge. Turn to the right side and, with raw edges together at the top edge, press the seam on the lower edge.

2 Finish ends and gather up the frill in the same way as for a plain frill (see opposite).

PLAIN DOUBLE FRILL

This type of frill is made from one piece of fabric folded in half lengthways, so that the frill lines itself, with the folded edge as the base. For a long frill join the number of widths of fabric required with flat seams and press them open.

1 Cut strips of fabric to make the required width and to twice the finished depth required plus 2cm/¾in allowances on all sides.

2 On the two short ends of the fabric, press under 2cm/¾in hem allowances. Then with the wrong sides together and with the raw edges matching, fold the frill in half lengthways. Press.

3 Gather up the frill along the raw edges using a gathering foot on the machine. Alternatively, use the largest stitch on the machine and pull up the bobbin thread gently. Work the gathering stitches within the 2cm/¾in seam allowance. (It might be easier to divide the frill into equal sections and gather each section in turn to prevent the gathering threads from breaking when pulled up. Then mark the edge to which the frill is to be attached into the same number of sections and match the sections together.)

4 To finish the frill, slipstitch the open short ends together.

Two of the fabrics on the left have been used for the unlined Austrian blind, below. The densely patterned main fabric is offset by a paler border frill, lined and edged in solid red cotton. The frill has been only lightly gathered so as not to hide the streaked design and crisp red edging.

MAKING AN AUSTRIAN BLIND

The instructions that follow are for making a lined Austrian blind with a frill at the base. If you prefer an unlined blind, simply ignore the references to the lining and neaten the side edges and base with standard double hems. For a blind without a frill, ignore the references to the frill and turn up a standard hem at the base (if the blind is unlined) or join the lining to the three sides of the blind. For a blind with a frill at the sides as well as the base, you can simply follow the instructions here, but start and finish the frill at one side of the blind, either at the finished drop line or just below the heading.

To produce the permanently ruched effect at the base, the blind is made from 50cm/20in more fabric than the finished depth of the blind. The cording of an Austrian blind is similar to that of a Roman blind, but you have to insert a ring on the drop cords to prevent the fabric dropping down to its full length. The instructions for fixing the blind are given on page 73.

MATERIALS
- Fabric and lining
- Timber support (see p. 73)
- Frill
- Piping run
- 2cm/¾in diameter curtain rings
- 7.5cm/3in pencil pleat curtain heading tape (to full ungathered width of blind)
- Sew'n stick Velcro (to finished width of blind)
- Fine polyester cord (for cording the blind)
- Drop weight and cleat
- 9mm/⅜in screw eyes

ESTIMATING THE FABRIC

To calculate the amount of fabric you need, work on the principle of two and a half times the width of the finished blind and 50cm/20in more than the finished depth. You will need a similar quantity of lining fabric (the lining seams must match the main fabric seams, as explained on p. 111), plus fabric for the frill (twice the finished width of the blind by twice the finished depth of the frill, plus seam allowances all round) plus a 5cm/2in strip of fabric, times the width of the fabric, for the piping. You will also need a backing strip of fabric to cover the heading tape (to the finished width of the blind plus the depth of the tape, plus seam allowances).

PREPARATION

Cut out the main fabric and join the widths together, pressing the seams flat. Repeat for the lining. Cut out the strip of fabric to back the heading tape. Cut out and make up the frill (see p. 88) and the piping run (see p. 125).

CONSTRUCTING THE BLIND

1 With right sides and raw edges together, apply the piping run (see p. 125) to the base of the main blind fabric (fig. a).

a

2 Working on the wrong side of the blind, position the top (raw) edge of the frill on the piping fabric at the base of the blind, raw edges together, and stitch as close as possible to the piping cord (fig. b), using a piping or zipper foot on the machine.

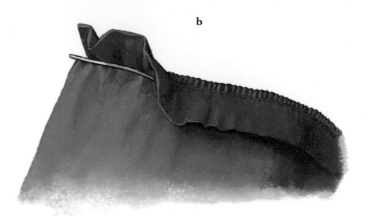

b

3 Place the lining on the fabric, right sides and raw edges together. Leaving the usual hem allowances, stitch the lining and main fabric together along the sides and the base of the blind, making sure that the frill does not get caught up (fig. c). Turn the blind inside out so that the right side of the fabric is on show.

c

MAKING THE SWAGS

1 Lay the blind, wrong side up, on a large flat surface. Working from the base to the top, position the rings, starting with a ring 5cm/2in up from the base of the lining and 5cm/2in in from the side of the blind. From the bottom ring, all vertical rings should be spaced 30cm/12in apart, leaving around 30cm/12in from the last ring to the finished drop line 3cm/1¼in down from the straight raw edge at the top of the blind.

2 To determine the spacing between the columns of rings, which will give the fullness in each swag, divide the number of swags required into the *ungathered* width of the blind (less 10cm/4in).

3 Then measure the vertical and horizontal positions of the rings using two rulers (fig. d). Where they meet sew a ring, at its top, through both fabric and lining. Measuring and sewing are done as one step.

d

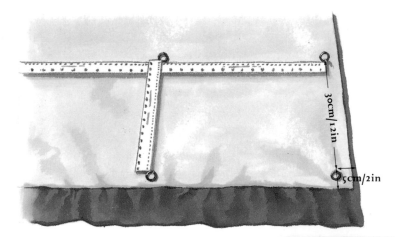

ADDING THE HEADING

1 When the rings are stitched in position, measure the finished drop from the top of the frill, add 45cm/17½in and mark this distance across the top of the blind, using pins. Press over the top edge of the blind at the line of pins to make a 3cm/1¼in deep turning and trim off any surplus fabric and lining.

2 Stitch the pencil pleat curtain heading tape to the back of the blind (see p. 113) and pull up the tape to the required finished width of the blind, before securing it (see p. 95).

3 Stitch one half of the Velcro to the long side of the backing strip and then press over a 2cm/¾in hem all round the strip. Place the wrong side of the backing strip over the heading tape and slipstitch it to secure it. (Be careful that neither the heading nor the gathering enlarges or decreases while you are stitching.)

FIXING AND CORDING

1 Cover the support as shown on p. 73, using a Velcro heading. Insert a screw eye under the support in line with each vertical row of cording rings (fig. e) and insert an extra screw eye 3cm/1¼in from the last one, at the side where the strings hang.

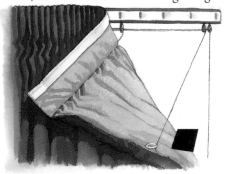

f

2 Thread the strings through each ring as for a Roman blind (see p. 79). Measure out the finished drop of the blind on a large flat surface, lay the blind on it face down and, with someone holding the blind heading, pull the strings simultaneously so that the blind ruches until the base is on the marked drop line. Mark the strings in pencil at this point, just beyond the last screw eye and secure a ring at this mark to all the strings. (It will catch on the screw eye when the blind is lowered, ensuring that the blind does not descend further than the finished drop and retains its characteristic ruched swags at the base.) Trim the cords evenly and thread a drop weight, securing the strings with a firm knot (fig. f). Fix the blind as shown on p. 73, fig. e.

FESTOON BLINDS

Similar in many ways to Austrian blinds, festoons have extra fullness in the depth and the width, and the fabric is permanently ruched from top to base on an integral set of gathering cords.

Most of the style characteristics of an Austrian blind apply to a festoon, if not more so. Festoons are intrinsically decorative and the ruching of the additional fabric makes them even more elaborate and extravagant. For this reason, the fabric and the form of the blind should be kept as simple as possible. Although you do see festoon blinds with frills at the base or even all round the blind, I think they look better unadorned.

Where festoon blinds are chosen to form part of a fully dressed window arrangement, it is as well to take particular care not to make the whole effect too fussy. If a festoon is to play the role of a sunscreen within a more elaborate scheme of draped curtains, it is better to keep a unifying theme throughout. An arrangement, say, in translucent, off-white or cream textured fabric, with a dark blue border on the curtains and cords of the same blue within the festoon, would help prevent the scheme from dominating the window, and possibly the room as well. For a small window, a simpler version of a festoon could be made with just one lightly ruched swag contained within a surrounding border of plain fabric.

Fabric

The earliest festoon blinds were muslin sunscreens used to protect more valuable draperies. Today, the most successful festoons echo this simplicity. Chinese silk, lustrous Egyptian cotton or even a thoroughly modern fabric, like translucent rip-stop nylon (see page 25), make an ideal choice. Heavier fabrics can be used, but are best left unlined as the extra weight tends to make operating the blind difficult. As with Austrian blinds, stiffer fabrics such as starchy cotton duck or ticking produce more sculptural swags and require less fabric, but beware of skimping on the quantity, which will alter the character of the swags and make the blinds look mean. Boldly patterned fabrics are best avoided as they can be overpowering when combined with the already ornate form of the blind.

Construction

The seam lines of the joined widths of fabric, and the points between them, provide the positioning lines for the gathering cords which are a decorative, as well as structural, element of the blind. You may want to bear in mind how these relate to any glazing bars in the window and adapt the formula for the number of swags and their spacing to suit a particular window. Ideally the finished width of each swag (the distance between the vertical cords on the finished blind) should be between 20cm/8in and 30cm/12in (50cm/20in and 75cm/30in at the sewing stage), but you could adapt this so that the cording lines fall in the best position on the window, balancing them across the width of the blind.

Richness of texture and finish combined with simplicity of design characterize the festoon samples displayed above. The bunched ones at the top are all of very fine translucent silk, which ruches beautifully. The red and grey checks and thin grey stripes to the left and right of this group are glazed pattern printed onto plain cotton, which produces interesting effects on impressive sculptural folds. The heavy texture of the charcoal grey printed cotton produces stiffer, rounded ruches.

Festoon blinds are more often noticeable for the depth and contours of their ruches than for their structural qualities. But the structural workings of the blind on the right are clearly visible: the closely pleated top and sides catch the eye along with the ridged seams enclosing the gathering cords, while the ruches lie neat and flat.

MAKING AN UNLINED FESTOON BLIND

In festoon blinds, the fabric is permanently ruched on gathering cords that are encased in French seams at the joins between the fabric widths, in the side hems and in artificially constructed seams at the mid-points between the fabric joins. To produce the gathered effect, the cords are the length of the finished blind (plus an allowance for knotting the cord) while the fabric itself is twice the finished drop of the blind. The fullness in the width is taken up by applying pencil pleat gathering tape to the heading (see below).

The instructions here are for an unlined festoon without a frill but if you want to add a lining and a frill, you can use the instructions for them contained in Austrian blinds (making the necessary adjustments to the fabric estimates). The instructions for covering and fixing the support for the blind are given on page 73. The blind is corded like a Roman blind (see page 79).

MATERIALS
- Fabric
- Timber support (see p. 73)
- 9mm/⅜in diameter curtain rings
- 7.5cm/3in pencil pleat curtain heading tape (to full ungathered width of blind)
- Sew'n stick Velcro (to finished width of blind)
- 3mm/⅛in polyester cord (for gathering the blind)
- Fine polyester cord (for cording the blind)
- Drop weight and cleat
- 9mm/⅜in screw eyes

ESTIMATING THE FABRIC

For the fabric width, allow for two to two and a half times the finished blind width. For the length, allow twice the finished length of the blind. An offcut can be used to cover the timber support for the blind (see p. 73) and to make a backing strip for the heading tape (see Austrian blinds, p. 90).

CONSTRUCTING THE BLIND

1 Cut out the fabric widths. Using French seams (see p. 204) join the fabric widths, wrong sides together, stitching only the first part of the seam at this stage.

2 On the wrong side, press a 4cm/1½in double hem on each side of the blind. To determine the position of the gathers, measure the distance from the folded edge of the side hem to the first seam. At the half-way point, press the fabric in half lengthways, with right sides together, to form the stitching guide for inserting the gathering cord (fig. a).

a

3 The first gathering cord is inserted at the side hem. On the wrong side of the blind, machine stitch 2.5cm/1in in from the side hem edge.

4 Place a length of 3mm/⅛in cord underneath the hem edge next to the first row of stitching. Knot the cord at the edge of the fabric and, using a piping foot, stitch down the blind, close to the cord, encasing it in the hem (fig. b). Because the cord is shorter than the fabric, you must gather the fabric onto the cord behind the machine foot as you stitch. Tie a knot in the other end of the cord when stitching is complete.

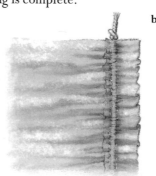

b

5 Complete the French seams by refolding the fabric, with right sides together, and, at each seam and each mid-point fold (fig. c), enclose a length of cord, tied in the same way as before, gathering the fabric as you stitch. Tie a knot at the end of each cord after you have inserted it.

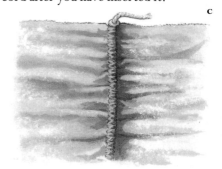

c

6 It is important that the lower ends of the cords are firmly secured by the 2cm/¾in double hem at the base of the blind. Sew over and over across the cord so that it is secured under the stitch lines (fig. d).

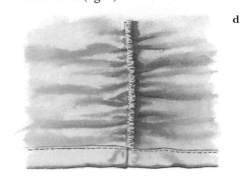

d

RUCHING THE BLIND

1 In order to pull up each cord to the required length for the finished drop of the blind, divide your finished blind width by the number of swags. This will give you the distance between the cords. Working on a table, position two adjacent cords parallel at this distance and weight them to keep them in place, with the lower end of the cord at the table edge, as shown, allowing the swag to fall over the edge (fig. e). Measure the drop of the swag from the table edge to the deepest point. Subtract this amount from the finished drop.

2 Place the blind, wrong side up, flat on the table and pull up each cord in turn to reach the required blind length, plus 2cm/¾in, keeping the last 7.5cm/3in (including the 2cm/¾in) of fabric flat at the top. 6cm/2½in down from the top of the blind (7.5cm/3in down from the raw edge), pull each cord through the fabric by splitting the hem in which it is encased. Knot each cord to hold it temporarily (fig. f).

3 Press over the 2cm/¾in hem at the top of the blind and apply the curtain heading tape to the top of the blind (see p. 113), catching in the tops of the cords with the lower line of stitching. Pull the heading tape up to the required width and secure the strings (fig. g) and cover the tape (see p. 91 *Adding the heading*, step 3).

COMPLETING THE BLIND

1 Check that the ruching is level and even on the cords before attaching the rings. It is easiest if two people hold the cords in position and stretch the fabric between them, levelling the gathering.

2 Attach the rings as for Austrian blinds (see p. 91), at roughly 30cm/12in intervals up each cord, with the first row of rings 5cm/2in from the base of the blind. Sew the rings through the gathering cords (fig. h).

3 Complete in the same way as an Austrian blind (see p. 91).

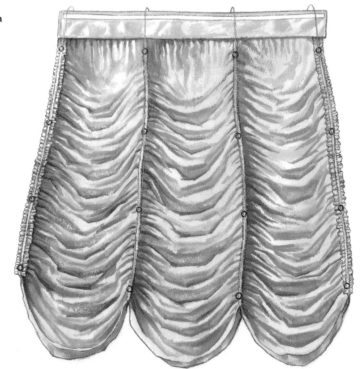

CURTAINS

The French were the first to exploit the decorative potential of curtains, in the second half of the seventeenth century. As symmetry became a desirable feature of fashionable interiors, pairs of curtains began to be used for the first time instead of single drapes, and pelmets were invented to conceal rods and rings. The single pull-up curtains and the forerunners of today's Austrian blinds described on page 69 were also much in vogue; although we now call them blinds, at the time they were thought of as curtains.

At the end of the eighteenth century the 'French rod' curtain made its appearance. It caught on all through Europe during the nineteenth century, to the virtual eclipse of the pull-up variety. The rod was in fact two rods, overlapping in the middle and fitted with cords to open and close the curtain – similar to the modern curtain track. It was almost invariably covered by some form of drapery or pelmet, which became elaborate, often excessively so, during the course of the nineteenth century. Lavish amounts of fabric were employed and much use was made of trimmings – braids, fringes, ropes and tassels. The practical accessories of curtaining, such as finials, rods and brackets, also took on decorative importance. Tie-bands in particular, both metal and fabric, were extremely popular; as well as holding back the curtains, they made it possible to achieve really grand draping effects.

This century has seen a reaction to the heavy and sometimes over-exuberant designs of the last. The trend has been towards less weighty arrangements, the most successful of which have preserved the elegance of the best old designs while eliminating the excess.

Planning a curtain arrangement

The choice of curtain fabrics and styles today is unparalleled. Curtains can be made to suit any type of window. They may be of any length, lined or unlined, full or taut, and they can either hang freely or be draped more formally. The way they hang partly depends on the heading, which can be a simple gathered top, or pencil pleats producing a sleek, linear effect or a more formal French pleat.

It is possible to have 'dress curtains', which do not have to close; they are there simply for show, to frame and embellish the window, and can be used in combination with shutters or blinds. But most curtains serve a practical purpose: they give privacy, keep out unwanted light, help to exclude draughts and retain heat. When making your decisions about the weight and opacity of the fabric, the

In this many-layered arrangement, the potentially old-fashioned use of velvet for the dress curtains has been offset and updated by the asymmetry of the design and by the cool feel of the roller blinds.

The arrangement relies for its effect upon the ruched lines of the fabric rather *than on voluptuous cloth. The finishing touches – gold braid edging both dress curtains and sheers, tassel braid on the base of the swags and gold tie-bands – are subtle rather than overwhelming, with the whole giving an agreeable impression of understated grandeur.*

fullness of the drapes and whether to have a lining, you need to consider these practical aspects. But not at the expense of appearance: once you have chosen your fabric (see pages 11–25), you need to plan the entire design, including the finishing touches, to suit the room in which the curtains will hang – its proportions, its colour scheme and its mood (see pages 46–66).

I think it worth repeating here that one of the simplest ways of enlivening a plain curtain and of making it personal is to add a border (see page 28). Flat braids were once the traditional curtain decoration, placed along the leading edges and often also along the base. Borders along the leading edge can be either flat, wadded slightly, or piped and frilled (see page 88).

If you live in an old house or flat, you may wish to find fabrics that are as close as possible to the original style of curtaining. Most of the larger fabric companies have an archive library that will give you some idea of the fabrics and patterns around at a particular period. Public libraries have books that illustrate both contemporary and antique fabrics. There are also specialist suppliers (see page 211) of antique curtains, fabric and trimmings.

The following pages, 100–7, discuss types of curtain lining, the choice of poles and tracks and other curtain accessories. If you have not yet decided on the style of your curtains and how they will hang, I hope you will find this information useful. Instructions for making up curtains in different heading styles are given on pages 108–23; finally, on pages 124–40, I discuss the shaping and finishing touches, including pelmets, valances, loose drapes and swags and tails, as well as trimmings such as tie-bands.

The hand-painted calico drapes on the right have been tailor-made for a very individual interior. Made to bunch stiffly on the floor, the curtains have had thinned-down emulsion paint streaked across them, producing a marbled look in perfect keeping with the paint effects on the walls.

The pillar-like quality of the stone-coloured curtains is helped by the fact that they do not close – the calico blind is the functional part of this arrangement. Even the heavy rope tie-bands are there to add colour rather than significantly to modify the impressive vertical lines of the drapes.

In the room below, the deliberately casual folding and draping of the heavy cream cotton curtains is in pleasing contrast with the solid pelmet arrangement above them. By fitting a soft valance under a shaped wooden pelmet, a formal focal point for the curtains has been created. The overall effect is gratifying, not distracting from the room's other attractive shapes and textures.

LININGS

There are five main practical reasons for lining a curtain or blind. First, the lining protects the main fabric, reduces everyday wear and tear and shields the fabric from the sun. (The sun's rays will, over time, fade most fabrics and eventually rot some: silk is especially vulnerable.) Second, applying a lining helps the curtain or blind to hang and drape better, by adding weight to the main fabric and giving the impression of extra fullness. Third, the lining encloses all the hems and gives a neater edge. Fourth, some linings effectively block out all light coming through a window. Last, lining and interlining make curtains more draughtproof and give a room some insulation. All lined and interlined curtains are best dry-cleaned.

Types of lining

Standard curtain lining is soft cotton sateen with a slightly shiny finish, usually inferior in quality to the furnishing fabric it will back. Colours are traditionally cream or white – ideal for backing light-coloured fabrics or for deflecting heat, but otherwise contributing little to the look of the window. There are coloured sateen linings available, and these come in a range of fade-proof colours that have a positive impact on window arrangements (see page 63).

Linings intended to shut out all light are known as blackout linings, the most effective of which is Roclon blackout. This fabric is not actually black, but cream or white. With a soft, rubbery feel on one side and a smooth outer surface, it is too heavy to line lightweight fabrics. It is also best used behind fabrics in a solid colour, because its opaqueness dulls surface pattern and obscures any translucency in the main fabric: I would never use Roclon blackout to line fabrics with a pale or subtle design. Another blackout lining, Italian blackout, is a heavy black cotton fabric that can be used on its own as a blind or as a backing for dark-coloured curtains or blinds.

Interlining is a soft, loose-woven, blanket-like layer sandwiched between the lining and the main fabric. As well as offering extra insulation, it can alter a curtain's appearance, softening the folds and making the surface of the fabric feel more luxurious. Since interlining is placed between two other fabrics, widths are joined with a flat seam to keep bulk to a minimum. Curtains that have been interlined must be hung from a strong track or a well-secured pole.

Joining lining to fabric

Standard lining widths match those of furnishing fabrics: 122cm/ 48in and 137cm/54in. European measurements are usually 130cm/ 51in. When joining lining widths, the seams should align with the fabric seam lines. Otherwise the lining seams will be visible through fine or very pale fabric viewed against the light.

When working with fabrics and linings of different widths, calculate the overall width measurement of the fabric when joined, and make sure all the lining widths add up to the same total. If you use part widths, place them on the back edges (see page 111, fig. a).

Red sateen

Yellow

Peach sateen

Curtain linings have to be 'locked in' at the seams (see page 112, step 4), so that the main fabric and lining lie together across the curtain and do not billow apart. The lining hem should also be caught to the main fabric hem with daisy chain stitches (see page 202).

Detachable linings

The advantages of a detachable lining are flexibility (see page 62) and easy washing. You make a detachable lining to the same width as your curtains but 5cm/2in shorter. The raw top edge is encased between the two sides of special detachable lining tape (see page 106) and the finished lining made to fit the exact width of the curtain heading. You then insert the hooks in the lining into the lower pocket of the curtain heading tape, preferably in the spaces between the hooks that fit the curtains to the track. You still need to catch a detachable lining with a stitch at intervals down the sides of the curtain, to prevent curtain and lining from parting untidily.

The dozen or so lining fabrics below span a perhaps unexpectedly wide range, both in terms of colours and weights – ranging from the heaviest cotton 'bump' to the lightest nylon sarill.

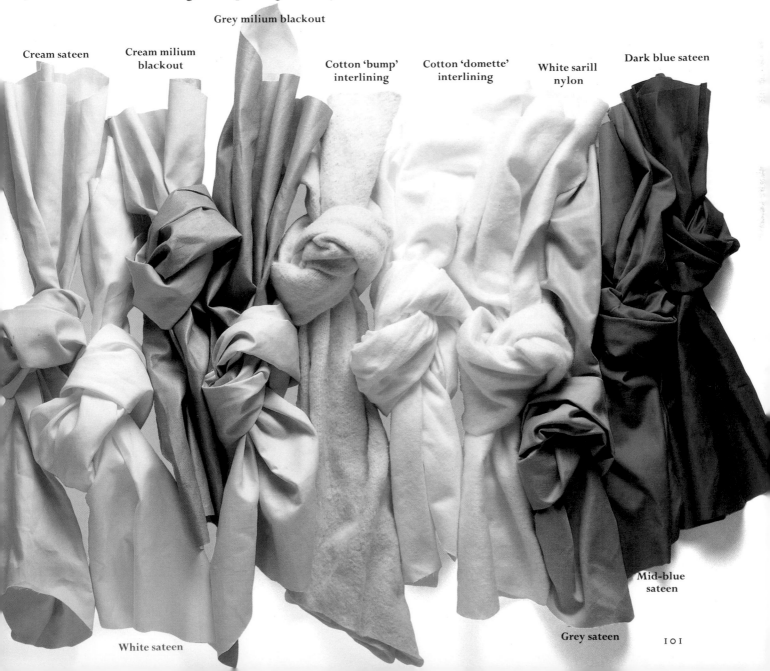

Grey milium blackout

Cream sateen

Cream milium blackout

Cotton 'bump' interlining

Cotton 'domette' interlining

White sarill nylon

Dark blue sateen

Mid-blue sateen

Grey sateen

White sateen

POLES & TRACK

Poles are intended to be seen and track is not; which you select is largely a matter of personal preference. To help you choose, either go and look at poles and track on display in a large haberdashery department or study the illustrated booklets produced by some of the larger manufacturers.

Track should be entirely concealed by the curtain heading when the curtains are closed, remaining unobtrusive when they are drawn back to the sides. Poles, on the other hand, are unashamedly decorative. The top of the curtain hangs either just below the pole, partly covering the rings, or right underneath the rings; in either case the pole is visible. If you are planning to have a pelmet, a valance or a swag and tail arrangement, you need a track.

Poles

Originally known as 'cornice poles' because they were fixed just below the cornice, these solid wooden or brass poles were popular in the nineteenth century and are currently back in fashion. The curtains hook into small metal rings in the base of the wooden rings encircling the pole.

Old cornice poles can still be found, but tend to be expensive. New ones are mostly made of brass or of natural wood that can be polished, stained or painted. They come in a wide range of lengths and diameters, and are usually supplied with all the necessary fitments. You can, of course, use almost anything you fancy as a pole as long as it is the right shape and length, especially for dress curtains that are not going to be drawn. Certain metal shops will make poles to your own design.

With most poles, the curtains have to be drawn by hand, but some corded ones are available. These are hollow and therefore very lightweight, with a rounded front concealing an inner track system that incorporates the cording mechanism. The 'ring slides' look like complete rings but are in fact only half the diameter; they glide along, efficiently operated by the cord system. Corded poles come in various wood finishes from pine to teak, as well as in plastic and metal finishes, and most of them are available either plain or decoratively ribbed.

Fixing poles to the wall

Pole brackets protrude from the wall, supporting the pole from underneath. There should be about 10cm/4in between the outer edge of the bracket and the inner edge of the finial; the outermost curtain ring sits in this space. You fix brackets about 15cm/6in out from the window frame on each side, by means of circular metal plates with screw holes, which fit flush to the wall and are concealed by the brackets. In the front of the brackets there are small screws, which, once the pole is in place, are screwed into the pole to secure it. You can also support poles on brass or metal brackets that fit in the wooden architrave of the window.

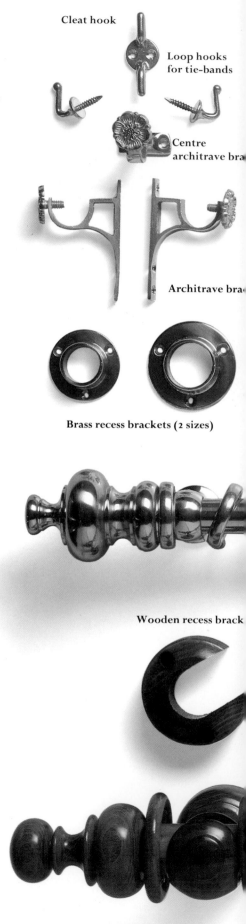

Cleat hook

Loop hooks for tie-bands

Centre architrave bra

Architrave bra

Brass recess brackets (2 sizes)

Wooden recess brack

Specialist manufacturers supply brackets that allow poles to go round corners, for a bay window. These are straight poles, with curved arms forming junctions for the straight pieces. Some manufacturers will bend brass poles for a bay, if ordered specially.

Café rods

These small brass rods, narrower in diameter than most poles and often without rings, come in the same range of finishes as ordinary poles. They are designed to take lightweight slot-head or scalloped curtains (see pages 119–21). Many versions are telescopic and extend to the required length, or you can have a rod cut to size. They are face-fixed into special brackets at the sides of a window recess or to the window frame itself.

Illustrated here is an assorted selection of poles and café rods, with a variety of brackets and finials.

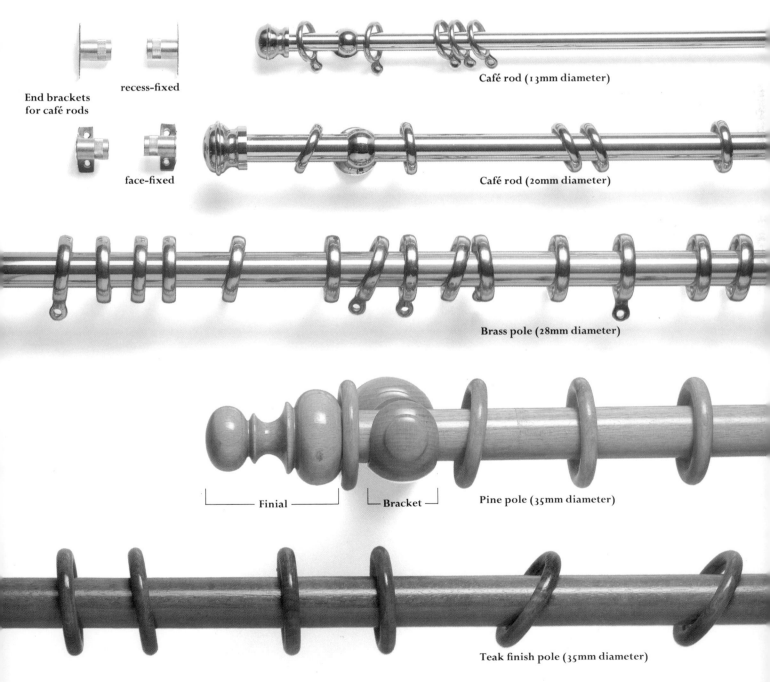

recess-fixed

End brackets for café rods

Café rod (13mm diameter)

face-fixed

Café rod (20mm diameter)

Brass pole (28mm diameter)

Finial — **Bracket** — **Pine pole (35mm diameter)**

Teak finish pole (35mm diameter)

Track

Track is made of plastic or metal and comes in many widths, lengths, weights and types of finish. Many manufacturers grade their track as being suitable for lightweight, medium or heavyweight curtains. I prefer and almost always use metal track, although more expensive, because it is stronger and longer-lasting than plastic, which is only really suitable for lightweight curtains.

Plastic track is usually white or off-white. Metal track is often stove-enamelled in white, cream or a wood effect. You either buy the length of track you need (or a bit longer – it can easily be cut to size), or extending track. This is sold for a particular length-range and you then pull it out to fit. When calculating how much you need, remember to allow enough at the sides of the window for the curtains to be drawn well back from the glass – 25cm/10in is standard, but you could leave anything from 15–40cm/6–16in, depending on the space available and the bulk of the fabric. A stiff linen, for instance, or a heavy slub cotton needs far more room than the same amount of calico.

Both plastic and metal track can be bent to fit bay or bow windows. The plastic type is pliable enough to curve round, provided it is carefully fixed to the wall in the right places. These are indicated in the instructions that come with the track. Metal track is either straight or specially designed to be curved. The latter type has to be bent at critical points around the bay, with the aid of a piece of metal that slots into the track. This is not an easy job: although a bending set and detailed instructions are included, I recommend getting professional help.

Most track comes ready corded (separate cording systems are available for track designed to be curved, but they require professional installation). Corded track is convenient and also saves the leading edge of the curtains from becoming grubby with use. The cording system is designed for two curtains but can be adjusted for a

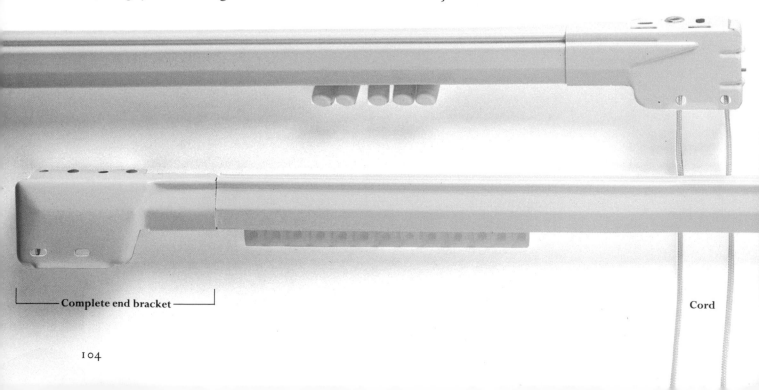

Complete end bracket

Cord

one-way draw if you have a single curtain or drape. Ideally the track should overlap in the centre to prevent curtains gaping in the middle when closed. Most track now has an 'overlap master runner' already built in, otherwise overlap arms are obtainable separately.

Fixing track to the wall

Each length of track comes packaged with fittings for securing it, and instructions and fixing details are also usually enclosed. However, I strongly recommend that you use a professional to fix track, or at least that you take expert advice. There are so many variables to consider, from the state of the plaster to the weight of the curtains.

Track can be fixed directly to the wall or ceiling (see page 66 for possible problems with ceiling-fixing). If the plaster is somewhat patchy, rather than fix track to the wall it might be better to face-fix it to a wooden support, or top-fix it under the wood of a pelmet board (see page 131). Alternatively, track can be hidden altogether behind a fascia board.

The track brackets are fixed at both ends and in the middle, according to the instructions supplied with the track. If the track is curved around a bay or is longer than 1m/3ft, you need extra support brackets, especially with plastic track. To find out exactly how many you need, give the dimensions of your bay to the person selling the brackets.

Should you need to clear a heavy architrave or protruding window sill, you can get special brackets that bring the track further away from the wall. This is also useful if you want curtains to hang clear of blinds already at the window. One type of extension bracket allows you to combine two separate tracks – a lightweight one for nets or sheers, say, and a medium or heavyweight one for the main curtain arrangement.

Special valance track that carries the valance in front of the curtain can be clipped on the main curtain track (see page 132).

Most track comes in kit form complete with everything you need; end and centre brackets, overlap arms, a cording system, curtain hooks and gliders. All these parts are also obtainable separately.

Gliders are usually made of plastic, although metal runners are still found on heavier-duty track. Some tracks come ready fitted with runners; on others you have to slide them on yourself, but this is not difficult. Gliders run in a channel at the base of some types of track, making it even neater and more unobtrusive. Runners are available with double hooks, enabling you to hang the lining separately (see p.101).

Plastic gliders

Standard bracket

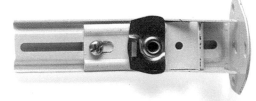

Long bracket for projecting track

White metal track

Overlap arm (master of two)

HEADINGS & HOOKS

The curtain is attached to the track or pole by means of a heading, which is the decorative top of the curtain. These days most people make curtain headings with the help of heading tapes, although some types of heading are best stitched by hand.

Heading tapes

These strips of fabric, bought by the metre, contain pockets and have an integral drawstring running through them. After sewing the heading tape on to the curtain, you pull up the drawstring to gather the fullness of the fabric in a decorative way. Curtain hooks are slotted into the pockets of the tape, then hooked on to the runners of a track or the rings of a pole.

Most types of heading tape take a standard one-prong hook, made in nylon, plastic, brass or aluminium. Plastic ones are fine for sheers or lightweight curtains, but metal hooks are preferable, especially

Gathering tape 2.5cm/1in deep
For 2–2½ times finished length.
This tape gives a shallow, random gathered heading suitable for informal or unlined curtains, especially at small windows. The tape has only one pocket for hooks, but is usually positioned at least 4cm/1½in below the top of the curtain, to conceal the track or partly hide the rings on a pole.

Pencil pleat tape 8cm/3¼in deep
For 2½–3 times finished length.
This popular heading tape gives stiff, regular, close-packed pleats. Its three rows of pockets allow you to adjust the height of the curtain: hooks in the middle or lower row will hide a track when the curtains are drawn, whereas hooks in the top row allow curtains to hang from rings and reveal the pole.

White plastic hooks   Brass one-prong hooks

Lining tape 2.5cm/1in deep
For 1½–2 times finished length.
This special tape is made for detachable linings (see p.101). It splits into two halves or 'skirts' to hold the lining firmly in place, enclosing the top raw edge. Hooks go through the lining tape and the curtain tape. Alternatively, you could use ordinary gathering tape and make a detachable lining like an unlined curtain.

Net tape 8cm/3¼in deep
For 2½–3 times finished length.
This fine, lightweight nylon tape is made for net or sheer fabrics; it forms pencil pleats, with only one row of pockets. If the tape is to cover a track or thread onto a stretch wire or café rod, sew it with the pockets at the bottom. If you want to suspend the sheer below a track, sew the tape with the pocket at the top.

Pin hooks   Sew-on hooks

The one-prong plastic and brass hooks above are intended for use with heading tapes, while the pin hooks and sew-on hooks below are for hand-sewn headings.

for heavier curtains. When inserting hooks into heading tape, remember to put them in the right pocket, depending on whether your curtains are going to hang from a track or a pole (see pencil pleat tape, opposite).

The heading you choose for your curtains dictates how much fabric you will need. Different heading tapes gather up varying amounts of fabric and significantly affect the appearance of the finished curtain. On the whole cotton tapes are preferable, as they give a firmer pleat and the cords both knot and unknot more easily. To attach and gather the various heading tapes, see pages 113, 118–23. Four of the most popular varieties are illustrated opposite.

Hand-stitched headings

More time-consuming than tapes, hand-stitched headings have many advantages, especially when used on formal headings such as French pleats (see page 114) or goblet pleats (see page 122). They are stiffer and can be stitched invisibly, which gives them a better, more professional finish. They can take heavy, interlined curtains and allow the interlining to be taken up to the top without sagging.

Hand-sewn headings need a special type of hook known as a pin hook. Pin hooks have sharp prongs that are pushed into the underside of each pleat on curtains without heading tape. Alternatively you can use solid brass sew-on hooks for hand-sewn headings and heavy curtains (see left).

WEIGHTING CURTAINS

Weights concealed inside the hems of curtains help the curtains to drape better, by holding them down and keeping the hems straight and even. Weights make a significant difference to the way some fabrics hang – particularly to heavy linens, which tend to be rather inflexible, and to lightweight, loosely woven fabrics.

You can buy either round or rectangular lead weights. The round ones generally have two holes in the centre, rather like buttons, so that you can sew them directly to the fabric. They are sewn inside the curtain hem, a weight at each mitred corner and one at each width or half width across the hem. Rectangular weights have no holes and cannot be sewn directly to fabric: for a neater result, I prefer to encase them in pieces of lining fabric (see right) and slipstitch these 'pockets' in place at each fabric join (see page 112, fig. b).

You can also buy 'lead-weight tape', which is a length of weighted chain sold in metre lengths or measured off a roll; it comes in three weights, the lightweight one being especially useful for sheers (see page 123).

MAKING 'POCKETS'

Cut two pieces of scrap material and join them with a line of machine stitching along the base. Then sew double lines of stitching at right angles to the first line, all the way across the joined pieces, making channels each wide enough for one weight. Slot the weights into the channels, one horizontal line at a time. Then sew a double line of stitching to secure and repeat, until a grid of stitch lines forms pockets that encase the weights. You then cut off pockets as you need them.

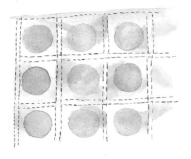

MAKING UP CURTAINS

The following pages, 110–23, set out all the processes involved in making up curtains. The first set of instructions, on making lined curtains with a pencil pleat heading, is the most detailed, with procedures common to making many types of curtain included, such as joining fabric widths and locking in lining to fabric. The next sequence, on making up curtains with a French pleat heading, includes interlining and hand-stitching the heading. Subsequent instructions do not repeat these procedures, so where necessary you will be referred back to earlier pages for fuller details.

Basic techniques – such as making hems and mitring corners – are grouped together at the end of the book on pages 200–5.

The pale curtains in the room below are given style and elegance by a French pleat heading. The curtains have been caught back formally to reveal undercurtains in lightweight blue cotton. A lath and fascia covering the curtain rail, combined with simple roller blinds for daytime use, complete the fully dressed effect, while a cream border on the leading edges of the undercurtains gives a trompe l'oeil *impression of yet another layer underneath.*

The exceptionally deep pencil pleat headings on the right, set high up above the windows, have been achieved by putting two 7.5cm/3in tapes one under the other. A yellow glazed cotton border runs round all four sides of the unlined butter muslin, adding definition and a subtle touch of colour. Informal tie-bands restrain the drapes at the level of the cross-bars, while fabric bunching on the ground balances the elegant window proportions.

MAKING A PENCIL PLEAT HEADING

The instructions on the next three pages are for making lined curtains with a pencil pleat heading. Pencil pleats are so-called because the narrow vertical folds, formed when the pulled tape gathers the curtain into the heading, are shaped like pencils. Standard pencil pleat heading tape (see page 106) is 8cm/3¼in wide and comes in different weights, to suit either lightweight and sheer fabrics or heavy velvets and linen. The tape has three rows of pockets for the curtain hooks. If the curtains are to hang from a track, position the hooks on the middle row so that most of the track is concealed. If the curtains are to hang from a pole, apply the tape as close to the top of the curtain as possible, with the hooks inserted in the top row of pockets.

Joining the widths of fabric and applying the tape are done by machine, but otherwise the method I describe mostly involves hand sewing. This is the professional way and gives a better finish, I think, when compared with the entirely machine-made, 'bagged' curtains, in which the lining and fabric are joined on three sides, then turned to right side out and treated as one.

MATERIALS

- Curtain and lining fabric
- Pencil pleat heading tape the length of the ungathered fabric
- Curtain weights
- Curtain hooks

A simple pencil pleat heading gathers the curtain fabric, left, into multiple, fluid folds. The curtains are caught back into crescent shapes which partly cover the outer two windows but leave the central door free to open and close.

ESTIMATING THE FABRIC

First measure the window (see p. 67), to give the finished width and length of the curtain. For a pencil pleat heading, you need $2\frac{1}{2}$ times the finished width of fabric.

If you are making a pair of curtains, and an odd number of fabric widths is needed in total, cut the odd width in half lengthways and join each half width on to the outside, or back edge, of each curtain. Always place a full width at the leading edge of the curtain (fig. a).

Add an extra 30cm/12in to the finished length of the curtains for a pencil pleat heading, to allow for a double 10cm/4in hem at the base and a 10cm/4in turnover at the top. (This turnover will eventually be trimmed to about 3cm/1¼in, but it is a good idea to start off with more fabric than you need.) Multiply this 'working drop' by the number of fabric widths to work out how much fabric you need.

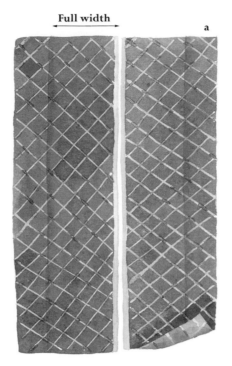

Full width

a

CUTTING THE FABRIC

Cut out the number of fabric widths required, allowing extra for pattern repeats if necessary (see p. 200).

It is essential that the fabric is cut straight and accurately, or the curtain will not hang evenly (fig. b). If possible, cut along a withdrawn weft thread (see p. 201). Mark the top of each width of fabric with a notch, so that any pile or shading will be matched across the widths. (For more detailed cutting instructions, also see p. 201.)

b

JOINING THE WIDTHS

Matching up any pattern, machine stitch the necessary number of fabric widths for each curtain, right sides together, using a straight 2.5cm/1in seam (fig. c). Press the seams open. Trim any surplus off the selvedges, particularly if they have any writing or symbols, which might show when the curtain is hanging.

Some fabrics tend to pucker, in which case clipping the seams will help the cloth to lie flat (see p. 205).

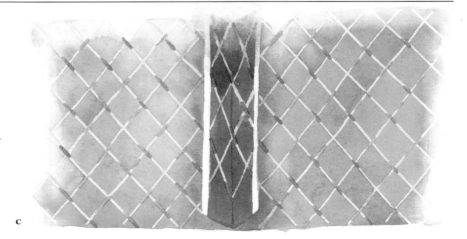

c

CUTTING & JOINING LINING WIDTHS

Cut the lining fabric into the same number of widths as the main fabric (I find this easier than trying to calculate the finished width of the lining and cutting it to fit exactly within the edges of the curtain). You can easily trim off any surplus as the back edges are pressed under.

If you have chosen standard lining fabric, try to buy it in the same width as the curtain fabric. If the lining, or the fabric, is a special width or you have assembled the fabric yourself,

make the lining 6cm/2½in narrower overall than the joined fabric widths.

The working drop of the lining should be the finished curtain drop plus 20cm/8in, allowing for a double 5cm/2in base hem (see p. 203) and for a 10cm/4in turnover at the top.

Join lining widths as for the main curtain fabric and press the seams flat. Press over a double 5cm/2in hem at the base of the lining and machine stitch in place (fig. d) along all the joined widths.

d

JOINING LINING & FABRIC

Lay the main fabric, wrong side up, on a table or other flat surface, with the base nearest to you and the leading edge parallel to one side of the table. (You can use the edge of the table as a guide to make sure that the hems are all straight.)

Always work from the bottom of the curtain to the top so that the fabric is kept flat for accurate measuring. You need to be able to move the fabric easily across the table without getting it bunched up, so aim to do as much as you can to the area of curtain on the table before moving on to the next section.

1 Press a double turning of 10cm/4in at the base hem along the entire width of the main fabric (see p. 203). Open out the fabric and press a 5cm/2in turning along the leading edge before opening out again (fig. a).

2 Mitre the corner (see p. 203) and fix a weight into it before sewing it up (fig. b). Slipstitch the double base hem in place a section at a time (stopping short of the opposite corner to be mitred), then herringbone stitch along the leading edge (fig. c).

3 Place the lining, right side up, on top of the main fabric so that the stitch line of the lining base hem is roughly level with the top of the curtain base hem. On the side hem, press under 2.5cm/1in of lining and slipstitch to the main fabric along the entire leading edge of the curtain and 5cm/2in along the base hem, leaving 2.5cm/1in of lining showing. The corner of the lining should be on or near the diagonal pressed line of the mitred corner, about 2cm/¾in from the edge of the curtain (fig. d).

4 Locking in the lining to the fabric is done at each fabric seam. Working across from the leading edge, fold back the lining in a straight line along its first width. Working up from the bottom, take the needle into the seam and pick up a single thread from fabric and lining. Locking in stitches are like enormous herringbone stitches, very loose and roughly 20cm/8in apart (fig. e). Stop each line of stitches 15cm/6in from the top of the curtain.

5 Continue to lock in the lining to the main fabric at each width of the curtain as you work across.

6 Before moving the curtain across the table to work on the next section, secure the lining to the main fabric along its length with pins at the point at which the fabric falls off the table. This will keep the two layers of fabric and lining from coming apart as you move them across the table in sections.

7 When you reach the other side, press under 5cm/2in along the back edge of the main fabric. Mitre the corner, inserting a weight first. Finish off the base hem with slipstitch, then herringbone stitch the side hem in place. Cut off any surplus from the side edge of the lining fabric and press under 3cm/1¼in. Slipstitch to the main fabric, leaving 2.5cm/1in of curtain showing. Loosely secure the lining to the base hem at every fabric seam with daisy chain stitches (see p. 202).

8 The lining is now secure along the base and two sides of the curtain. Measure up the finished length from the base of the curtain and mark it with a line of pins. Press over the top of the joined curtain at the pin line, and mitre the corners (a few stitches can be undone along the side hem if necessary). The turnover should be concealed by the curtain tape, so trim off any fabric in excess of 8cm/3¼in.

a

b

c

d

e

ADDING THE HEADING TAPE

1 Position the tape on the underside of the curtain close to the top, folding under about 12mm/½in of tape at one end. Secure the strings with a knot under the tape on the leading edge of the curtain and leave the ends loose for pulling up on the back edge of the curtain.

2 Machine stitch the tape in place along the top edge, A–B, then stitch the end at which you started, A–C. Turn the needle in the fabric and stitch along the lower edge of the tape, C–D. Keep the fabric smooth beneath the tape, or it will pucker.

3 With the strings together, pull up the tape to the required width, anchoring one end of the curtain heading so that you have something to pull against, and distributing the pleats evenly (fig. f). The finished width for each curtain of a pair is half the length of the pole or track, plus, if relevant, any overlap or return.

4 Secure the strings with a knot (fig. g). Wrap them round your hand into a sausage shape and stitch roughly but firmly in place on the tape, parallel to the pleats (fig. h). If the 'sausage' is too bulky to slot into

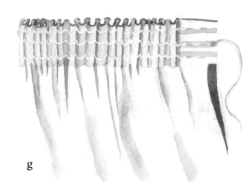

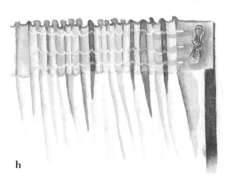

the fold of a pleat and would otherwise get in the way of the track bracket, you should sew it just beneath the heading tape. Alternatively you can buy a 'cord tidy' around which you wind the strings and which then slots into the heading tape. It is essential that the excess strings are not cut off, as the curtains could not then be pulled flat again at a later date for cleaning.

5 Place the hooks in the correct row of pockets at intervals of approximately 5–8cm/2–3¼in, with a hook positioned at each end of the curtain. Fit the same number of gliders or rings as there are hooks on to the track or pole and hook the curtain into them. Pull the curtain across the window to check that the width of the heading is correct, and make any adjustments by loosening or tightening the heading cord.

MAKING UNLINED CURTAINS

I think that most curtains and fabrics should be lined: adding a lining has many advantages (see page 100). But sometimes an unlined curtain is more appropriate, perhaps at a small window in a bathroom or scullery, or where something simple and unobtrusive is wanted (see page 48). Even dress curtains can be left unlined if their function is solely to frame the window.

Unlined curtains also come into their own for summer window furnishings; they can be made to take a detachable lining (see page 62) for the winter months. Billowy fabrics unlined, such as cream poplin or Egyptian cotton, can look glorious.

The method I describe here again uses a pencil pleat heading, so allow two and a half times fullness in the width and an extra 30cm/12in allowance in the finished length (the base hem can in fact be cut down to a double 5cm/2in hem if you prefer). Gathered, box or slot headings (see pages 118, 119, 122) are also appropriate. French pleats, however, really need the added weight of lining (and preferably interlining) to hang well.

MAKING UP THE CURTAIN

1 Join the widths by French seams (see p. 204) and press. Then press a double 2.5cm/1in hem along the side edges of the curtain and machine or hand stitch.

2 Press a double 10cm/4in (or 5cm/2in) hem at the base of the curtain. Mitre the corners (see p. 203) and secure weights into them (see opposite, fig. b). Slipstitch or machine stitch the base hem in place.

3 Measure off the finished drop with pins and attach the heading tape as shown in steps 1–5 above.

MAKING A FRENCH PLEAT HEADING

A French pleat heading (also known as pinch pleat) is a deep, formal heading in which the flat curtain is punctuated at regular intervals by pleats in groups of three (see page 108 for photograph).

As discussed on page 107, this type of heading is best sewn by hand. You can buy tapes for French pleat headings, but I much prefer to stitch them by hand; otherwise they tend to sag, especially if the curtains have the added weight of interlining. Most hand-sewn headings are stiffened with tarlatan applied beneath the fabric, so that the pleats stay neat and vertical and the top edge makes a sharp, smooth line.

I recommend interlining all curtains with French pleat headings; the soft, blanket-like layer (see page 100) gives extra insulation, as well as helping the fabric to hang in deeper, more luxurious folds.

ESTIMATING THE FABRIC

First measure the window (see p. 67). For a French pleat heading, $2\frac{1}{2}$ times the finished width of the curtains generally gives enough fullness.

Add an extra 40cm/16in to the finished length for the working drop of the main fabric, to allow for a double 10cm/4in hem at the base and a further 20cm/8in for the heading at the top.

The working drop of the lining should be the finished length plus 15cm/6in; this allows for a double 5cm/2in base hem and 5cm/2in surplus at the heading.

CUTTING OUT & JOINING WIDTHS

Cut and join the main fabric widths (see p. 111).

Cut the lining fabric into the same number of widths as the main fabric (see p. 111). Join lining widths as for the main fabric and press seams open. Press over the double 5cm/2in base hem and machine stitch in place along all joined widths.

Cut the interlining to the same width and length as the lining and join the widths together using a straight seam (see p. 204).

MAKING UP THE CURTAIN

1 Lay the main fabric wrong side up on a large, flat surface, with the base nearest to you and the leading edge parallel to one side of the work surface. Press over a double 10cm/4in hem at the base and 5cm/2in on the leading edge, leaving the hems unstitched (fig. a).

2 Place the interlining on top of the fabric. The base of the interlining should lie along the pressed line of the main fabric nearer the bottom raw edge and its side edge should be in line with the leading edge (selvedge) of the main fabric.

3 Fold the interlining back on itself along the leading edge of the curtain at the pressed hem line. Herringbone stitch along this fold to secure the interlining to the fabric, taking only a thread at a time so that the stitching is invisible from the front (fig. b).

4 Lock in the interlining across the width at each seam (see p. 112, *Making up the curtain*, step 4).

Move across the curtain one section at a time, alternately locking in and using herringbone stitch to secure the interlining at the base hem (fig. b). When you reach the other side, herringbone stitch the interlining to the back edge of the curtain in exactly the same way as to the leading edge.

a

b

c

5 Once the interlining is locked in across the entire width, and both sides have been secured, fold the base hem of the main fabric along the pressed line nearest the base. Then secure the top of this part of the hem to the interlining beneath, using large tacking stitches (fig. c).

6 Mitre the bottom corners (see p. 203). Sew weights into each corner and at every width (see p. 112, fig. b), then slipstitch the top of the base hem in place. Herringbone stitch the side hem in place, stitching into the interlining (fig. d).

Move across the curtain a section at a time, alternately slipstitching the lower hem and applying the lining to the main fabric (see p. 112, *Making up the curtain*, steps 3–7).

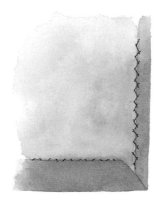
d

MAKING THE HEADING

1 Once the lining is secure on three sides, measure the finished drop of the curtain up from the base and mark it with a line of pins. Stand at the top of the curtain, with the heading on the table. Press over at the pin line.

2 Cut the lining and interlining, but not the main fabric, level along the pin line. Herringbone stitch lining and interlining to the main fabric along the cut edge (fig. e).

3 Place the tarlatan stiffener with its lower edge against the raw edges of the lining and interlining and its short side edges under the side hems (fig. f). Mitre the top corners. Press the surplus main fabric down over the tarlatan (fig. g).

4 When the tarlatan is fully secured, fold the stiffened heading down over the lining. Slipstitch the side edges in place (fig. h).

e

f

g

h

CALCULATING PLEATS & SPACES

1 Measure the width of the flat curtain, now made up, along the heading. Subtract from this the width of the finished curtain (allowing about 8cm/3¼in on each side for any overlap or returns). The difference between the two widths is the amount left over for pleats.

2 Allow, as a guide, four pleats for each width of fabric used. Divide the amount available for pleats by the total number of pleats. Not including an overlap and return at either end, there will be one less space than pleat. Therefore, if each curtain is, say, 1½ fabric widths, there will be 6 groups of pleats and 7 spaces per curtain (fig. i). Two of the spaces, situated at either end of the heading, are for the overlap and return and are usually 8cm/3¼in wide.

To calculate the size of the spaces, divide the number of spaces into the finished width of the curtain, less the return and overlap.

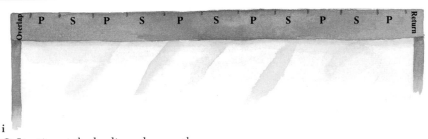
i

3 Starting at the leading edge, on the wrong side of the curtain, mark the pleats (p) and spaces (s) with pins at the top of the curtain (fig. i). Bring each pin to meet the next and join them, thus making single large pleats along the front of the curtain.

4 Machine stitch these single pleats, from the top of the curtain where the pin is to where the tarlatan ends, using a ruler to keep the stitch line straight and parallel to the folded outer edge of the pleat (fig. j).

5 Neat oversewing at the top and bottom of each stitch line is essential. Tuck the fold of the pleat inwards to make a triple pleat (fig. k).

6 Pin hooks or special sew-on hooks (see p. 106) can be placed in each pleat on the underside of the curtain.

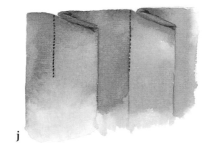
j

k

Using different headings

The slot heading on the right is refreshingly plain and unfussy. Prettily casual, it is intended to support the curtains, not to distract from them.

In contrast, the goblet pleats at the window below are exceedingly formal, creating deep ruches all down the curtain. (Note the less formal pencil pleats on the bed-curtains.) The overall effect is cool and textured, with welcome splashes of colour on bedspread and tablecloth.

The white drapes on the far right lack any conventional heading. Unlined curtains in crisp, paper-thin cotton have been stiffened at the top, with hooks for rings simply sewn on some way down. The inflexible fabric has been moulded at the base in the same way as at the heading.

SIX ALTERNATIVE HEADINGS

Illustrated here are finished versions of the six commonly used headings for which instructions are given on the next few pages. They range from the enjoyably casual to the extremely formal.

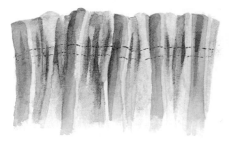

Gathered heading

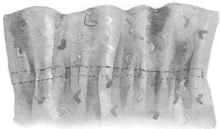

Bunched heading

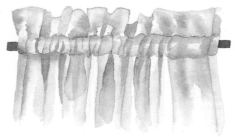

Slot heading

Scalloped heading

Box pleat heading

Goblet pleat heading

MAKING A GATHERED HEADING

The instructions below are for lined curtains with a gathered heading, the most casual of all headings and the easiest to make. I also describe a variation that gives a fuller heading with softer folds. Gathered heading tape is 2.5cm/1in deep (see page 106).

ESTIMATING THE FABRIC

Allow 2½ times the finished width of the curtain. For the working drop, add to the finished length enough for a double 10cm/4in base hem and for the heading (the depth of the tape itself plus the distance it is set down from the top of the curtain, which should be at least 2.5cm/1in). For an interlined, stiffened variation see *Bunch heading*, opposite.

Make the curtains as described on p. 112, *Making up the curtain*.

ADDING THE HEADING TAPE

Mark a line in tailor's chalk (or lightly in pencil) on the underside of the curtain heading, the distance you have allowed from the top of the curtain to the tape. Align the top edge of the tape with this line and machine stitch the tape in place. Pull up to the required width (fig. a) and secure the tape (see p. 113, steps 3 – 5).

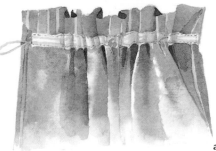

a

MAKING AN INTERLINED GATHERED HEADING

To achieve a slightly more formal look without interlining the whole curtain, you need a strip of interlining as long as the width of the flat curtain and as wide as the heading tape plus an extra 4cm/1½in. Place the heading tape about 4cm/1½in from the top of the curtain and position the interlining in the top of the curtain, its lower edge beneath the heading tape. Herringbone stitch it in place along the finished drop line before the top of the curtain is pressed down.

MAKING A BUNCH HEADING

This is a variation on a gathered heading. The same tape is used but set down some 10cm/4in from the top of the curtain. The heading is stiffened with tarlatan and also interlined to give a fuller and sharper effect.

ESTIMATING THE FABRIC

For a bunch heading, 2½ times the width of the curtain gives enough fullness. Add 35cm/14in to the finished length for the working drop: this allows for a double 10cm/4in base hem and 15cm/6in for the heading. Make the curtains as described on p. 112, *Making up the curtain*. If you are interlining the whole curtain (see p. 114, steps 2–5), there is no need to insert further interlining at the top.

ADDING THE HEADING TAPE

1 If you are not interlining the whole curtain, place a single strip only in the heading, cut to the required size (as long as the width of the flat curtain and wide enough to cover the whole of the heading area down to the base of the tape). Herringbone stitch the strip at top and bottom to the underside of the curtain (fig. b).

b

2 Place the tarlatan stiffener on top of the interlining, with its upper edge along the drop line and its short side edges under the side hems. Press the main fabric down over the tarlatan.

3 Mark a line in pencil or tailor's chalk, 10cm/4in down from the top of the curtain, on the underside of the heading. Align the top edge of the tape with this line and machine stitch the tape in place.

4 Pull up to the required width and secure the tape (see p. 113, steps 3–5).

MAKING A SLOT HEADING

This type of heading (also called a cased heading) is mainly used for nets or sheer fabrics, but it is just as suitable for a lined curtain made of lightweight fabric. The casing slots on to a narrow rod or, alternatively, onto a length of plastic-covered stretch wire fixed to the wall or the window frame with screw-in metal 'eyes'. The method described is for an unlined curtain.

ESTIMATING THE FABRIC

Sheers can be up to three times as full as the width of the curtain rod or wire, as long as the fabric is fine. The working drop should be 21cm/8½in more than the finished drop of the curtain to allow for a double 5cm/2in hem at the base, and a double 5cm/2in turnover at the top (this provides the casing). A further 12mm/½in is taken up as the curtain slots over the rod. (For curtains hanging from a wire, this extra 12mm/½in allowance can be ignored.)

MAKING UP THE CURTAIN

1 Cut out the fabric and join widths, using French seams if the curtain is unlined (see p. 113). Press, then machine stitch, a double 12mm/½in hem down each side of the curtain and a double 5cm/2in hem across the base edge, first threading chain weights along the inside of the base hem (see p. 123).

2 Measure the finished drop up from the base and turn over a double 5cm/2in hem at the top. Press and pin in place.

3 Sew two lines of top stitching parallel to each other, on the wrong side of the curtain, one 2.5cm/1in below the top of the curtain, and the other 2.5cm/1in below that (fig. c). This makes a channel wide enough to take a wire or narrow rod; if you are using a thicker rod or pole, adjust the fabric quantity and turnover accordingly.

4 Slot the curtain on to the rod or wire. It will gather up naturally into folds.

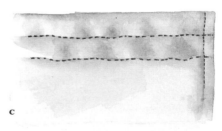

c

MAKING A SCALLOPED HEADING

This effective and eye-catching heading has traditionally been used to make the half-curtains known as café curtains, and is especially suited to curtains covering the lower half of a sash window, where the eye is at heading level.

The detailed instructions are for making plain unlined scalloped curtains. These are lined with a facing at the heading only, to give extra strength, and are then hung along a pole or rod by rings attached to the top of the curtain. There are instructions for lined or pleated variations as well. I also describe an alternative hanging method, involving fabric loops made by extending the strips of fabric in between the scallops.

ESTIMATING THE FABRIC

For a completely flat curtain, the fabric width should be the same as the length of the pole on which it is to hang, plus 4cm/1½in at either side. If you want the curtain to be slightly gathered, allow 1½ times the width of the pole for the fullness of fabric. The fabric length should be the finished drop of the curtain plus an allowance of 10cm/4in for the base hem and 2cm/¾in at the top. You also need to allow about an extra 20cm/8in of fabric for a facing, which can be in either the same or in a contrast fabric; the exact length depends on the depth of your scallops (see below), and whether you hang the curtains by rings or fabric loops (see opposite).

These calculations apply to unlined curtains; for lined curtains, see opposite.

ESTIMATING SCALLOP SIZE

1 Join the fabric widths, using French seams (see p. 204). Cut out the fabric as described on p. 111.

2 The scallop size will depend on the dimensions of your curtain but, as a general guide, 12cm/4½in is an average scallop width, with a 5cm/2in space, or strip, in between. To determine the total number of scallops, divide the width of the finished curtain by the sum of a scallop and a strip, in this case 17cm/6½in. There should always be one more strip than scallop, with a strip at either end (fig. a).

Scallop depth also varies according to the size of the curtain. Try and make each scallop roughly as along as it is wide, so it looks attractively 'square'. (If you intend to hang the curtain by fabric loops, you will need longer strips in between the scallops – see *Making fabric loops*, opposite.)

3 Because the curtain is unlined, the heading needs to be faced, in a matching or a contrast fabric. Cut the facing to the same width as the curtain fabric, and 8cm/3¼in longer than the finished scallop depth.

MARKING THE SCALLOPS

1 You need to cut a template out of stiff card for the scallop edge. The shape of the scallop is based on a circle with the top end squared (fig. a).

2 On the wrong side of the fabric, starting 6cm/2½in from the end, with the help of the template mark out the shape of the scallops with tailor's chalk; position them 12mm/½in down from the raw edge and leave 5cm/2in between each curve. It is important that the top of the fabric is cut straight and square to the selvedge (see p. 201), and that you keep the template level.

APPLYING THE FACING

1 Cut out the facing. Turn over a double 2cm/$\frac{3}{4}$in hem across its lower edge and machine in place. With right sides together, match the facing to the top of the curtain and pin in place at top and bottom. Mark a line on the facing round the scallops, 2cm/$\frac{3}{4}$in from the top of the curtain.

2 Machine stitch the facing to the curtain, starting from the bottom of the facing and stitching 4cm/1$\frac{1}{2}$in away from its raw edge. Machine stitch along the line which marks the scallops. Cut out the scallops 12mm/$\frac{1}{2}$in from the stitch lines (fig. b) and clip the curves (see p. 205).

3 Press a double 2cm/$\frac{3}{4}$in hem on both sides of the curtain and machine or slipstitch in place. Turn up the base hem, using a double 5cm/

b

2in hem. Mitre the corners (see p. 203) and machine or slipstitch to secure. Turn to right side and press.

4 Stitch curtain rings in the middle of each strip between the scallops and thread on to the pole.

MAKING FABRIC LOOPS

If you want to hang your curtain from fabric loops, carry out the instructions for plain unlined scallops, with the following alterations.

1 Add a further 10cm/4in to the fabric length (see *Estimating the fabric* for other allowances).

2 When cutting the template, extend the straight sides by a further 10cm/4in.

3 Instead of *Applying the facing*, step 4, turn under 5cm/2in and stitch to the back of the faced curtain, creating a loop for the pole to go through (fig. c).

c

MAKING PLEATED SCALLOPS

Carry out the instructions for plain unlined scallops, with the following amendments.

1 To calculate the total width of fabric you need: decide on the width of scallop you will be using (see *Estimating scallop size*) and multiply the number of spaces, or strips, by 8cm/3$\frac{1}{4}$in to find out how much fabric the pleats will take up. Add this figure to the width of the curtain pole, then add 4cm/1$\frac{1}{2}$in at either end.

2 To make the pleats, mark two vertical lines each 6−12mm/$\frac{1}{4}$$\frac{1}{2}$in away from the edge of a scallop. Join these two lines, wrong sides together, to form a single fold, and secure it at the base. Make triple folds (see p. 115, *Calculating pleats and spaces*, step 5).

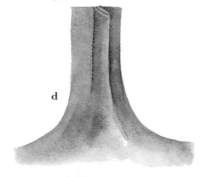

d

MAKING LINED SCALLOPED CURTAINS

1 Estimate the fabric as for plain unlined curtains, opposite, allowing an extra 2cm/$\frac{3}{4}$in for a hem on either side of the fabric width for both main fabric and lining, and an extra 4cm/1$\frac{1}{2}$in to the finished drop of the curtain (2cm/$\frac{3}{4}$in for base hem and the same amount for the top).

2 Estimate the scallop size and make a template as for plain unlined curtains, opposite. With right sides together, pin the fabric to the lining, and mark the scallops on the wrong side of the lining. Machine stitch the fabric to the lining along the sides and across the top of the curtain, following the scalloped edge; also machine stitch along the base, but leave half the width of the curtain unstitched in the middle.

3 Cut out the scallops, then clip the curves (see p. 205) and turn the curtain right side out. Press well. Slipstitch the remaining unstitched base hem. Stitch curtain rings as for plain unlined curtains, step 4, above.

MAKING A BOX PLEAT HEADING

Box pleats give a neat, flat finish to the top of curtains. They are hand-sewn, without a curtain tape, and stiffened with tarlatan. Very bulky fabric – such as heavy woollen cloth or springy quilting – is not suitable, as it has to press easily to form successful pleats. The method described is for a lined curtain.

ESTIMATING THE FABRIC

You need three times the length of the curtain track to give the correct fullness for box pleats. Allow standard amounts for any returns and for side hems.

First, determine the finished width of each pleat – the flat part at the front. Multiply it by three and make sure that the result divides exactly into the finished curtain width. An average pleat width is 10cm/4in, in which case the curtain width should be divisible by 30cm/12in. If it is not, make an adjustment either to the curtain width or to the pleat width so that the two are compatible.

For the working drop allowances, see p. 111, *Estimating the fabric* for the main cloth and *Cutting and joining lining widths* for the lining. Make the curtains as described on p. 112, *Making up the curtain*.

MAKING THE HEADING

1 To decide where the folds for the pleats will come, mark the top of the curtain across the fabric with pins.

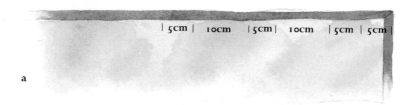

Assuming the pleats are to be 10cm/4in wide, make the first mark 5cm/2in from the leading edge of the curtain and the next mark 5cm/2in from that. Then make marks at alternate 10cm/4in and 5cm/2in intervals across the top of the curtain (fig. a), ending with two marks 5cm/2in apart.

2 Join the pin mark 5cm/2in from one end to the one 20cm/8in further along from it (fig. a). Pin them together. Leave a 10cm/4in space and join up the next 20cm/8in length to form another single pleat. Repeat across the width of the curtain, finishing 5cm/2in from the other end.

3 To secure the pleats in place, machine stitch a 10cm/4in line across the front pleats only, from the top of the wrong side of the curtain. Flatten the pleats and pin them in position (fig. b).

4 To secure the back of the pleats on the underside of the curtain, slipstitch through both lining and fabric. Sew-on hooks (see p. 106) can be attached to the back of the curtain. Alternatively, stitch Velcro as for Austrian blinds (see p. 91, *Adding the heading*, step 3).

MAKING A GOBLET PLEAT HEADING

Curtains with goblet pleat headings are formal and imposing. They look especially impressive if each 'goblet' has a piece of contrast fabric inside it. This can simply be a ball of cloth sitting on top of the stuffing and visible above the goblet edge.

MAKING THE CURTAIN

1 Follow the instructions for making a curtain with French pleat heading on p. 114, as far as *Calculating pleats and spaces*, step 4. Instead of making a triple pleat, secure the single fold at the base into a cup or goblet shape.

2 To keep the pleats rounded and cylindrical, insert a piece of scrap interlining or cotton wadding into each one.

MAKING UP SHEERS

Most sheers are slot-headed (see page 119) and hung on a narrow pole, rod or wire. You can also pleat them with a lightweight, nylon heading tape, hooking them on to a lightweight track fitted beneath the main one.

Cutting out and measuring need particular care (see page 201). Sheer fabric often comes in widths of 3m/10ft or more, as it is intended to be drawn up very full, so there may be no need to join widths. If you do join widths, make sure that you use French seams (see page 204).

Take care to make neat hems – double 12mm/½in side hems and either double 5cm/2in or 10cm/4in base hems, depending on the length of the curtains and your own preferences. It is advisable, but not essential, to press side hems in advance of sewing; it is possible to fold as you sew. The base hem does need pressing and another pulled thread (see page 201) at the 10cm/4in point is often a good idea. Press the seams well after stitching. The side hems can be machine stitched, using a long, fairly loose stitch so that the fabric does not pucker. But if the edges of the fabric show signs of twisting when you machine (as may some stiffer silks), it would be better to slipstitch all hems by hand. Any really delicate fabric, such as old lace, should be hand-stitched. Hems may be chain-weighted (see right).

5cm/2in

Some voiles and nets come with ready chain-weighted hems in set lengths, so you need only work at the heading of your curtain. Chain weight can be bought by the metre and is threaded into the hem to run the whole width of the curtain; it needs to be 'caught' to the fabric with a daisy chain stitch or two at intervals inside the lower hem (see p. 202).

Here is a pretty sheer for a tiny window, an unlined, open-weave, self-striped cotton. A pencil pleat heading has been set well down from the top for a ruffled effect, balanced by the deep chain-weighted base hem.

Though undoubtedly softening the stone wall around it, the curtain has a lovely ice-like quality.

TIE-BANDS

Tie-bands are at once practical and exciting. They can hold curtains tightly, letting in maximum light and creating straight angular lines, or more loosely, so that the curtains are allowed to drape into full deep swags, covering the top part of the window and framing it decoratively.

The basic hand-made tie-band is generally a straight strip of fabric, made firm with buckram or similar stiffener, with a brass ring sewn on to either end. The rings loop over a hook, which is fixed to the wall or window frame. But there are many variations on this, both in shape and styling. Shaped tie-bands usually have rounded edges, curve upwards from the centre and taper to a point at either end. The wider the tie-band, the more of a feature in its own right it becomes; the narrower the band, the less it interrupts the flow of the curtains.

Experiment with colours and decoration. You might use the same fabric as for the curtain in a different colour, or a plain fabric picking up one of the colours of a patterned curtain. (If you are working with patterned fabric, make sure that you position the part you want to see at the front of the tie-band.)

There is a great deal of scope for borders – in fact, the most basic decoration is simply to add a contrast piping around the outside edge of the band. If the same piping also runs along the edge of the pelmet and along the leading edge of the curtain, it draws together all the elements of the arrangement.

Tie-bands do not have to be made of fabric. Anything that will loop round a curtain will do – perhaps a fine brass rosette. And your tie-bands do not have to be expensive to look good: to hold back lightweight curtains, especially sheers or lace, try using a simple length of ribbon. Ready-made cord or rope tie-bands are often, I think, the neatest way of tying back a curtain. Obtainable from major department stores and specialist suppliers, they add luxury, holding the curtain firmly and allowing for swagging above the rope.

ESTIMATING THE FABRIC

To calculate the finished length of any tie-band, hold a cloth tape measure loosely around the hanging curtain at the desired height. Add 5cm/2in to allow for positioning the rings. Drawing the curtain back against the wall, mark the position of the holding hook at the same time. It should be behind the back edge of the curtain.

The width of the tie-band will vary according to the proportions of the curtain and the shape of the band itself, but an average width is 10cm/4in. Add 3cm/1¼in all round for hems.

For each tie-band you need enough fabric to cover the back as well as the front; you can either use the same fabric for both or cover the back with lining material.

The options available when considering tie-bands are numerous, as is clear from the photographs below.

On the left, padded strips have been made out of three different fabrics (one of which is the same as the curtain border) and plaited together for a well-stuffed effect. In the centre, a very simple rope tie-band restrains the curtain with ease, showing off the fabric beautifully. And, on the right, a brass French tie-band looks like a delicate arm, which the curtain simply tucks behind.

MAKING A STRAIGHT TIE-BAND

The instructions below are for making a straight piped tie-band, interlined and stiffened with buckram. If you want to make a straight tie-band without piping, omit steps 4 to 7. I also describe how to make a template for a shaped variation.

MAKING UP THE TIE-BAND

1 Cut the buckram to the finished length and width of the tie-band. If you want rounded corners, use a cotton reel as a template, making sure that all four corners are the same. Place the buckram on top of the piece of interlining.

2 Fold the interlining over the buckram, trimming off excess fabric at the corners. Stick firmly in place, by wetting the buckram (fig. a) or following manufacturers' instructions for other stiffeners.

a

3 Place buckram and interlining on the wrong side of the main fabric and tack the hems of the fabric to the interlining (fig. b), mitring the corners (see p. 203).

b

4 For the piping, cut strips of fabric 2–3cm/¾–1¼in wide and long enough to go all round the tie-band, plus 5cm/2in for hems. (You may need to join several strips together to achieve the right length.)

5 Encase the piping cord inside the fabric strip, using a piping foot or a half-foot on the machine (fig. c).

c

6 Put the tie-band on top of the piping, with the right side facing you. Apply the piping to the front of the tie-band, slipstitching about 12mm/½in away from the raw edge of the piping, and as close to the piping cord as possible (fig. d). The raw fabric edges of the piping should be behind the tie-band.

d

7 Join the piping all around the tie-band, clipping corners where necessary. Join the two ends together by inserting one raw edge inside the other with a folded hem and finish neatly (fig. e). The joins in the piping should not be visible from the front.

e

8 Slipstitch the fabric or lining to the back of the tie-band, close to the edge, turning under the hems as you stitch (fig. f).

f

MATERIALS
- Fabric and lining for tie-band
- Interlining same size as fabric
- Buckram or other stiffener same size as finished tie-band
- Fabric for piping and piping cord
- 2 brass rings about 12mm/½in diameter, or large enough to go over hook

9 Sew a ring to the underside of each end of the tie-band, using blanket stitch. The ring at the front half of the tie-band should be hidden; the ring for the back half should protrude about halfway over the edge of the tie-band (fig. g).

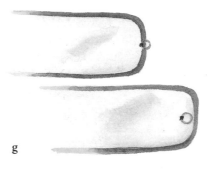

g

SHAPED TIE-BAND

Work out the finished length of the tie-band and the width at its widest point (see opposite, *Estimating the fabric*). Draw a template on folded paper, so that the two halves of the tie-band are identical. Curve both sides upwards from the centre and narrow the ends into a crescent. Fit the template around the curtain to check that the measurements are correct.

Place the template on the fabric and lining and cut out two pieces, allowing an extra 3cm/1¼in for hems all round. Then follow instructions for the straight tie-band. (Rather than mitre corners, ease the fabric round the curved edges, clipping it where necessary.)

MAKING A PADDED TIE-BAND

Padded tie-bands add texture and a three-dimensional feel to your curtain arrangement. It is entirely up to you how tubular or how flat you make them. The softer the tie-band, the more flexible it is.

Instead of using a single fabric, you could make a striped tube. Simply stitch some contrasting strips of fabric together until you reach the required length (see *Joining fabrics* on page 33 for ideas). Then continue as below.

A stiffened, shaped style of tie-band, with scarlet fringe, right, admirably restrains the long, heavy curtains bunching on the floor and complements an already formal interior. The crescent-shape of each tie-band is emphasized by an inset border in printed fabric, which also runs down the length of the curtain edges.

ESTIMATING THE FABRIC

Work out the finished length of the tie-band (see p. 124, *Estimating the fabric*).

Decide on how wide you want the 'tube' to be: the fabric will be the circumference of the tube plus an extra 4cm/1½in for seam allowances. The interlining should be about the same size as the fabric – the more interlining the fatter the tube and the wider the fabric must be.

MAKING UP THE TIE-BAND

1 Roll up the fabric and interlining together, with the fabric on the outside, and slipstitch a hem to secure the roll (fig. a).

2 Flatten the ends of the roll slightly and neaten them with a slipstitched hem, turning under the raw edges (fig. b).

3 Position the rings at each end of the roll on the inside (seamed) edge (fig. c – see p. 125, step 9).

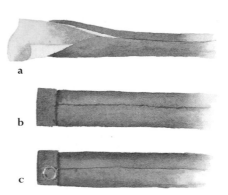

a

b

c

MAKING A PLAITED TIE-BAND

For a padded rather than a flat plaited effect, follow the instructions for making a padded tie-band, step 1. Repeat twice. Then, to plait the tie-band and secure the ends, follow the instructions below, which are for making a flat plaited tie-band, steps 3 and 4.

ESTIMATING THE FABRIC

Work out the finished length of the tie-band (see p. 124, *Estimating the fabric*).

Cut each of the three fabrics to the finished length, plus 4cm/1½in for hems. If you want the finished width of each strip to be, say, 2cm/¾in, make each one 5cm/2in wide, including 12mm/½in for a seam allowance. You can vary these dimensions according to style.

MAKING UP THE TIE-BAND

1 Fold each strip of fabric in half lengthways, right sides together. For a quick method of stitching and turning right side out (figs d and e), see p. 204.

2 Press the three tubes flat, with the seam in the middle (fig. f).

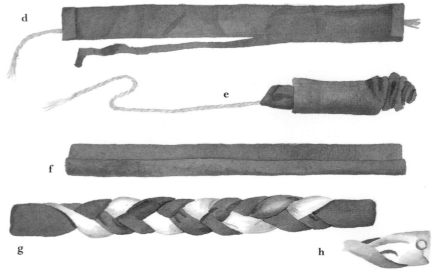

d

e

f

g

h

3 Slipstitch and neaten one end of each strip and hold the three ends together. Secure them with a heavy weight, or ask someone to hold them, while you plait the strips (fig. g).

4 Secure the other three ends together and neaten with a slipstitched hem. Turn under the raw edges and position the rings at each end (fig. h – see p. 125, step 9).

PELMETS & VALANCES

Pelmets and valances should not be dismissed as merely formal cover-ups for track and curtain headings. Their slightly stuffy image is a thing of the past: modern versions with inspired design and clever choice of fabric can utterly transform an otherwise ordinary curtain arrangement.

Pelmets are usually cut from plywood or buckram stiffener into the desired shape, then covered with fabric. The cloth is stretched over the pelmet, which is then mounted on a wooden board that sits above the curtain heading. Because of the buckram, fabric pelmets have to be steam cleaned. (Pelmets can, of course, be made entirely out of wood, perhaps painted to match the room.)

The lower edge of a pelmet can be shaped. A decorative edging can enhance the surface appearance of the curtains and help define their overall shape. There are all sorts of possible trimmings; a border of horizontal stripes, for instance, looks most effective at the base of a plain shaped pelmet, either in the form of fabric-inset borders or of braid applied on top of the fabric. You can sew braid or fringing on to the base edge of the finished pelmet by slipstitching it into the fabric using a curved needle; you may also have the option of applying braid by machine before the fabric is stretched over the buckram, but this will depend on the thickness and intricacy of the braid – for some braids machine stitching is not suitable.

Valances are softer in effect than pelmets, usually gathered or pleated, rather like short curtains. Their shape is determined largely by the choice of heading tape. They can either be fixed on to a timber board or hung from a special valance track.

Valances can be cut, shaped and made more interesting in many of the same ways as stiffened pelmets. You need to spread shaping evenly across the width of the valance: keep any design in proportion with the curtains, never losing sight of the window style and architecture of the room.

The pelmet on the right is a delightful example of the way shape can evolve naturally out of fabric pattern. The fabric has been turned 90° (so that the length becomes the width) and the design of the cotton print has been used as a template to dictate the shape of the pelmet. This device is very simple, yet very effective.

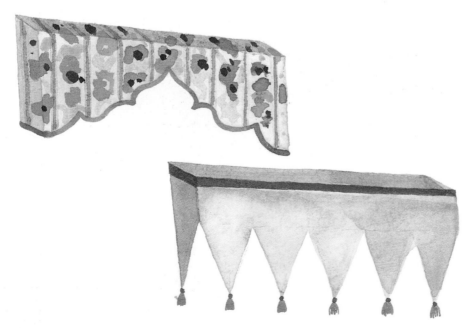

Illustrated on the left are two shaped pelmets, their widely differing appearance giving some idea of the great selection available.

MAKING A STIFFENED FABRIC PELMET

The instructions below describe how to make a straight fabric pelmet, stiffened with buckram and interlining. The covered pelmet is then attached to a timber board (see opposite) and fixed to the wall or window frame above the curtains (see page 73). I also explain how to make a shaped variation. Pelmets can be either dramatic or subtle in effect, depending on whether the fabric covering is chosen to blend in or contrast with the main curtain fabric.

MATERIALS
- Fabric
- Lining and interlining same size as fabric
- Buckram or other stiffener same size as finished pelmet

ESTIMATING THE FABRIC

The pelmet drop should be in proportion to the length of the curtains and must at least cover the track mechanism and the soffit of the window. As a general rule, one-eighth of the overall curtain drop is about right for fabric calculation. Add an allowance of 10cm/4in on to the finished drop (and a hem allowance of 4cm/1½in all round).

Calculate the amount of fabric you need by dividing the width of the pelmet (including the returns, unless it is a recess pelmet that does not have any), by the width of the fabric you will be using.

Carefully cut the fabric, lining, interlining and buckram to the correct dimensions.

MAKING THE PELMET

1 Cover the buckram with the interlining (see p. 125, *Making up the tie-band*, steps 1–2).

2 Join the fabric and lining widths, if necessary (see p. 111). Make sure that any patterning in the material is positioned evenly along the length of the pelmet and that the repeats are placed centrally. A full fabric width should be placed in the centre, with any part widths at each side. Press the seams flat.

3 With right sides together, join the fabric and lining with a machined seam at the top (fig. a). Turn to right side out and apply a line of Velcro just beneath and close to the seam line on the right side of the lining (fig. b).

a

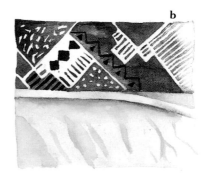

b

c

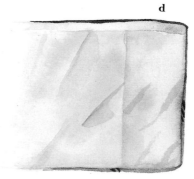

d

4 Insert the covered buckram between the lining and fabric, placing the interlined side of the buckram against the wrong side of the main fabric and ensuring that the fabric is smooth and even across the front (fig. c).

5 With the pelmet flat on the table, take the fabric over the base edge of the buckram and tack it in place to the interlining (fig. c). Then fold over and tack the fabric at the sides of the buckram, mitring the corners (see p. 203). You will need to make a crease in the stiffened pelmet at the corner of the returns (fig. d).

6 Fold under the hems of the lining and slipstitch the lining to the fabric through the interlining all around the edge. Throughout this procedure, keep the Velcro at the top of the underside of the pelmet straight and level.

MAKING A SHAPED PELMET

This stiffened fabric pelmet is shaped with the help of a paper template. Having estimated the fabric as described, opposite, proceed in the following way.

USING THE TEMPLATE

1 Make a paper template of the desired outline, taking care that any repeated shape divides evenly across the width of the pelmet. If making a scallop, for example, take the returns into account and make sure that each corner of the pelmet board ends in a complete scallop. (See p. 201 for how to draw perfect curves).

2 Pin the template on to the fabric, making sure that any patterning in the material is going to be effective after the fabric has been cut out.

3 Carefully cut out the fabric, lining and interlining, allowing for returns and an extra 4cm/1½in all round for hems. Cut out the buckram to the template shape, plus returns.

4 Follow the instructions for making the pelmet, left. When tacking the fabric to the buckram (step 5), clip the curves of the fabric (see p. 205) to ease it around the shaped buckram.

FIXING THE PELMET TO THE TIMBER BOARD

The pelmet board must be made of a timber that does not bend, such as pine or plywood. How far above the top of the window you place the board depends on how high the track is and on whether there is a cornice or other restriction – an average is about 5–8cm/2–3 in. To fix the board to the wall you will need several angle brackets spaced evenly across the width, 30–40cm/12–16in apart.

The stiffened fabric pelmet is fixed to the edge of the board with a strip of Velcro attached to each surface and secured at each end of the pelmet with a small hook, slotted into a small screw eye attached to the wall.

MATERIALS
- Timber board cut to size
- Velcro strip the length of finished pelmet (including any returns)
- 2 curtain rings
- 2 small hooks

ESTIMATING THE BOARD SIZE

About 12–25mm/½–1in thick, the timber board generally needs to be about 12–18cm/4½–7in deep, so that it projects far enough beyond the track for the curtains to move freely, with plenty of space for them when drawn back. The board should be the same length as the curtain track, plus 5cm/2in (2.5cm/1in at either end).

ATTACHING THE PELMET

1 Cover the pelmet board with fabric stapled to its underside (see p. 73). Alternatively, stick the fabric to the board with glue (fig. e).

2 Fix the reciprocal strip of Velcro all along the narrow edge of the pelmet board with long 12mm/½in staples, and then secure the fabric pelmet to the timber board (fig. f).

3 To secure the stiffened pelmet firmly at either end, place a small screw eye in the wall at the edge of the underside of the board. Then sew a curtain hook to the pelmet, which should return to the wall, around the ends of the timber board.

It is sometimes better and neater to finish the end of the fabric pelmet *behind* the timber board, so that there is a firm edge close to the wall. If you want to do this, the stiffened fabric pelmet should be made about 4cm/1½in longer.

MAKING A VALANCE

To make a valance, you first need to decide on what type of heading you want. Pencil pleats (see page 110), French pleats (see page 114), box pleats (see page 122) and slot headings (see page 119) are all appropriate. The instructions below show how to make a valance in simplified terms: for more detail about each stage, turn to the instructions for making curtains with your chosen heading.

Most valances can be hung either from a timber board or from a special valance track, which is hooked on to the main curtain track. A slot-headed valance is fixed rather differently, by being slotted on to a metal track which has been curved to fit the required dimensions. I recommend using a professional for this tricky procedure. To fix the timber board to the wall, see page 73.

ESTIMATING THE FABRIC

Determine the finished drop of the valance: as a rough guide, it should be about one-fifth or one-sixth of the finished curtain drop. Allow for a single base hem of 2cm/¾in and a turnover at the top of 5cm/2in.

Calculate the width of fabric required by multiplying the length of the track (including returns) by the amount of fullness required. The latter will depend on which heading you choose (see pp. 108–22).

The lining is cut to the same dimensions as the fabric. Interlining is not essential but gives the valance a softer look; if you are having a French pleat or other formal heading, interlining is advisable.

FIXING THE VALANCE TO A BOARD OR TRACK

If you are fixing the valance to a pelmet board, the method depends on the type of heading.

A slot heading secures the valance to a track or pole. For other types of heading, attach a Velcro backing strip as for Austrian blinds (see p. 91, *Adding the heading*, step 3). Then apply the reciprocal strip of Velcro to the narrow edge of the timber board and secure the valance to it.

If you are fixing the valance to a special rail or track, fix hooks to the back of the heading and attach to the track in the usual way. See p. 105 for fixing track to the wall.

MAKING THE VALANCE

1 Join fabric widths and lining widths (see p. 111). Press seams open. Lock in the interlining, if used, to the fabric before attaching the lining (see p. 112, steps 4 and 5).

a

2 With right sides together, join the fabric and lining at the base and up the sides. Machine stitch along the base edge first, starting 2cm/¾in from one side and ending 2cm/¾in from the other side (fig. a). Then lift up the base so that the lining meets the sides of the fabric, forming a small triangle of fabric at the corner, which will be the mitred corner (fig. b).

b

3 When the sides are stitched, turn to right side out, press down the mitre and slipstitch it in place (fig. c). Press the whole valance.

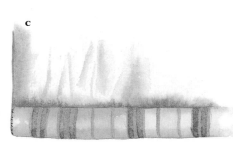

c

4 Measure the finished drop up from the bottom and mark with pins, then press over the surplus and apply the heading (see p. 113, *Applying the heading*).

Here the shape of the valance is being used to reinforce a very staged and theatrical look, 'dressing' the window in the most costume-like way.

Plain sheers, with appliquéd braid applied to the leading and base edges, are overhung by a bright red valance, whose subtly scalloped heading has hooks for rings sewn in between each scallop. The shape is echoed by the rope cord caught up at regular intervals in front of the valance and by the wavy flow at the base caused by the slight fullness in the valance fabric. The brass rosette tie-bands and the pole, with its spear-shaped finials, make the overall effect yet more elaborate.

LOOSE DRAPES

Loose drapes, the informal alternative to swags and tails, are less structured and far easier to make. If you are going to hang loose drapes at the same window as a working pair of curtains, you must fit a separate pole for them. If a drape is a window's only dressing, simply take it up from the floor, across the width of the window at the top over a pole, and then return it to the floor.

There are several variations. Loose drapes can be made to swag or 'snake' around a pole, in an even or a less regular way, or a central length of fabric over the pole can be caught back to the sides, imitating curtains.

ESTIMATING THE FABRIC

Assuming that the drape is to hang over a pole fitted above a track holding curtains, first determine the length of the tails. If the window is a sash type, the halfway point is a good guide to tail drop.

For a full drape or swag in the centre of the window, add to the length of two tails the finished width of the curtain plus 1m/3ft. This gives you the length you need, to be cut in one piece; a normal fabric width provides enough fullness. If you want the fabric to snake round and round the pole along its length, add $1\frac{1}{2}$ times

the finished width of the curtain to the length of the two tails.

It is not essential to line the drape, but better to do so if the curtain has been lined. Coloured or contrast linings (see p. 63) can be used to wonderful effect here: the drape can be twisted along the pole to show off the contrast lining, and the long 'tails' can be draped so that they also display sections of lining. If the drape is unlined, why not choose a textured fabric with a noticeably different reverse side?

MAKING A LOOSE DRAPE

1 With right sides together, join the lining and the fabric on all sides, leaving a small opening so that you can then turn the drape right side out. Press the seams and slipstitch the opening closed.

2 According to your taste, just drape the fabric length several times around the pole. You can secure it on to the pole with small tacks, if necessary, but it should stay in place during normal use.

The curtain arrangement on the right is an example of truly architectural draping, quite casually executed but planned with some style.

Lavish quantities of calico have been used, both for the basic curtains and for the superimposed 'swag' knotted back at its

edges. The gatherings and folds have been informally worked out and then tacked in place. The result fills the window recess, creating an impressive focal point yet blending in, with the help of the thoroughly functional Roman blinds, to the otherwise deliberately neutral room.

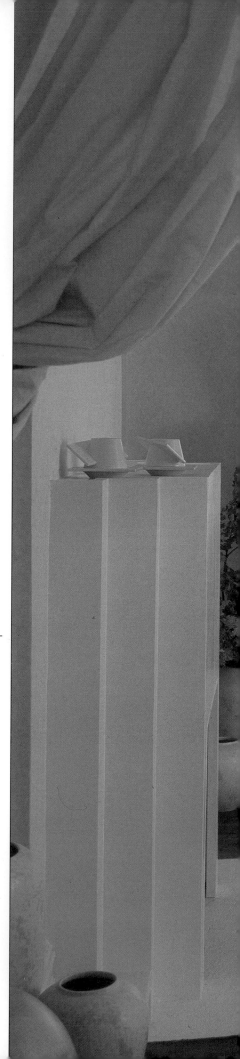

MAKING SWAGS & TAILS

I describe on the following pages how to cut and make a single lined swag and one pair of tails. The sewing involved in making swags and tails is not complicated; the skill lies in estimating and cutting the cloth correctly. Without wasting fabric, you want the finished results to have the right degree of fullness and shaping. As a guide to the finished drop of the swag at its deepest point, allow one-sixth to one-eighth of the window height (or for each 30cm/12in of swag width allow 50cm/20in of length).

My method is versatile and flexible: by adjusting the proportions of the template or the width of the pleats, you will end up with different depths of swag and varying degrees of fullness.

A single swag is cut and sewn so that it makes deep folds and falls in a semi-circle from the top of the window. The fabric is cut on the bias, which helps it to drape naturally into folds. Each long side of the lined fabric has to fold up into pleats on either side of the centre of the window, to fill the finished width measurement.

Tails are made separately (see page 139). The finished swag and tails are then attached to a pelmet board (see page 140). Try making tails with a coloured or contrast lining (see page 63). Soft fabrics – silk noil or cotton-satin, for instance – that fold easily into the form of swags and tails can be interlined for a fuller, firmer effect. Other, less fluid, fabrics – stiff cottons or heavy velvets – are best not interlined, to avoid unnecessary bulk.

The cut swags and tails on the right are designed to stamp a formal imprint on the room. Plain glazed cotton curtains are overhung with three cut swags and two tails lined and bordered in navy blue, which has also been used to define all the edges of the swags and tie-bands. The result is both pretty and practical, showing off the window shape and interior.

The window arrangement below left has been made (as shown on the following pages) from three pieces of cotton jacquard weave. Formal and elaborate though they are, these swag and tails retain a simple and austerely classical appearance.

The window dressing below right, on the other hand, relies far more on the way it has been shaped. The pole and the tie-bands are decorative, while the heavily glazed cotton is moulded to emphasize its lustrous quality.

ESTIMATING THE FABRIC

The main fabric for the swag is cut on the bias. Allow $1\frac{1}{2}$ times the finished width (the length of the curtain track plus 2cm/$\frac{3}{4}$in) of the swag by $2\frac{1}{2}$ times the finished depth, plus the usual hem allowances. Measure out the swag to the proportions shown (fig. a), placing any join necessary in the fabric widths in the lower corner of the swag.

CUTTING OUT

1 Place the lining fabric, wrong side up on a flat surface and mark out the measurements for the swag in pencil on it. Cut out the lining fabric to these measurements.

2 Using the lining as a template, lay it on the main fabric, on the bias. Pin it in position and cut it out carefully.

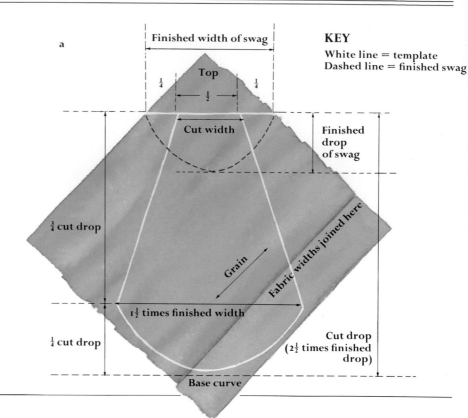

a

Finished width of swag

KEY
White line = template
Dashed line = finished swag

Top

$\frac{1}{4}$ $\frac{1}{4}$

$\frac{1}{2}$

Cut width

Finished drop of swag

$\frac{3}{4}$ cut drop

Grain

Fabric widths joined here

$\frac{1}{4}$ cut drop

$1\frac{1}{2}$ times finished width

Cut drop ($2\frac{1}{2}$ times finished drop)

Base curve

MAKING UP THE SWAG

1 Remove the template. Press a 12mm/$\frac{1}{2}$in hem round all the edges of the main fabric and secure with herringbone stitch.

2 With wrong sides together, slipstitch the lining to the main fabric swag along the base curve (the only edge visible on the finished swag), turning the lining fabric under as you work. Tack the remaining edges of the lining to the sides of the main fabric (fig. b).

b

3 The next step is easier if you have the fabric hanging over the edge of the table, rather than flat. Attach some spare fabric to the edge of the work surface, then pin to it the top edge of the swag fabric. Mark on the work surface the centre of the fabric and the finished width of the swag.

↓ Centre

c

4 Working inwards from the outer edge, fold up a long side of the fabric in rough pleats, to one side of the centre point (fig. c). Allow the last fold (nearest the centre) to lie across the top edge of the swag. Repeat with the other long side. You can space the pleats, or folds, as you wish, completely covering the top edge of the swag or allowing that to remain uncovered. 8−10cm/$3\frac{1}{4}$−4in per fold is a rough guide; any surplus can be absorbed into the underside of each pleat across the top to fit your finished measurements.

5 When you have made all the folds on either side of the centre mark, pin them so that they are secure. Machine stitch across the top, securing all the folds in place (fig. d).

d

MAKING TAILS WITH PARALLEL FOLDS

Although apparently a natural extension of the swag, the tails have to be made separately. They are then fitted on to the pelmet shelf so that they fall in front of the swag. As well as balancing the swag at each end of a window, tails can also be used more elaborately in between several swags.

Here I show how to make the right-hand tail of the pair; for the left-hand one, cut the template back to front.

ESTIMATING THE FABRIC

First you need to decide on the finished length of the tail, from the top to the pointed base. As a guideline, tails are generally just under half the length of the window itself, though some people prefer very long tails. The length of the short vertical edge is a matter of personal taste; on average it is about 15cm/6in.

To determine the length of the top horizontal edge (fig. e), first work out the number of folds required (usually four) and double this number. Then multiply the doubled number by the width of each fold, which should be the same as the width of the timber shelf (because the top of the tail returns to the back wall of the window along this width – in most cases 10cm/4in). This figure is the cut width of the tail at the top.

Using these measurements, cut a full-size template out of lining fabric. Think of the cut shape as a triangle with the top corner sliced off.

If your fabric is patterned, you will need to allow, for a pair of tails, a length of fabric twice as long as the finished length of the tail. With plain fabric, often you only need one finished length, as the triangle shape can simply be inverted.

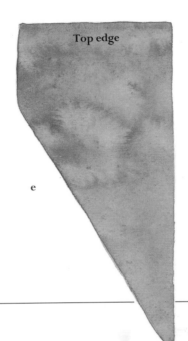

MAKING THE TAIL

1 Cut out the fabric to the dimensions of the lining template. Apply a line of piping along the shaped edge of the fabric (see p. 125).

2 With right sides together, pin the lining to the fabric, then machine stitch the three lower sides (fig. f). Trim the seams, then turn the tail right side out, press carefully and secure the top edge with tacking stitches (fig. g).

3 Mark the finished fold width along the top of the tail and place a pin in the corresponding place along the lower, diagonal edge. Fold from the short edge to the back edge with the fabric facing you (fig. h). Keep the last fold open, as this will be fitted around the edge of the timber board.

4 When you have finished folding, bind the top edge as for the swag (fig. i – see p. 140).

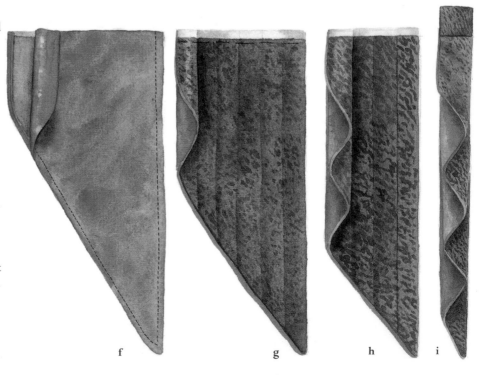

f   g   h   i

FIXING THE SWAG & TAILS TO THE BOARD

The finished width of a single swag is the length of the curtain track plus 2cm/¾in at either end. Cut the pelmet board to this length, using 10 × 2.5cm/4in × 1in timber (or whatever width is necessary to allow the swag to hang free of the curtains). Cover the board with matching fabric and secure the fabric with tacks or staples.

MAKING THE BINDING

Cut a strip of fabric twice the width of the timber board times the finished width of the swag. Machine stitch the strip along its length to the top of the swag, right sides together (see p. 205), stitching over the first row of tacking.

Fold over the strip of binding and slipstitch it to the underside of the heading, covering all the edges. Bind the top edge of the tails in exactly the same way and position the tail binding at the corners of the pelmet board.

FIXING THE BINDING

With the right side of the tails flipped up against the top of the board, fix the binding at the top of each tail with tacks to the corners of the pelmet board. The tacks are then hidden underneath the binding. Take the returns along the short edge of the timber. Fit the swag in the same way before flipping down swag and tails.

Fit the timber shelf to the wall or window frame by means of angle brackets (see p. 73).

As the focal point of its interior, the bay window below warrants the choice of elegant swags and tails as a heading to long, fine drapes. Although not always appropriate for French windows, here the swags can lie undisturbed as the upper section of each of the windows is a fixed pane of glass. The swags have been casually and unevenly draped but the overall arrangement retains an air of graceful elegance, in keeping with the rest of the interior. Deep fringing stitched onto the edges of the swags and tails forms an attractive defining border.

BEDS
& BEDDING

CHOOSING A STYLE
• Dressing the bed • drapes & hangings •

COVERS & LINEN
• Throwover bedcovers • fitted bedcovers •
• valances • duvet covers • pillowcases • bolsters •

CHOOSING A STYLE

Bedrooms offer an exciting chance to use fabric on a large scale. The very size of a bed makes it an important element in a room. A floor-length throwover bedcover – or even a simple duvet – represents a considerable expanse of fabric. If you opt for one of the decorative bed hangings that echo the historical importance of the 'state bed', the display potential of the bedroom is intensified.

Beds have for centuries been valued among the most prestigious possessions of a household, and a bed may still be the largest single item of furniture in your home. Complete bed hangings around four-posters originally performed the necessary function of excluding draughts, but substantial curtaining became increasingly decorative from about 1600 onwards. Skilled upholsterers combined sumptuous draperies with intricate trimmings to turn beds into extravagant status symbols for those who could afford them. In the nineteenth century, prosperous and fashion-conscious middle-class households took up the theme on a domestic scale, adorning contemporary tent or four-poster frames with 40 or 50 metres of fabric.

Manuals of style have always given a great deal of emphasis to the more flamboyant styles of bed, just as books and magazines do today. In the past only the wealthiest people had ornate, fully draped beds, but today it is very much a matter of taste whether you choose to 'dress up' a bed in the grand manner or opt for a more understated and tailored treatment. Although I dislike both the frillier extravagances and the studied, self-conscious look of some of the styles derived from the past, bed hangings undoubtedly offer irresistible opportunities to drape and hang attractive fabrics.

Finding the right fabric

At windows, fabrics are chosen to be visually pleasing as well as practical: light diffuses through the weave and illuminates the contours of folds and drapes. On the bed itself, fabric needs to be just as attractive to the eye, while the bedclothes should also send tactile messages suggesting warmth and smoothness against the skin. A plump downy duvet or the snug layered weight of blankets and crisp linen both promise comfort.

It is important to plan a bedroom that serves your own particular needs: bedrooms have to look good by day as well as at night. Decorative fabric ideas can complement or transform the architectural character of the room, or create an appropriately luxurious setting for your bed.

The imposing four-poster bed frame threatens to dominate this small bedroom completely. But, by the use of blues and whites only, a potentially sombre setting has been transformed. Precisely because they are linked by colour, the patterns embroidered onto the bedlinen and painted onto the walls, although all different, work harmoniously together.

The embroidery itself is intricate: fine old fabric has been delicately worked. (Note the tactile appeal of the bedcover's reverse side and the skilled open-work stitch on its inset border.)

143

Swags of fabric behind the bed can enhance its status with an interesting frame, while panels of plain or gathered fabric hung on a wall next to the bed soften the acoustic in the room. In a large room a fabric setting for the bed creates a 'room-within-a-room' feel; conversely, in a small space, the fabric around the bed can be attached to walls and ceiling so that the whole room becomes an extension of the bed.

Different kinds of drapes as well as different fabrics can be used to recreate period styles – from 'empire' coronets with heavy sculptural folds of fabric to end-of-the-empire mosquito-net effects of diaphanous muslin – or more generally to suggest seclusion, spaciousness or whatever other intangible qualities are important to you. At the other extreme, the bedroom may be treated as a living room in which the bed is just another piece of furniture.

The dressing of the bed comprises two distinct parts: on the one hand, the decoration provided by the cover, the valance or skirt (if used) and any hangings above or around the bed and, on the other, the more practical, but equally important, linen for the bed – pillows, sheets and duvet covers. I have outlined my ideas for different types of bed decoration on the following pages but have concentrated on showing how to make covers and linen on pages 162–72. Many of the hangings shown in this chapter are variations of the curtains discussed on pages 108–23, the techniques for which are shown there in detail.

The lengths of old lace so carefully draped around the frame and legs of the four-poster on the right appear dazzlingly white against a background of mellow surfaces – the leather day-bed, the worn carpet, the wooden steps leading up to the bed and the piece of old fabric that has been lovingly draped at the bedhead. The highly starched whitework of the bedcover also stands out from this background, its opaque solidity contrasting effectively with the fragility of the lace.

At first glance, the bed in the room below looks understated. In fact, the symmetry of the interior is very deliberate, while the bed is more like a chopped-off four-poster than a simple rectangle.

Though unfussy, the cotton sheeting is exceptionally inviting, its simple grid pattern echoing that of the floor covering. The bedcover has been cut at the corners for a neat fit, and moulds snugly around the thick bedposts, confirming the impression of comfort given by the quilting and the overstuffed pillows.

DRESSING THE BED

The most basic form of cover is a rectangle of fabric thrown over the bed. The fabric moulds itself to the form, perhaps draping over it so that its edges hang down or rest on the floor, or tucks in neatly round the shape of the mattress. The effect can be economical in both senses: think of inexpensive white ticking bunching on to a simple jute rug for example. On the other hand, quite special sorts of 'fabric' such as old quilts and kelims also just drape over the bed's form and are not manipulated in any new way. Duvets and wadded bedcovers mould over the mattress and round off its square corners.

Whether a simple bedroom is casual or austere in the mood it creates, the design is often deliberately planned to keep extraneous details out of the picture. (The apparent simplicity of a Japanese bedroom conceals deep philosophical deliberations.) It also demands discipline in everyday upkeep to stop personal clutter interfering with the clean unbroken lines and smooth surfaces.

The most basic bed shape is that of the divan, but even ornate beds can be treated simply. The cottage look of a quilt combined with a traditional iron bedstead allows you to enjoy the quiltmaker's skill undistracted by its setting. An empire-style daybed needs simple bedclothes that will tuck in round the mattress so that the polished wooden frame can be fully appreciated.

Two crisp white cotton sheets are the only covering for this beautiful bed. Nothing is allowed to distract the eye from the bed's fluid lines and its delicate caning at head and foot. For the same reason, there is no colour anywhere that might compete with the glowing tones of the wood. The light diffusing softly through the screen adds to the relaxed, yet almost wistful mood.

The most obvious simple coverings to make are throwovers (see pages 162–63) and duvets (see page 168). Fitted bedcovers (see pages 164–65) can either just be tailored and perhaps piped, with plain or striped fabric underlining the smooth outline of the bed, or they can be made into a feature – so that the bed becomes a focal point in the room. Patterned fabrics, contrasting piping and borders and accessories such as tailored bolsters help to create a quiet grandeur that is particularly flattering to beds of classic style and proportions, but that enhances even a simple divan shape. Pleating or gathering the skirt adds to the decorative effect.

Traditionally the dressed bed used ordinary furnishing fabrics, often ornately patterned chintzes, but you can achieve an equally handsome result with other less conventional fabrics of varying weights and textural qualities. Consider using crisp ticking with emphatic contrasting borders, or painting a plain sailcloth in an all-over design to give an opulent look.

A bed of specific character can be the obvious starting point for a decorative fabric effect. Four-posters will often dictate the way you suspend the fabric on the frame, though you are still free to make unexpected choices – flimsy silk instead of thick velvet, perhaps. The shapely head and foot of an empire-style daybed are too fine to mask in complicated folds, though they make ideal supports for the wings of a simple canopy hung over a pole: you could bring a

The basic bed below looks both smart and inviting. A double futon lies directly on the floor, covered by quilt, bolsters and pillow. With the only decorative touch the tassel on the pillow, the effect is practical, austere yet tactile. The use of colour is pleasing – the bolsters and pillow tone exactly with the wall grid.

freshness to your interpretation of this time-honoured style by using cambric or cheesecloth instead of the more predictable brocades. With plainer beds, even divans, there are ways of creating similar effects, without all the business of frames and testers, by suspending fabric from curtain rails or poles attached to walls and ceilings.

Most rooms offer little flexibility in positioning something as large as a bed, and attaching a decorative framework of fabric to walls and ceiling will make the position more permanent. On the other hand, architectural elements may offer a structural shape that makes a useful starting point for a design with fabric – perhaps a chimney breast that is transformed into a half-tester, or a picture rail to which you can staple an improvised canopy – and fabric used as a decorating tool makes wonderful camouflage, distracting the eye with a flourish from less attractive areas. I know of a room where the bed is flanked by two doors of unequal size; the doors are painted to match the walls, and a fabric canopy above the bedhead forms a pronounced triangular shape that draws attention away from the imbalance.

Fabrics used around beds are often echoed or repeated at the windows. I like to see this done subtly by picking up a detail or trim from the curtains, say, and using it in larger quantities around the bed – or vice versa. This sounds like the 'mix-and-match' technique beloved by so many interior designers, but I prefer the 'coordination' to be slightly open-ended. You could even create a bazaar effect by juxtaposing single widths of different fabrics that have something in common without joining them with seams or separating them out with borders. I find it exciting to keep a tension in the contrast between two fabrics so that they balance, rather than dovetail together too predictably. On the other hand, there does need to be *some* relationship between different fabric elements in a room – otherwise they will fight or cancel each other out.

The essential grandness of a four-poster like the one on the right, set in a spacious room, can be reinforced by the fabric treatment. Here a mellow floral glazed cotton is given real strength by the use of a contrast border along all visible edges. Especially decorative because of the border are the corners of the fitted diamond-quilted cover, cut away on either side of the bedposts.

The box pleats of the valance recur in the lining fabric used at the head of the bed, and two lined working curtains are fitted on rings at the head of the bed. Double tails at all four corners and pretty double swags on three sides show off the painted detail on the bed frames.

When there is colour and pattern in the fabric, the setting automatically becomes more formal. In the pleasant room on the left, the floral fabric of the valance and tucked-in bedcover covers the bolsters and cushions, and is even continued in the upholstered panelling of the head- and footboards. The bolsters are serving their traditional purpose of supporting the pillows.

DRAPES & HANGINGS

A framework of decorative drapes and swags offers plenty of scope for enjoying the appearance of large quantities of fabric. Canopies over a bed hang in a three-dimensional triangle or cube, which is seen from inside and below as well as from the outside, offering opportunities to use contrast linings creatively (see page 63) – or, indeed, to experiment with translucent fabrics.

Most bed hangings, moreover, are not functional. If you need to keep out draughts or yearn to sleep in a fabric tent, you can furnish a four-poster bed with curtains that actually draw: otherwise it is acceptable to hang dress curtains, which save on yardage. There is no need for your fabric to be particularly hard-wearing or light-resistant. You can show glimpses of a fragile or partly worn treasured old fabric by using it as a lining or a trim with a more robust companion (see page 35). There is plenty of opportunity to use decorative edgings and borders (see page 28). Fringes, in particular, will show to best effect.

History provides the inspiration for many of the canopies that are being revived today, as well as the patterns for a mass of reproduction half-tester, tented and four-poster bed frames. Unless you are much concerned with period authenticity and have a room of the right proportions, the best approach is not to take the old designs too literally. 'Read' them for the lines the fabric makes, its qualities of stiffness or suppleness and the general effect, and then reinterpret them with a personal twist.

For the simpler canopies that suit most of today's settings, use fabrics in only one or two colours. Better still, concentrate on texture. For a lightweight unlined fabric appropriately attractive to the touch, consider a perforated silk noil, or a white linen in an interesting slubby texture or a fine shirting linen. The whiteness and slight translucency of a fine canopy keep the room spacious: if you want a more solid-looking shape, try using one of these lightweight fabrics as a lining beneath something heavier and coarser. With a simple curtain canopy suspended in a triangular shape from a pole, it has an attractive 'underskirt' effect.

The space in the very small room on the left (c. 4×4m/13×13ft) has been used to productive effect. The bed is built on a plinth painted white. In complete contrast, the working curtains are made from old kelims, rich in colour and detail. Heavy and solid, they can enclose the bed space completely. The owner's delight in texture is obvious – not only from the kelims but from the rug and cushions, the floor, the elaborate carving on the chair and from the highly personal collection of objects and sculptures.

Fixings for bed canopies can be very straightforward. For an empire-bed look (fig. a), screw a pole about 50–60cm/ 1½–2ft long into a recess end bracket (see p. 102). You can simply drape fabric over the pole or make a slot heading for it (see p. 119).

For more complex draperies (fig. b), you could use two poles as long as the width of the bed, either wall- or ceiling-mounted. If the poles are wooden, tack the fabric to them to secure it.

The height of poles above the bed will depend on the architecture and proportions of the room, but they are usually fixed about 30cm/12in below the ceiling.

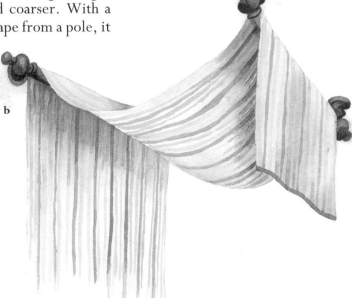

I find that choosing cool clear colours, especially white- and grey-based, steers you away from the traditional bedroomy look. Canvas cotton ducks make beautifully sculptured folds for simply draped canopies and tented effects. For finer drapes, use thick muslin for soft folds and poplin for crispness.

If you want to create a dramatic or opulent effect, opt for silk taffeta in rich jewel-colours, which glints with light, or checked fabric with a moiré finish in good deep colours. Both lend themselves to extravagant treatments echoing those of the fully dressed window (see pages 52–3), and go with the sheen of a highly polished wooden bedstead. You can take advantage of dress widths: dyed shot silk is available at reasonable prices, markets often have bargains in so-called exotic materials and shops selling sari fabrics can provide a rich source of unusual fabrics.

The design of the room below has been built around its centrepiece – the wooden bed and its patchwork quilt bedspread. A cool green in the quilt appears in the rug, the wallpaper, the paintwork and in the minimal curtains.

The bed hanging is the perfect finishing touch: it stresses the importance of the bed and emphasizes room height by drawing the eye up to cornice level. The hanging is made from two pieces of fabric, a lightweight organza and a heavy dark cotton, again green. The two are not joined together but simply draped over a pole fixed to the wall.

Remember that sumptuous fabric effects need to be matched by the scale, style and textures of other furnishings in the room. Grand effects need space to carry them off – rooms of generous proportions, and preferably substantial furniture to lend weight to their frivolity. Simpler effects, with inexpensive materials and do-it-yourself support systems, are not so demanding.

Styling details

The traditional furnishings used around four-posters and half-testers – curtains drawing along poles or tracks; or swags, drapes or pelmets; or tie-bands and so on – share both the same fixings and the same styling techniques as window dressings. For a curtain hanging against a wall at the head of the bed, for example, the decisions are much the same: whether to hang the curtain from cornice height to make the fabric extend the full drop of the wall or to create a more localized fabric area, perhaps using swags to suggest a frame. You choose the heading that suits the texture and draping qualities of your fabric (see pages 108–23).

Remember that hangings around the bed are viewed from both sides. Either choose fabrics with both sides the same, or make the

The setting of the room above is traditional, but this treatment (unlike the one on the left) would equally well suit a modern bedroom. Again, it is the addition of fabric at the bedhead that makes the impact.

A half-tester attached to the wall and ceiling holds a fabric arrangement that dominates an otherwise plain bed with a fabric-covered headboard. The plain bedlinen and the white moiré eiderdown show off the quilting without detracting from the elaborate bedhead. Helped by the matching window- and bed-curtains, the mood is welcoming and cosy.

most of the need for a lining (see page 100). For the same reason avoid headings that are made with curtain tapes (see page 106), because they can be seen from the inside.

When sketching out your ideas for canopies to be hung above the bed, get a builder to confirm that the hardware you are planning to use can be fixed securely to the wall or to a ceiling joist and will take the weight of fabric you want to use. It is often necessary to adapt your design to accommodate such structural practicalities.

Wall canopies

The simplest canopies consist of a strip of fabric slung in an inverted V-shape over a projecting pole. The drapes can be caught back on either side with some suitable tie-band (see page 124), but quite often they rest on the bed's frame, which takes some of their weight. The classic form is combined with an empire-style bed set lengthways against the wall, with the curved ends of the bed taking the weight of the heavy fabric and helping it drape beautifully.

A single width of fabric often gives the cue for the length of the pole that will be the depth of the canopy; the lining may be attached or separate. The same lining fabric is often used to fill the V-shaped space against the wall, perhaps gathered or pleated at the top and raying out in a fan at the bottom.

Ornamental tie-bands, braiding, borders, tassels, rosettes and other decorative touches can be added to create a neo-classical or exotic mood. The slot heading through which the pole passes can have a contrasting border to add height.

Half-testers

The support for a traditional half-tester is usually a continuation of the frame at the head of the bed. Drapes at either side make a shallow three-dimensional effect that can be exploited with a contrast lining also running across the width of the bedhead.

To make your own version of a 'ceilinged' half-tester, you could have a board cantilevered out from the wall on brackets (hidden by the two wings of fabric). Alternatively, a framework of curtain track or poles could be suspended from a structurally sound ceiling.

Half-testers often tend towards folksy prettiness but by using thick, firm fabrics such as sailcloth you can create a quite different atmosphere; lustrous cottons with fine stripes make an unfussy alternative in a lighter weight. Another approach is to twist fabric around a pole as for loose drapes (see page 134).

Even a fabric as plain and inexpensive as this sheeny parachute silk can look stunning when used with imagination.

The perfectly ordinary bed on the right has a ticking self-striped duvet cover and self-bordered pillows that provide a welcome splash of colour. Around and above it, a modern version of the four- *poster has been constructed from photographers' poles, over which quantities of parachute silk have been draped. The fabric has just been casually caught around the poles and knotted, lending the end result a deliciously spontaneous air — in spite of all the effort that obviously went into it.*

Fabric cubes

The four-poster is the extreme example of a fully dressed bed, its framework supporting a valanced ceiling and four vertical walls of fabric in full sail. It was the fabrics and the way they were arranged that people admired about most old beds: the timber frame was often concealed completely, or glimpsed between the rich hangings. The completely furnished four-poster is a period piece in most contexts now and many people like the look of the frame unadorned. A handsome frame can also look attractive with just twisting swags of fabric softening its outlines (such as the lace dress curtains on page 145).

Alternative treatments

A suggestion of the overhead canopy can be achieved with curtain poles suspended from the ceiling; swags or sheets of fabric can be draped and hung in mid-room around the bed as if defining an invisible cube. Or, in an alcove or small space, the fabric walls and the walls of the room may more or less coincide. One historic precedent for this was the old curtained box bed, with panelled wooden ends and base, standing alongside a wall and often built in. The idea of the bed as a self-contained interior, temporarily screened or curtained off, gives excellent scope for fabric – swathes of soft Irish linen, creamy muslin or strong striped awning-like canvas. Children in particular love these spaces where they can hide or play secretly together, and bunk beds can be arranged to give the room-within-a-room illusion.

In the room on the right, the rich, heavily patterned fabric makes the impact, with no help here from a stunning bed frame. The use of only two colours tones down the complexity of the design, simultaneously reinforcing its strength.

The bedcover is tucked under the mattress, allowing access to the built-in drawer underneath and encouraging the use of the bed as a couch by day. The matt surfaces of walls, woodwork and carpeting play a strong supporting role, with a hint of further complexity in the rug. The shape of the swag and tail at the window adds an eye-catching final touch.

The solid oak bed frame on the left dominates its setting; nevertheless the intricate carving on the bedhead and frame is superbly partnered by the lavish detail on the bedspread, cushions and bolster.

The central panel of the bedspread and circles on the cushions are cut from an original piece of Turkish goldwork embroidery, while the side panels of the bedspread are black velvet, dyed by the owner and joined to the original pieces. The background fabric of the cushions and bolster is heavy black wool. The owner also added the braid and tassels to the cushions and bolster. Rich and grand though the overall effect undoubtedly is, this is not at the expense of comfort.

COVERS & LINEN

The bed itself provides a specific framework for fabric. In assessing its potential, you can divide the bed area into 'sections' – the basic rectangle of the mattress, the vertical lines of any head and/or foot, plus the adjacent space in the room.

Futons, plain divans and straightforward beds with low-profile modern frames are flattened cubes that you can treat as you please, keeping them simple or dressing them up. Other styles are more explicitly beds – divans with conspicuous headboards, and ornate bedsteads in wood or metal. The extreme form of the more obvious bed shape is where the head grows upwards into a half-tester, or where both head and foot meet overhead in a four-poster.

Simple beds

Simple beds give you a rectangular cube to dress up or down as you please. The understated shape can be unobtrusive.

Divans can be completely covered with throwover or fitted bedcovers. If you use a duvet, without a bedcover, the sprung base (and any under-bed storage) needs to be concealed by a valance of some kind. Covers for divans can go round all four sides, though it is not necessary to cover a side placed permanently against a wall.

Divans used as seating areas during the day need the minimum of decoration – perhaps just contrasting piping. A tailored valance and a throwover tucked between mattress and base can be made in robust fabric: grey flannel is smart and unfussy.

Futons often double up as sofas during the day. Concentrate on a sheet, a duvet cover and one or two pillows or bolsters and make these work as a whole. Simple stripes and plain colours retain the simplicity of the futon style: your own hand-painted stripes on an understated cotton fabric could look stunning and very individual.

Beds with frames

Unless it is just a simple fabric-covered headboard, a frame almost always links the bed to some particular style, besides introducing a material that is not fabric. The style of cover and choice of fabric should not be fussy, but they need to emphasize the obvious decorative qualities of the bed frame. With traditional bedsteads in brass, iron or old polished hardwood, I think it is quite important to choose natural fabrics that are in keeping: tickings with white or black piping and striped poplin shirtings are good, but nothing really beats crisp white slightly starched cottons.

This exquisite bed is shown off perfectly by its silky soft cotton bedcover and self-bordered pillow. The puckering of the fabric all over the quilt, normally undesirable, is here a most attractive feature. The simple grid pattern, created by a single stitch line interrupted by fabric flowers, is surprisingly understated, even though the fabric is offset by toning Austrian blinds. The bedcover is thoroughly decorative, yet in no way detracts from the shape of the bed.

In the room on the left, the bed hangings establish the mood, falling gracefully from a tester on the ceiling to loop casually round the elaborate bedposts. But the throwover bedcover, although less immediately eye-catching, is playing a strong supporting role. Plain white linen with a delicate edging along its border, the cover's inviting expanse of fabric reflects and increases the fresh, cool, crisp feel of the bedroom.

In contrast, nothing in the modern bedroom below is allowed to distract from the semi-circles of alcove and window recess or from the rectangle of the bed. The fitted deep blue cover shows off the outlines of the bed, while the self-consciously casual bunching of fabric onto the floor brings out the form of the fabric as well as the bed. The only decoration is in the seam joins, which have been made into a special feature on the bed skirt.

Bedsteads in brass and iron are often high off the ground. A fitted cover with a box section over the mattress and a straight or gathered skirt beneath will exaggerate that height; proportions are better with a generously sized duvet or a three-quarter-length throwover, plus a valance between bed frame and floor.

Whether or not there is a well-turned leg to reveal, a valance or skirt section needs to be split at the corners to accommodate the frame. An attractive border emphasizes the split and draws attention to the bed frame. A traditional long bolster is a good solution to the gap that often yawns on this type of bed between mattress and frame. **Bed frames** with a 'solid' footboard will also need a split in any valance or skirt section. For a modern bed where the proportions are low and streamlined, a duvet makes a convenient cover, in a colour and texture that complement the material of the bed.

Empire beds also have solid footboards, which show off the beautiful quality of the polished wood. The shape of such beds is so special that it needs only the simplest tucked-in throwover or tailored bedcover, with no skirt to spoil the lines. Firm bolsters, tailored or trimmed with rosettes, are flattering and quite in keeping with the dignity of the bed.

Four-posters are special cases of beds with frames. Bedcovers need to be sympathetic to any curtaining or drapes, but almost all four-posters look their best with their height counterbalanced by bed-coverings which bridge the gap between mattress and floor.

Divan

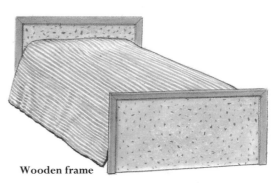

Wooden frame

Futon

Brass frame

Steel frame

Four-poster

THROWOVER BEDCOVERS

The detailed instructions that follow are for making a lined throwover bedcover with rounded corners. I also include a variation, which involves extending the lining round to the front of the main fabric to form a broad border with mitred corners. As long as you use appropriate fabric for the lining, the bedcover is potentially reversible.

There is no shaping involved in the method I use, apart from rounding the corners. Although it is possible to add intricacies such as a pillow flap or a T-shaped base to suit a bedstead, I prefer a throwover to be a simple rectangle of fabric draped over the bed. It touches the floor on either side and at the foot of a divan, and is tucked under the mattress if the bed has a decorative wooden frame so as not to conceal it.

The simplicity of the throwover need not make it dull. Such a large expanse of fabric offers the opportunity to be creative, perhaps in one of the ways described on pages 27–44. Use a soft, draping fabric that moulds to the bed, or a stiffer fabric for a crisper, squarer outline. A thick or lightly quilted fabric creates more rounded contours. Shape, however, is subordinate to the colour, pattern and texture of the chosen fabric.

MEASURING THE BED

Measure the bed with the usual bedclothes on it, including pillows. The finished length, A, runs from the bedhead to the floor at the foot end. Allow an extra 25–30cm/10–12in of fabric to go behind the pillows. The finished width, B, runs across from floor to floor at either side of the bed (or to the desired height from the floor).

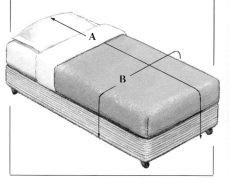

Throwover bedcovers offer wonderful opportunities for borders. Here are just three suggestions.
Top: The flat cotton canvas striped cover is bordered with dull red glazed cotton.
Centre: The cover is made from marbled beige cotton, with the inset green cotton border slightly raised.
Bottom: Two borders decorate the edges of this dark glazed cotton, a simple red edging and a double red and cream stripe. The stripe is made up first and then inset into the green.

ESTIMATING THE FABRIC

Unless you are using sheeting for a single bed or have joined strips of fabric together, you will need to join fabric widths (see p. 111). Centre the main width and add the usual seam allowances. Press all seams open.

Allow extra for any pattern repeat (see p. 200). Add 4cm/1½in all round to the finished length and width of fabric and lining.

MAKING A THROWOVER WITH ROUNDED CORNER

1 Cut the fabric and lining to the required length and width, positioning seams in the lining to match up with those in the main fabric. Place the fabric on top of the lining, right sides together.

2 Use a plate or saucer to mark a cutting line on the wrong side of the fabric for the rounded corners (fig. a).

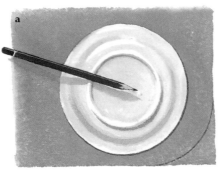

3 Allowing 2cm/¾in all round, machine stitch fabric and lining together, following the marked curve at the corners. Leave an opening of about 40cm/16in in the middle at the head end. Trim away the surplus fabric at the corners (fig. b) and clip the curved corners to help them lie flat (see p. 205).

4 Turn the bedcover the right way out through the unstitched opening and press. Slipstitch along the opening to finish.

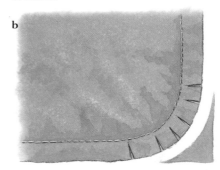

MAKING A THROWOVER WITH A LINING BORDER

1 Cut two pieces of fabric, the top piece to the size of the finished bedcover, and both the width and length of the base piece to the size of the finished cover plus twice the width of the border plus twice 2cm/¾in seam allowances.

2 Centre the top piece on the base piece with right sides and bottom raw edges together. Machine stitch the two bottom raw edges along the 2cm/¾in seam allowance, starting 2cm/¾in from the corner of the top piece and finishing 2cm/¾in from the opposite corner (fig. c). Press the seam away from the top piece. Sew the top raw edges in the same way.

3 Centre the top piece of fabric over the base piece, creating a loose fold at either side, equal to the finished width of the border (fig. d). Press along the fold lines and press seams open.

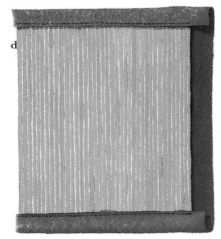

4 Move the top piece so that its raw side edge lies along the raw side edge of the base piece, keeping the 'fold' of fabric thus created out of the way (fig. e). Machine stitch along the 2cm/¾in seam allowance down the side of the cover. Press the seam away from the top piece.

Sew the other side edges in the same way, leaving a gap in the middle of 40cm/16in.

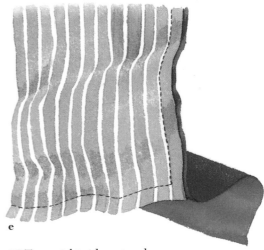

5 Turn right side out and press. Folding under surplus fabric, press corners flat. Slipstitch the mitred corners (fig. f) and the 40cm/16in opening.

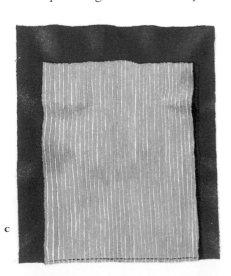

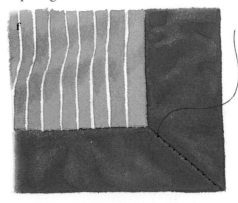

FITTED BEDCOVERS

Unlike the simple throwover, a bedcover tailored to fit an individual bed is relatively complicated to make. For the look of understated elegance, especially when offset by plain, textured fabrics or those with subtle motifs rather than bold patterns, the effort is well worthwhile.

The method of making an unlined fitted bedcover that I describe here divides the cover into three parts: a flat top panel, a box strip corresponding to the depth of the mattress and a straight skirt with inverted pleats at each corner. The box strip and skirt run along three sides of the bed, extending neatly about 20cm/8in round the corners at the bedhead.

Designed for a divan with its head against the wall, the instructions for this bedcover could easily be adapted for a divan set lengthwise against the wall. To use the cover on a bedstead rather than a divan, simply omit the inverted pleats, cut the corners and hem these vertical edges of the skirt's panels so that they fall on either side of the legs at the foot of the bed.

You can further emphasize the tailored look by adding piping, between the main panel and the box strip and between the box strip and the skirt. A matching pair of bolsters (see page 172) placed at either end of a plain bed would look very smart. For a softer line, on the other hand, double the amount of skirt fabric and gather it into the box strip, as for the valance on page 166.

ESTIMATING THE FABRIC

If you are using stripes or a one-way fabric, run the pattern as shown (fig. a), positioning seams joining widths as inconspicuously as possible.
Top panel: Add 4cm/1½in to the distances A and B. (If you need to join widths, centre the main piece and press seams open as on p. 111.)
Box strip: This is made in four sections. For each of the two side pieces, add 4cm/1½in to the distance A and the same to C; for each of the two end pieces, add 4cm/1½in to the distance B and the same to C.
Skirt: This is made in three sections. For each of the two side pieces (which carry allowances for the box pleats), add 90cm/38in to the distance A and 4cm/1½in to D; for the end piece, add 10cm/4in to B and 4cm/1½in to D.

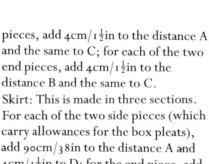

a

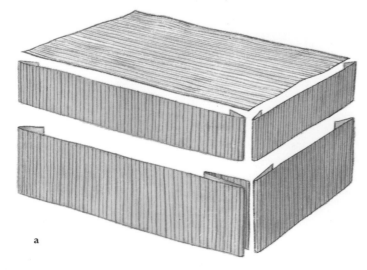

MEASURING THE BED

Measure the bed with the usual bedclothes on it, without pillows. Divide the bed into three sections. For the top panel and the box strip, measure the length and width of the mattress, A and B. For the box strip, measure in addition the mattress depth, C. For the skirt, measure in addition the distance from the base of the mattress to the floor, D.

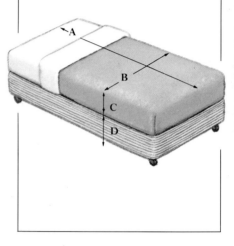

JOINING THE BOX STRIP TO THE TOP PANEL

1 Cut out all the pieces of fabric to the correct measurements. On the top panel, mark the centre point of the corners on seam allowances.

The ideas on the right apply to valances (see p. 166) as much as to fitted covers.
Left: This ticking cover has a box-pleated skirt below a box strip. Piping runs all around the cover between the main panel and the box strip. The inverted part of the pleat is contrast lined in deep red.
Centre: This simple grey flannel cover has no box strip and inverted kick pleats on the corners only. Red piping adds colour.
Right: A heavy blue linen main panel has been fitted with a lightly gathered skirt in a pretty pattern.

2 To make the box strip, machine stitch the short edges of the end pieces to the short edges of the side pieces, right sides together. Press the seams open.

3 With right sides together, pin the box strip to the top panel, matching the seams in the box strip to the marked centre point of the top panel corners. Machine stitch box strip and top panel together, taking a 2cm/$\frac{3}{4}$in seam allowance (fig. b).

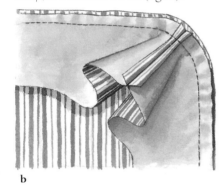

b

4 Clip the corners (see p. 205) through both layers and press seams towards the box strip.

MAKING UP THE SKIRT

1 Machine stitch each short edge of the end piece to a short edge of a side piece, right sides together, taking a 2cm/$\frac{3}{4}$in seam allowance. Then press seams open and slipstitch or machine stitch a double 1cm/$\frac{1}{2}$in hem all along the base edge of the skirt.

2 With the skirt right side up, fold the fabric as shown (fig. c) to form an inverted pleat, so the centre of the pleat matches the corner seam on the box strip and so the seam is invisible inside the pleat. Press the pleat and keep it in position with tacking stitches. Measure the correct distance and make the second pleat in the same way, and so on until all are completed.

c

JOINING THE SKIRT TO THE BOX STRIP

1 Match the centres of the pleats to the corner seams of the box strip and pin. With right sides together and allowing for 2cm/$\frac{3}{4}$in seams, from the head machine stitch the top of the skirt to the bottom of the box strip.

2 Remove the tacking stitches from the secured inverted pleats. Slipstitch the raw horizontal edge of the box strip and the vertical edges of the skirt at the head end of the top panel (fig. d). On the wrong side of the fabric, trim all the raw seams and neaten with binding or pinking shears.

d

VALANCES

The instructions given here are for a lined valance with a gathered skirt, finished with a piping run. Accurate measuring and cutting out of the separate pieces is the complicated part of this; the sewing is not difficult. For a professional fit, my method uses a panel of inexpensive lining fabric beneath the mattress, bordered by strips of the main fabric, the only part of the panel to become visible if the mattress shifts. This panel is then lined to enclose all raw edges of the skirt and to give firmer support. The lined skirt is continuous round three sides of the bed, returning round the head end at least 15cm/ 6in from each corner, as for a divan with its head against the wall. (For a bedstead, make sides and base sections in separate panels so that they hang on either side of the bed's legs.)

Since the valance is visible below the duvet or bedcover, use fabrics that work together. You could choose the same fabric as for the bedcover, perhaps with a contrasting border. The skirt is best lined, unless the fabric is very thick.

A valance need not be a flouncy, over-decorative affair. Made in a tough fabric such as ticking or cotton canvas or drill, without too much fullness, the skirt looks substantial and falls in heavy moulded folds. I think it looks particularly attractive if allowed to sit on the floor rather than hanging just above it. A tailored alternative is to use a firm fabric capable of holding box pleats (see page 122). The result is smart and crisp. For an even more tailored look, try making a valance with no fullness in the skirt, but inverted pleats at the corners – like the skirt of the fitted bedcover on page 165.

MEASURING THE BED

Measure the bed base without bedclothes. The finished length, A, runs the length of the bed base. The finished width, B, runs the width of the bed base. The finished depth, C, runs from the top of the bed base to the floor.

MATERIALS

- Fabric and lining
- Piping cord twice the length of the bed plus width plus 30cm/12in

ESTIMATING THE FABRIC

If necessary, join widths (see p. 111) of lining fabric for the panel.
Bottom panel: Using lining fabric, cut one piece as long as A plus 4cm/1½in and as wide as B plus 4cm/1½in.
Upper panel: Cut a second piece of lining fabric 30cm/12in smaller each way than A and B, plus 2cm/¾in.
Border strips: Cut four strips of main fabric 15cm/6in wide; two strips should be as long as B plus 4cm/1½in less 30cm/12in, and two as long as A plus 4cm/1½in.
Skirt: Cut a piece of fabric as deep as C plus 4cm/1½in. The basic length of the valance skirt is B plus twice A plus 30cm/12in for turns at the bedhead: depending on the fullness, multiply this figure by 2, 2½ or 3. Allow for this quantity in main fabric and in lining. Allow for pattern repeats (see p. 200) and allow extra fabric for piping.

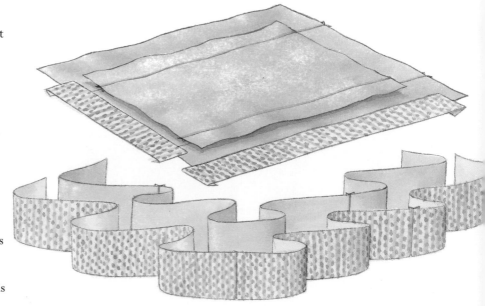

MAKING THE MAIN PANEL

With right sides together and allowing 2cm/¾in for seams, machine stitch the two shorter border strips of main fabric to the short edges of the upper panel of lining fabric, and press seams open (fig. a). In the same way, machine stitch the long border strips to the long edges of the upper panel and press (fig. b).

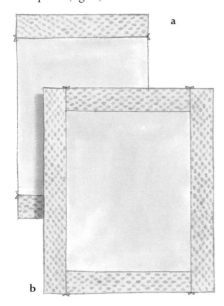

MAKING THE SKIRT

1 Prepare a piping run (see p. 125) to fit round the bed sides and foot, as well as 15cm/6in round each corner at the bedhead.

2 Make the skirt as you would a lined frill (see p. 88). With the frill turned right side out, pin the raw edges of fabric and lining at the top.

JOINING THE SKIRT TO THE MAIN PANEL

1 Starting at the head end, 15cm/6in in from the corner, apply piping to the right side of the main panel along the 2cm/¾in seam allowance (see p. 125). Clip to ease at the corners (see p. 205) and finish 15cm/6in along the head from the opposite top corner.

2 Press under a 2cm/¾in seam allowance on each vertical end of the skirt. Starting at the head end, 15cm/6in in from the corner, apply the skirt over the piping run, right sides together, and machine stitch through all layers (fig. c). (With such a long frill you need not be scrupulously accurate unless you are working with very little fullness;

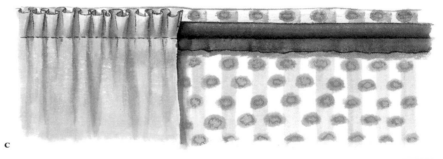

adjust the gathers as you go, allowing plenty of fullness at each corner. If you find you have a surplus length of frill to trim off at the end, keep a 2cm/¾in seam allowance on the vertical edge of the skirt, and press under.)

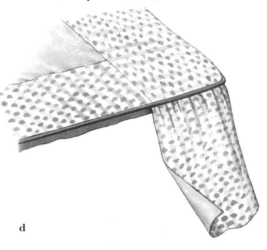

3 Finish off the raw vertical edges of the skirt at either side by turning under and slipstitching the seam (fig. d).

LINING THE MAIN PANEL

Fold back the skirt to lie on top of the main panel, right sides together. Lay the bottom panel of lining fabric on top of the main panel, right sides together, sandwiching the skirt. Machine stitch the edges of the two panels together with a 2cm/¾in seam allowance, pushing the fullness of the skirt towards the centre so as not to catch any skirt fabric as you sew (fig. e). Leave a gap at the head end of 40cm/16in.

Turn the valance right side out, and slipstitch the gap closed.

DUVET COVERS

The instructions that follow are for an unlined duvet cover, which is simply a bag sewn from two rectangles of fabric, with the opening fastened either with Velcro or with press studs. You can fold sheeting fabric over in a single piece, in which case only the sides need seaming. If you are using fabric in narrower widths, centre the main panel and join part widths on either side as for curtains (see page 111).

The undersurface of a duvet cover should be smooth against the skin, but the upper side can be embellished – with borders, joined strips of fabric or a lightweight textured weave. Keep fabrics soft. The only restrictions are that the top fabric should not be uncomfortably heavy and that it should be compatible with the underside for washing.

ESTIMATING THE FABRIC

Measure the dimensions of the quilt, which should overlap the bed by about 25cm/10in. Cut out two pieces of fabric for the duvet cover, each quilt length plus 6cm/2½in and quilt width plus 4cm/1½in.

(If you are using one length of fabric folded, cut it to twice quilt length plus 8cm/3¼in and quilt width plus 4cm/1½in.)

MAKING THE COVER

1 Using French seams (see p. 204), machine stitch the two pieces of fabric along both sides and across the top, clipping corners after the first stage of stitching. Turn right side out.

2 Press under a double 2cm/¾in hem along both open long edges.

ATTACHING PRESS STUDS

Machine stitch the hem. Then sew the press studs at intervals of about 20cm/8in across the opening (fig. a), taking care not to let stitching show on right side of fabric. Make sure that pairs of studs line up exactly. With studs closed, topstitch an X-shape at either end through all layers to secure the corners of the opening.

a

ATTACHING VELCRO

Place the two halves of the Velcro along the hems on either side of the open edge, and machine stitch along both long edges of the tape (fig. b). This stitches the hem as well as securing the Velcro. With the Velcro closed, topstitch an X-shape at either end through all layers to secure the corners of the opening (fig. c).

b

c

This streamlined, modern room with its clean, sharp lines has clearly defined ground colours – white, pale grey and charcoal grey. The duvet cover is made from white starched ticking, but the pattern has been organized to break up the large expanse of white with colour. Joined strips of glazed cotton, charcoal grey and red, have been inset as a border.

DECORATIVE SEAMS

When making duvet covers (and bedcovers generally) you usually have to join widths of fabric (see p. 111). If the fabric is plain, the seams are very noticeable. Why not insert a contrast fabric border between the two widths of fabric you are joining?

You could have two plain colours next to each other (for instance, blue and black strips on a plain white cover). Then again you could put stripes or checks within the seam space. Try setting patterned fabrics in between a plain fabric ground, or selecting two or three different fabrics in the same colour for your cover and using two more different textures for the inset border. Use old fabrics (see p. 35) or painted fabrics (see p. 36) that you make first, then cut into strips and insert into the seams. Simple additions like this will make all the difference.

PILLOWCASES

The instructions below are for plain pillowcases, which are simply made from one length of fabric with a pocket on the inside (although you can use up remnants, with separate pieces for top, bottom and pocket flap), and for self-bordered 'Oxford' pillowcases. The latter have a 5cm/2in border all the way round, formed by folding extra fabric in one layer over the other. Made from crisp, white or navy cotton, for instance, these square pillowcases can look stunning.

The lines of the classic sofa below are broken up by a profusion of pillows and bolsters. The shapes, textures and fabrics – including Thai silk, moiré, Toile de Jouy and butcher's striped ticking – all complement each other in an inviting way.

A PLAIN PILLOWCASE

1 Measure the width and length of the pillow. If you are making the pillowcase from a single folded length, add 4cm/1½in to the pillow width and 25cm/10in to twice the pillow length, to allow for seams, hems and the pocket flap. Cut out the fabric.

2 Turn under a double 12mm/½in hem on one end (which will become the pocket flap inside the pillowcase). Make a hem on the opposite end by turning under first 12mm/½in then 5cm/2in. Machine stitch both hems.

3 With wrong sides together, fold down the pocket flap 17cm/6½in and fold as shown (fig. a). Stitch along the two long edges in the first stage of a French seam (see p. 204).

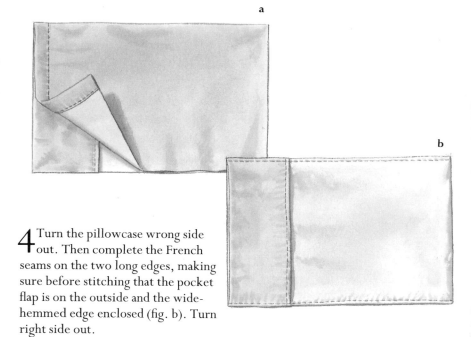

4 Turn the pillowcase wrong side out. Then complete the French seams on the two long edges, making sure before stitching that the pocket flap is on the outside and the wide-hemmed edge enclosed (fig. b). Turn right side out.

A SELF-BORDERED 'OXFORD' PILLOWCASE

1 Measure the sides of the square pillow. Cut out the three pieces: a top piece, pillow width plus 4cm/1½in and pillow length plus 5cm/2in; a square bottom piece, pillow width and length plus 24cm/10in; a pocket flap, pillow width plus 4cm/1½in times 20cm/8in.

2 At the base end of the top piece, turn under 12mm/½in, then 2cm/¾in, and machine stitch to make a hem. Make a double 12mm/½in hem along one long edge of the pocket flap.

3 On the bottom piece, fold under all the edges 2.5cm/1in, then 5cm/2in, and press. Open out the second fold and mitre corners (see p. 203). Refold to form the border (fig. c).

4 With wrong sides together, tuck the seam allowance on the three raw edges of the pocket flap evenly beneath the folded edges of the border at the opening end of the pillow. Sew in position by zigzag stitching along the long edge; the stitches will at the same time catch the inner edge of the adjacent border (fig. d).

5 With wrong sides together, place the top section of the pillow on the bottom piece, so that its hemmed edge is level with the zigzag stitching at the pocket end. Keeping the layers flat, tuck the seam allowances on its three raw edges evenly beneath the folded edges of the border. Zigzag or satin stitch into position round all three sides (fig. e).

c   d   e

BOLSTERS

Traditionally, bolsters are used as firm cushions on chaises longues, daybeds and similar couches. A bolster made with a well-stuffed feather pad is often placed along the width of a bed as support for other pillows (this is especially useful on bedsteads where there is a gap between mattress and bedhead). Bolsters also make popular pillows for futons.

The instructions below are for a neatly geometric cylinder, formally edged with a piping run. But a bolster can also be a soft sausage shape, perhaps with ends simply knotted – it all depends on the firmness of the pad, the texture of the fabric and the style of the finish. The ends can also be gathered into a central tassel. As with all cushions, the choice of fabric influences character: bold stripes and bright colours make bolsters more fun and informal, while smooth, silky fabrics – particularly embellished with tassels and ties – make them grand and luxurious.

MATERIALS

- Fabric
- Bolster pad (see p. 190)
- Zip about three-quarters of bolster's length
- Piping cord twice bolster's circumference

ESTIMATING THE FABRIC

The bolster is made from three sections of fabric – a main piece and two ends. Measure the length and circumference of the bolster. This gives you the dimensions of the main piece, plus 4cm/1½in all round for seams.

For the end pieces, cut two circles each the same diameter as the bolster, plus 2cm/¾in all round. Make a paper pattern as a cutting guide.

You also need enough bias-cut fabric (matching or contrasting) for the piping runs – the circumference of the circle times two plus the usual allowances.

MAKING THE BOLSTER

1 With right sides together, machine stitch the long edges of the bolster together at either end to make a cylinder of fabric, leaving three-quarters of the length open for the zip to be inserted. Press the seams open. Insert the zip (see p. 205).

2 On the right side of the end pieces, draw a line in chalk 2cm/¾in in from the circumference as a sewing guide. Machine stitch a piping run with a piping or zipper foot to each circle, clipping the piping runs to ease them smoothly round the curved edges (fig. a).

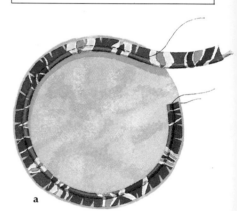

a

3 With right sides together and taking 2cm/¾in seams, pin and machine stitch each end of the bolster tube to a piped circle (fig. b). Clip the curves of the other two layers as you go. Turn the bolster right side out and insert the pad.

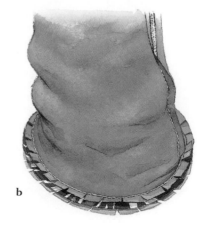

b

BOLSTER STYLES

As an alternative to a fitted bolster, simply make a long tube the circumference of the bolster pad. Neaten the ends with narrow hems or decorate with contrasting borders. Depending on the thickness and flexibility of the fabric, you can create a Christmas cracker effect, leave a floppy tail of fabric or twist a casual-looking knot. The ends can be tied with ribbon or be self-knotted. (This last option can take up a lot of fabric, so test it before you calculate and cut out. You are likely to need at least twice the length of the bolster pad.)

COVERINGS

CHOOSING A STYLE
• Pattern mixing •

FABRIC SURFACES
• Room dividers & screens •

FABRIC FURNISHINGS
• Seating • throws • dining chairs • cushions •
• tablecloths •

CHOOSING A STYLE

So far in this book I have concentrated on fabrics as hangings — at windows and on beds. In this chapter, I want to discuss the ways, whether on a small or a large scale, in which fabric can be used to transform the surfaces of a room. Fabric panels on the wall, for example, can emphasize architectural detail, while tent-like swathes of fabric can alter a room's shape and feel. Fabric can complement or contrast with the shapes of the furniture — imagine a floor-length cloth softening the hard-edged outline of a circular table, or a colourful throw breaking the harsh straight lines of a modern sofa.

To demonstrate the very different effects you can produce, let me create two interiors. In one — a sharp-edged, black and white kitchen with ceramic tiles, white-painted cupboards, wooden slatted blinds and marble surfaces — plain white kitchen chairs have been given padded seat cushions covered in black and white gingham, secured with ties. The fabric, although still monotone, contributes a tactile softness that reinforces the contrasts of the hard surfaces. In my other example, a bedroom lacking any distinguishing architectural features has been turned into an Arabian tent, using a mixture of richly patterned brocades and dazzling stripes, each with the same density of background tone, but in vibrantly different colours — magenta, indigo and emerald green. The walls and ceiling are completely hidden under a neat tented shape. Minimal window blinds contrast with the exuberance of the interior. To be inside this room is to be caught up in a world of fabric, at once welcoming, dominating and exotic.

Pattern mixing

Nothing dictates that you have to use one fabric pattern only. A method popular in the nineteenth century was to use two different patterned fabrics on walls, alternating them to create vertical stripes, but I have seen several fabrics used inspiringly, with different patterns but toning colours.

Indiscriminate mixing of patterns and fabrics seems to work best in rooms that are otherwise fairly bare, perhaps with plain pale walls and unobtrusive polished floorboards. If you want to cover several surfaces in a room — walls, windows, furniture — with fabric, juxtaposing different patterns, it pays to keep to a limited colour

The elegant furniture in this large, formal interior has, perhaps surprisingly, been disguised with white loose covers. Single pieces of fabric shaped only very slightly have been tucked in around chairs and sofa. The effect is to reinforce the feeling of light and space in the room, with the covers echoing the white mouldings on the ceiling.

The deep fringe on the shawl over the daybed provides a vivid touch of textural interest, while the pale rug successfully links the white covers and the antique carpet. This could be the permanent look of the interior — or it could be seasonal, temporary protection for grand furniture only on display at certain times.

palette and pattern design, following colours through from one fabric to another. Otherwise the impact is lost in the sheer excess, and the dazzling display of rich colours and textures becomes jarring and overwhelming.

For more subtle but equally interesting effects, you could keep to one colour – say pale grey – and mix texture and pattern only; rough linens on walls and raw silks over chairs, for instance, with a formal window arrangement in heavy damask contrasting with flimsy organza would be texturally exciting.

Practical points

I have limited the technical information in this chapter to items that can be easily made, and that do not require a great deal of precise tailoring. Loose covers (or, more accurately, fitted removable covers) need careful measurement, accurate pattern cutting and very precise making up if they are not to look amateurish and disappointingly baggy. Unless you want to embark on a specialized upholstery course, far better to limit yourself to making simple, genuinely loose covers and throws that look good without especially skilled effort.

The interior on the right has been painted to dramatic effect, with fabrics carefully selected to enrich the colour scheme. The striped curtain, the paisley shawl and the puffy layers of damask over the table enhance each other, their textures and weights as crucial as their patterns and colours. It is the interplay between fabrics and setting that makes this clever room so appealing.

The interior below, on the other hand, is clever to the point of being contrived. The formal lines of the classical trompe l'oeil, *helped by stagey lighting, produce the effect of an exquisite backdrop, to be observed rather than inhabited. The covers casually flung over the chairs like dustsheets reinforce this view. Although tied at the sides to prevent them from slipping, these loose covers were surely never meant to be used.*

FABRIC SURFACES

Fabric makes an unusual covering for walls and even ceilings. This aspect of interior decoration is dominated by paint and paper nowadays, but fabric was once the rule in grand houses. In medieval times, the earliest forms of fabric covering were free-hanging tapestries. These could be taken down easily and carried off by the household if it had to decamp in a hurry. As society stabilized, more permanent fabric wall coverings became popular, in a variety of fabrics – silk, satin, velvet, damask and canvas, and even stamped and figured leather. The fabric was normally either fixed to panels or glued directly to the plaster. Later, in the eighteenth century, when printed fabrics came into popular use, including the handsome striped Empire designs and the famous Toile de Jouy (now appealing to younger tastes and enjoying a revival), these, too, were used for highly successful all-over treatments on ceilings and walls, and at windows.

It can be great fun to transform a room by covering the walls, and perhaps the ceiling, with fabric. There is maximum scope for imagination – but remember that such large quantities of cloth can be overpowering. Choose fabrics carefully, keeping to the style and period of your house. As a general rule, avoid large-patterned fabric; stripes nearly always work, and equally good are small motifs or geometric designs. Dark-coloured fabric, plain or printed, will add strength to an interior, while making a large room seem smaller and more intimate. In contrast, translucent fabrics, loosely gathered and draped, provide light ethereal effects, and give a feeling of air and space.

Ambitious, tent-like effects, covering the ceiling as well as the walls, can be created using the 'marquee' principle, where the fabric is gathered from a central point. In a high-ceilinged room, you could construct an internal 'roof' from translucent fabric, so creating a second space. A loosely woven slubby Indian cotton would also look splendid, pinned from ceiling to floor in informal folds, altering the proportions and creating a room within a room.

If the concept of a permanent fabric room strikes you as daunting, why not try using fabric on this scale for something more short-term? Wonderful temporary effects can be achieved for parties and special occasions, using sheeting for overhead canopies, indoors or out. Eyelets round the edge of the fabric can take ropes and cords,

The shape of this airy conservatory has been the inspiration for the fabric arrangement. A tented ceiling dominates: widths of dipped cotton voile have been joined into a large fabric cylinder, gathered at one end into the centre of the ceiling and pinned at the other all the way round the edge.

The short slot-headed curtains are made to look as if the ceiling is continuing down the sides of the room. Softened with silk edging, the straight lines of the curtains are also broken by flowing swags and tails. The room can take these quantities of fabric without being oppressive, because its bare surfaces give it a spacious feel.

attached by screw eyes to walls or ceilings – or a pergola in the garden – to make a suspended awning.

If you simply want to cover the walls, fabric can be stapled to thin wooden battens screwed into the wall, or clipped to a dado rail if there is one. On a smaller scale, fabric can be successfully hung on individual panels around the room or used to draw attention to an alcove. Imagine a length of dyed shot silk in a rich emerald blue, caught at ceiling height and hanging behind a shelf on which one or two pieces of glass or painted ceramics are displayed to great effect. This would be equally eye-catching in a classically plain, formal room or a pristine, white modern interior.

Some of the ideas for original fabrics mentioned on pages 27–44 would look particularly good displayed on panels, including the painted and dyed effects on calico, canvas or unbleached sheeting. Or fabric could be treated with stiffeners like wallpaper paste (see page 44) to produce a material that has a rigid, more paper-like quality.

To create a successful wall or ceiling treatment, you need a sure colour sense and a good understanding of the qualities or shortcomings of the architecture of the room. If you are in any doubt about

Fabric can be used on walls to create very different moods. In the room on the right, fine, translucent, lightly gathered, silk voile curtains hang on the walls suspended from thin battens. By falling in front of the pictures and doorways, these hangings are softening the contours of the room; subtle and unobtrusive – their colour the same as that of the walls – they quietly extend the mood inspired by the bed to the rest of the interior.

The room below could hardly be more different. The choice of a modern glazed cotton, casually gathered on a 2.5cm/1in tape and hung on the wall by picture hooks, makes an inspired setting for the many older fabrics, like the paisley shawl and tapestry cushions. As a result, the décor exactly captures the mood of a Victorian drawing room. (See p. 63 for a surprisingly altered summer version of the same interior.)

your ability to achieve the effect you want, seek advice from an interior designer whose work you respect. Even a small room covered in inexpensive fabric can cost a substantial amount.

Practical points

Fabric has the advantage that it can be draped, cut and pinned to cover awkward spaces, for example under a sloping ceiling or in a narrow alcove. Any wrinkles or ruches simply add to the charm of the effect. In the same way, fabric has an immediate ability to cover imperfections in the wall's surface, provided of course that the wall is strong enough to take the fixings required for attaching the fabric to its surface.

The amount of fabric will need to be estimated in the same way as wallpaper, matching patterns and joining widths, and allowing for fullness where relevant. Edges will need to be neatened with hems if clipped to the wall or, if stapled to a batten, with a finishing such as braid glued over the top. A rolled strip of fabric can be used like piping, to cover edges at ceiling and skirting height. On a tented ceiling, the central point from which the gathered fabric fans out will need to be finished with a rosette (see right) or with a flat fabric-covered shape.

A principle often used for covering walls and ceilings is here adapted, I think more appropriately, to make a tented 'roof' for a bed. Clearly defined pleats radiate outwards from a central rosette.

The rosette, top, is simply a cut circle of fabric, gathered round the edges and then pulled up into a 'shower cap' shape. This ruching is secured by stabbing stitches before the raw edges are attached, on the underside, to a circle of tarlatan, which is sewn or stapled to the ceiling fabric.

The rosette, bottom, is joined to the ceiling in the same way. Initially a square piece of fabric, contrast lined, is folded equally at all four corners, which are then secured with invisible stitching under a decorative button.

ROOM DIVIDERS & SCREENS

Fabric can be used successfully both to make movable screens or to divide a room into different functions. Free-standing screens are wonderfully versatile, dividing room space or acting as a backdrop to a specific item of furniture – a particularly handsome chaise longue, perhaps. Whether of solid wood, or simple wooden frames, screens display fabric to advantage. Bear in mind that they are also a good medium for showing off a fabric that you have created yourself – whether stitched and pleated or painted and dyed.

The sides of a screen can be covered identically or with contrasting fabrics. The latter allow great flexibility, linking two rooms with different colour schemes. A plain white linen on one side of a screen backed with a brilliantly coloured striped cotton on the other would be interesting, especially on a frame screen, where the light would be able to shine through.

For permanently positioned room dividers, a series of roller blinds offer a good solution, as they can be drawn down or pulled up to varying heights. Their functional and unobtrusive nature makes them suitable not only for modern interiors – like the one below – but also for rooms that are formal and classical.

The living and sleeping areas of the large split-level room below are clearly defined by a line of four roller blinds. Visual interest is lent to the plain blinds by the neat wooden pelmet concealing the roller mechanisms at the top. In addition, a light shining from behind the pelmet casts atmospheric shadows, both on the floor and onto the slightly overlapping blinds. Made of strong fabric and heavily weighted in the base to keep them vertical, when down the blinds make an effective fabric wall.

COVERING A SCREEN

The instructions that follow are for a solid wooden-frame screen (as opposed to one with a 'hospital' frame that might take a curtain with a slot heading at top and bottom).

Your approach to covering the screen will depend on how it is hinged and panelled. Before following the instructions below, you will probably either have to remove layers of fabric from an old frame or make a new one. However your screen is made, the golden rule is to work on one panel at a time, first making sure that no part of the mechanism, such as hinges, protrudes beyond the edge.

If the screen has a front and a back, start by covering the back, so that the front's neat edges conceal the raw edges of the fabric attached to the back.

MATERIALS

- Wooden frame or solid screen
- Fabric
- Dacron or interlining same size as fabric
- Braid long enough to go round all sides of all panels, no wider than the width of the narrow edge
- Fabric glue
- Tacks or staples and staple gun

ESTIMATING THE FABRIC

Measure the length and width of each panel of the screen. Cut out two pieces of fabric and two pieces of interlining for every panel, each the length and width of the panel plus 2cm/¾in seam allowance all round.

COVERING THE SCREEN

1 With the screen flat on a table or floor, cover the back of one panel with interlining. Starting in the middle of the top edge, tack or staple the interlining to the frame (fig. a).

2 Stretch the interlining taut across and down the frame, and staple or tack it to the middle of the panel's bottom edge, then down the middle of each side edge. Trim the interlining accurately around all four edges, so that it does not extend beyond the back of the panel to the narrow edges.

b

4 Cover the back of one panel with fabric, right side up. Tack or staple the fabric to the frame as for the interlining, this time going into the narrow edges (fig. b). Trim the fabric around all four edges of the panel.

5 Turn over the panel. Tack or staple fabric in the same order to the front of the panel, pressing under a neat 12mm/½in hem allowance that covers the raw edge of fabric on the back (fig. c). Repeat for all panels.

6 Starting from an inconspicuous point towards the base of the frame, stick braid in position, using a fabric glue according to the manufacturers' instructions. Unroll the braid as you go along. When you have gone all round one panel, press the end under and stick it to the first so that the edges do not fray.

a

3 Repeat steps 1 and 2 for both sides of all panels of the screen.

c

This four-part screen has been covered in ticking after being stripped of layers of old fabric down to the bare frame. Its edges finished off with toning braid, the neutral screen can either be a very plain and functional space divider, or, appropriately draped with fabric throws, it can stand as a piece of furniture in its own right.

In the austere modern room below, multiple linen screens on a metal frame make an appropriate covering for the large picture windows. One piece of fabric doubled over is stretched taut at top and bottom, with eyelets punched into the hems serving as a decorative inset border. The fabric is then slotted onto battens that run by the eyelets.

FABRIC FURNISHINGS

Most upholstered furniture comes complete with its fabric surface, although these days there is a growing trend to take covers only to their cambric undercover, allowing the customer to choose fabric for a removable or fitted cover. Both upholstery and fitted covers are beyond the scope of this book, since they demand expert cutting and fitting. This chapter is concentrating instead on the many exciting coverings that you can create without any particular experience but which will, just as successfully, transform a piece of furniture and, together, the look of a whole room. Most are covers for seating but cloths for tables are also included.

Fitted and loose covers

If you are having fitted covers made, try to make sure that the style is in keeping with the design of the chair or sofa it is covering. If it is period furniture, why not try to establish the kind of fabric or pattern that was once used for the upholstery and make sure that the fitted cover retains some of this quality, in either texture or pattern? Fitted removable covers are first and foremost a practical item, safeguarding the upholstery from damage.

A simple combination of textures always looks interesting. Consider a plain smooth off-white fabric on a light-wood chair, contrasting with a richly textured one – heavy ribbed cotton, say – in a similar colour for the cushions.

Piping helps to define the shape, and a line that contrasts with the main fabric defines it even more clearly. Consider, in the same room, austere white armchairs piped in black next to a solid black sofa defined with white piping. Add to this an assortment of contrasting plain cushions, and the effect is both dramatic and eye-catching.

Throws

The simplest form of fabric cover-up is to leave the fabric uncut and unshaped, a two-dimensional textile that drapes over and partly hides the form it covers. The idea is to create an effortless display, but fabrics and furniture treated in this way have to be appropriate

Pattern and texture, formal and informal, are cleverly mixed in this large room, giving it a lived-in but restful feeling. There is nothing at the windows to distract from their classic proportions, from the mouldings on the ceiling or from the elaborate cornice work. Yet this cool grey and blue background is set off with patches of warm rich colour, in the shape of throws casually draped over elegant upholstery, lending significance to the form of the furniture. The paisley shawl draped over the double-sided sofa in the foreground, so striking against the pale striped upholstery, could also be functioning as room divider.

for the purpose. A simple white sheeting dust-cover throw looks best on furniture that retains the elements of its form even when very loosely covered. Temporary-looking covers of this kind can perfectly well become so popular that they remain as a permanent feature of the room.

Chairs and sofas look good when only partly covered – if the fabric is draped casually, like a shawl, over the back or an arm. This works particularly well with strong, richly patterned fabric on a plain ground. In practical terms, throws are a wonderful device for giving an old or worn cover a few more years of life.

Dining chairs

One of the best ways of transforming a junk shop chair, or of protecting a valuable upholstered one, is to make loose slip covers for the back and seat. A particularly effective-looking fabric (although not hard-wearing) is inexpensive gingham – black and white for a town-house dining room, perhaps, and blue and white for a less formal interior. The back cover is just two pieces of fabric joined at the top with a seam and at the sides with matching ties. The seat is a single piece of fabric with the corners cut out at each leg, similarly fastened with ties.

The modern chair on the right has been transformed by its carefully designed and constructed cover. The cream linen has a multi-layered look, with the double and even triple pleats at the corners giving it weight and substance. A line of applied braid runs along the hem. The result is both loose and fitted, simple and complex.

In contrast, the salon chairs and sofa of the period interior below have merely been protected, rather than disguised, with faded and bleached fabric slipcovers. Cut in sections to fit the furniture, the covers are held on with numerous ties, which have been caught in the hems of the main sections. This method of securing can be adapted easily to almost any form of covered chair.

CUSHIONS

Although tailored, these are relatively easy to make as the form is regular. They must be measured and cut accurately, to ensure a good fit (see pages 200–1). Scatter cushions are the small square, rectangular or round cushions that provide decorative focal points and spots of comfortable support on plain expanses of seating. They provide opportunities for using up scraps of fabric in imaginative borders and trimmings. Squab cushions are more functional, strategically placed on hard seats and against chair backs.

A glorious alternative to the very tailored look is to use the cushion like a parcel, draping loose fabric around; this works particularly well with bolsters (see page 172). A simple soft bleached calico is as good as a hand-dyed raw silk in the right surroundings.

Another original idea, popular in France in the nineteenth century, was to have cushion covers attached at the four corners only, revealing an inner cover sandwiched between. A similar effect was also created for bolsters, with the circular ends 'bursting' open to reveal an inner cover underneath. Made in brocade, and adorned with tassels and cords, a modern-day version could be created in ticking with a black piped edge, open to reveal a scarlet inner cover.

Most fabrics make good cushion covers, although very fine ones, like muslin, in time strain at the seams. It is best to choose fabric on the basis of the likely wear the cushions will get.

Cushion pads

All cushion pads need an inner cover or casing for two reasons; the inner one remains intact when the outer one is removed for cleaning, and it can be thrown away complete when the time comes. Foam pads eventually start to disintegrate, and crumbs can then collect inside the inner cover.

Inner covers can be made from lining material – calico, ticking or cambric – in the same way as outer covers (see pages 194–97), omitting decoration and slipstitching the opening after filling.

Cushion fillings

Feathers are the best filling and the most expensive. Feather pads can be bought to size and in different degrees of firmness. Soft ones are comfortable and can be reshaped again and again; 'over-stuffed' ones have the solidity required of a seat pad.

Plastic or latex foam chips are cheap, but need to be used with care. Unless packed evenly, they become lumpy. Non-absorbent, they are practical outdoors. Foam blocks are ideal for solid squab or 'hamburger' cushions. They can be shaped with a Stanley knife.

An attractive setting is made even more inviting by the cushions, linked by pattern yet so diverse in their shapes and densities. They make the two sofas look like one unbroken line of seating. There are three self-bordered cushions, a square scatter cushion and two shaped hamburgers. Note too the unusual role of the tiny bolsters, acting as space dividers in between the big squab sofa cushions.

TABLECLOTHS

In seventeenth-century interiors, tables were often covered with a fringed table carpet, over which was laid a smaller, washable white linen cloth, often finely embroidered. Contrary to current convention, curiously enough, a round table covered with a square cloth emphasizes the roundness of the shape.

The layered look works best when the lower layer is solid and weighty-looking; a dark-coloured, substantial fabric looks best. It can be made more substantial by lining, interlining and even quilting, and by padded borders or chunky braiding and fringes. The top layer can either pick up one of the colours of the base layer, or make a contrast with it, although a crisp, starched linen top with exquisite drawn threadwork takes a lot of beating.

Another idea is to cover a round table with an excessively large white cloth and to knot up the four ends, so that the cloth billows and bunches onto the floor. Just as tables themselves vary in character, their fabric coverings can be organized to suit the situation, changing the effect when you change the cloth.

These two layered tablecloth arrangements are performing similar roles as focal point cloths. On the left, the colours in a restful bedroom are restricted and neutral. A beige linen undercloth drapes on the floor, with a square white cotton cloth as the top layer. Four lines of decorative satin stitching border the top cloth and intersect at its corners.

The cloths on the right are far more dramatic. The circular undercloth bunches on the floor next to the curtains, its stunning blue contrasting powerfully with their bleached pallor. The rich colours of the patterned topcloth extend into its edge — almost like a solid selvedge — and then on into the fringing. This alternate-coloured border adds bold definition to both layers of cloth.

PIPED & SELF-BORDERED CUSHION COVERS

The instructions that follow are for two types of square scatter cushion (the principle can be adapted to other shapes of pad). Both types are suitable for ordinary pads fairly loosely filled.

The basic method involves making a permanent opening, usually a zip. If ease of cleaning is not essential, you can of course omit the zip, simply slipstitching the cover closed once the pad has been inserted.

The piped cushion is just a bag with piping in between the two sides. It can take textural treatments, such as strips of fabric combined to form one surface (see page 33). Try offsetting multi-seamed main surfaces with piping in one of the joined fabrics. Or keep the main surfaces plain, but use stripy textured piping.

In contrast, the self-bordered cushion cover makes an impact by virtue of its simplicity (as with the similar pillowcase on page 171), and I would be reluctant to use joined or textured fabrics. Smooth 'classic' fabrics – silks, linen, plain-weave cottons – best suit the shape and feel of the bordering flap. You could always make the flap out of a neatly mitred border in a contrasting colour.

MATERIALS
- Fabric for cover and any piping runs
- Square cushion pad
- Piping cord, if used, the length of the four sides of the pad
- Zip 4cm/1½in shorter than one side of the pad

MAKING A PIPED COVER

The cushion cover should be fairly tight. Measure the length and width of the pad. Cut two square pieces of fabric to the finished size of the pad, plus 2cm/¾in seam allowances all round.

MAKING THE COVER

1 Make a piping run and apply it to the right side of one square piece of fabric, along the seam allowance all around the edges (see p. 125). This becomes the underside of the cushion. Clip the piping fabric at the corners (see p. 205).

2 With fabric right sides together, lay the second piece over the first (fig. a).

3 Make an opening for the zip on the underside of the cushion, setting the opening 2cm/¾in in from two corners. Stitching as close to the piping as possible and parallel to it, machine stitch through all layers for 3cm/1¼in at each end. Insert the zip into this seam (see p. 205), topstitching along the zip on the unpiped square of fabric (fig. b).

4 With fabric right sides together, and leaving the usual seam allowances, machine stitch the remaining three sides of the cushion cover. Remember to leave the zip open so that the cover can be turned right side out. Clip the corners and trim the seams with pinking shears (fig. c). Turn to right side out.

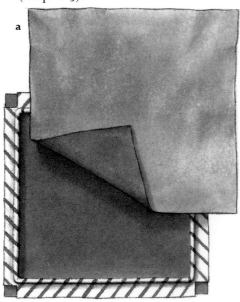

a

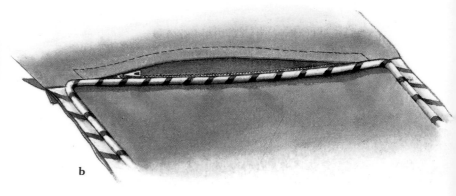

b

MAKING A SELF-BORDERED COVER

Measure the cushion pad. For the top side of the cushion, cut one piece of fabric to the size of the pad, plus twice the width of the border plus 2cm/¾in seam allowances all round.

For the underside of the cushion, cut a second piece, to the same length as the first piece but with an allowance in the width of an extra 3cm/1¼in for a zip.

INSERTING A ZIP

Make an opening for the zip in the second piece of fabric, setting the opening in 2cm/¾in from two corners. Machine stitch across the seam and border allowances and 12mm/½in into the main panel of fabric. Insert the zip into this seam (see p. 205).

MAKING THE COVER

1 Join the two squares of fabric along the seam allowances all the way round, right sides together (fig. d). (Be sure to leave the zip open so that the cover can be turned right side out.) Clip off the corners and trim the seams with pinking shears.

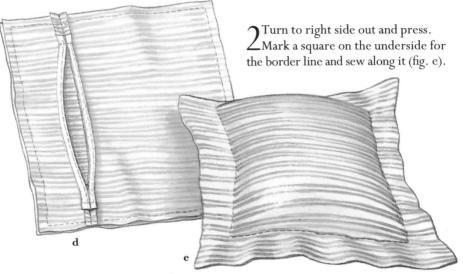

d

e

2 Turn to right side out and press. Mark a square on the underside for the border line and sew along it (fig. e).

In this welcoming study, the loosely filled scatter cushions are the perfect finishing touch. The fabrics in the room are all different tartan checks and plaids in earthy colours — ochre, terracotta and brick set off against deep blue. They make the room warm and appealing, comfortable and lived in. Showing off a variety of patterns, the cushions sit invitingly on the chair and window-seat.

SQUAB CUSHION COVER

The presence of a gusset, or welt, in between the upper and lower panels of fabric means that a squab (or box) cushion effectively has six facets like a cube. For this reason it needs a firmer, more block-shaped pad than the two cushions so far described.

The following method has the zip running along the fourth side or 'back' of the gusset. The proportions of the gusset can be adjusted to allow for a longer zip, which would make it easier to insert the pad. If you have to join fabric to make the long gusset strip, try to avoid positioning seams where they will be visible.

Because a squab cushion is often substantial (compared with ordinary scatter cushions), it can take thicker fabrics and textured weaves, as well as fabric made from joined strips. Piping round the edges of the upper and lower panels defines the shape well and strengthens the seams. Make sure that any bold stripes or checks are symmetrically placed, running from the top into the gusset.

MATERIALS

- Fabric for cover and piping runs
- Box-shaped cushion pad
- Zip 10cm/4in shorter than one side of the pad
- Piping cord twice the length of four sides of the pad

ESTIMATING AND CUTTING THE FABRIC

You need to cut out four pieces of fabric, one for the upper and one for the lower panel, and two for the gusset strip (fig. a).

Upper and lower panels: Cut out two pieces of fabric the size of the pad plus 2cm/¾in seam allowances.

Long gusset strip: Cut a piece the length of three sides of the pad, plus 10cm/4in plus 4cm/1½in seam allowances. Its width is the depth of the pad plus 4cm/1½in.

Short gusset strip: Cut a piece the length of one side of the pad less 10cm/4in, plus 4cm/1½in seam allowances. Its width is the depth of the pad plus 4cm/1½in seam allowances plus 3cm/1¼in for the zip.

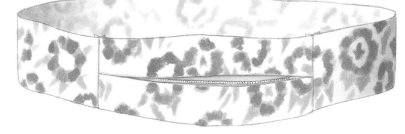

b

MAKING THE COVER

1 Apply a piping run to the edges of the two main panels of fabric (see p. 125).

2 Cut the short gusset strip in half lengthways and apply the zip (see p. 205), running the ends of the zip off the ends of the fabric.

3 Right sides together, machine stitch the short ends of the short gusset strip to the short ends of the long gusset strip (fig. b). Press all seams open.

4 Right sides together, machine stitch one long edge of the gusset strip to one of the piped panels along the seam allowances, matching the centre of the zip to the centre of the back of the panel (fig. c). Clip the gusset seam at the corners.

5 Join the other long edge of the gusset strip to the other piped main piece in exactly the same way. (Be sure to leave the zip open so that the cover can be turned right side out.) Trim seams and turn right side out.

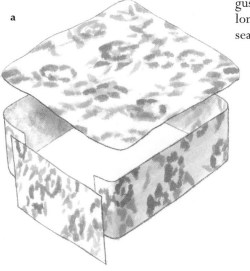

a

c

'HAMBURGER' CUSHION COVER

The shape of this soft-edged, solid cushion gives it its name. A cross between the squab and the simple piped cushion, it has a classic elegance, with definite depth, yet rounded contours. The rounded look is achieved either by using an all-purpose simple feather pad, fairly densely stuffed and with the corners poked inwards, or by using a foam block with its hard edges shaved off.

In the instructions that follow, the zip is inserted along one seam as with the piped cover on page 194, although it can also be set across the centre of the cushion underside. The latter position is preferable when cushions are stacked in pairs for a 'pouffe' effect, because a couple of strips of Velcro can be sewn to the centre of the underside of one cushion and the top side of another, to keep them together.

The solid and often large-scale nature of a 'hamburger' cushion means that all the fabric suggestions for squab cushions, left, apply. Thick fabric often puckers attractively where piped.

> ## MATERIALS
> - Fabric for cover and piping runs
> - Box-shaped cushion pad, with rounded corners
> - Zip 4cm/1½in shorter than one side of the pad
> - Piping cord the length of four sides of the pad

ESTIMATING AND CUTTING THE FABRIC

Measure the pad. Cut an upper panel of fabric the length and width of the pad top, plus half the pad depth plus 2cm/¾in seam allowances. Cut a lower panel of fabric the same width as the first piece, but allow an extra 3cm/1¼in in the length for the zip.

MAKING THE COVER

1 Make an opening in the lower panel of fabric for the zip. At each end machine stitch across the seam allowance and the pad depth allowance, extending 12mm/½in into the central fabric. Insert the zip into this seam (see p. 205).

2 Lie the cushion pad on the wrong side of the upper panel of fabric and mark the position of the corners with chalk. Cut away from each corner a square of fabric, the length of whose sides equals half the pad depth plus allowances (fig. d).

3 With right sides together, fold the upper panel of fabric so as to machine stitch together the newly cut edges of each square, stopping short at the seam allowances (fig. e). This makes a dart to the chalk marks (fig. f).

4 Repeat steps 2 and 3 with the lower panel of fabric.

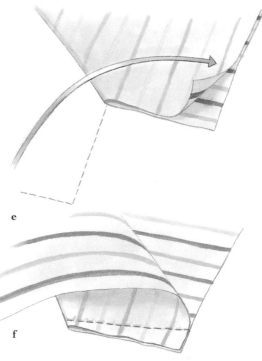

e

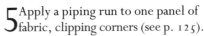

f

5 Apply a piping run to one panel of fabric, clipping corners (see p. 125).

6 Right sides together, join the other panel of fabric to the piped panel, taking care to position the darts on both panels so that they are aligned when the cover is turned right side out. Machine stitch along the seam allowances all the way round, remembering to leave the zip open so that the cover can be turned right side out. Trim the seams with pinking shears and turn to right side out.

d

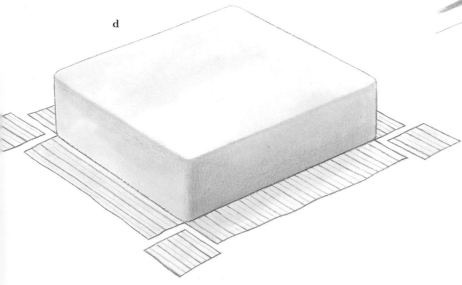

TABLECLOTHS

As with the skirt of a long dress, the edge of a tablecloth needs to brush the floor but also to push out of the way at the touch of a toe. The instructions opposite are for lined circular cloths (although a square cloth looks especially pleasing on a circular table, a simple square needs no special making instructions). You can adapt the circular method to make an oval cloth, by drawing a template based on the tabletop and adding the drop all round. Depending on the fabric width and table size, the seaming can run lengthwise or crosswise.

Simple hems are difficult to execute smoothly around the curving bottom edge of the cloth, and I find it easiest to machine stitch the main fabric and lining together round the edges, clip the curves, and then turn right sides out. This quick method is ideal for cloths where fabric and lining are of similar weights. You also have the option of making a border out of bias-cut strips of fabric, which mould themselves to the curve of the tablecloth.

Occasionally hand stitching gives a better finish, with the chance to apply braids or fringes. This more time-consuming method is an advantage with particularly shiny fabrics or if there is a significant difference in weight between fabric and lining (if the main fabric is interlined, say, and decoratively stitched or quilted).

MEASURING THE TABLE

Measure the diameter of the table, A, and the distance from top to floor (or whatever the required drop), B. For the full working diameter of the cloth, add A to twice B. To this add a 2cm/¾in seam allowance all round.

The hem of a full-length cloth should just brush the floor. If the cloth is to drape onto the floor, add 5–10cm/2–4in. Subtract the depth of any fringe or border.

Pale light and blue-grey walls show off this layered arrangement to advantage. The circular undercloth bunches stiffly on the floor, its damask goldwork full of delicate detail. The topcloth takes the form of a large rectangular Kashmir shawl, which has been positioned so that its corners also reach the floor. Elsewhere it has been carefully shaped to expose plenty of the undercloth. The cloths add depth to a cool corner, drawing attention to the books and objects displayed on the table.

ESTIMATING THE FABRIC

Unless very small, most circular cloths take more than one width of fabric. If the cloth needs two widths, the fabric length you need is twice the working diameter (see left).

Split a second width in half lengthways and join the halves to either side of the first width (fig.a). Allow extra fabric if you have to match any stripes or bold patterning.

Calculate lining in the same way.

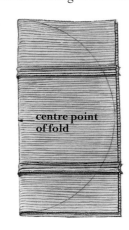

a

centre point of fold

CUTTING THE CIRCLE

Fold the fabric in half crossways, right sides together, keeping any seams even. Mark the centre point on the fold with a pin. Using string and pencil, carefully draw a semicircle on the fabric and cut through both layers along the pencil line (fig.a – see p. 201). As a guide for the seam allowance, draw a second line 2cm/$\frac{3}{4}$in inside the first.

MACHINE STITCHING A LINED CLOTH

1 Cut two identical circles, as fig. a, for fabric and lining.

2 With seams aligned and right sides together, stitch the lining to the main fabric around the circumference seamline. Leave a 30–40cm/12–18in gap for turning the cloth right side out. Trim the seam allowance all round and clip curves. Turn the cloth right side out and press carefully, so the lining does not sag at any point. Press under the seam allowances along the gap and slipstitch closed.

HAND STITCHING A LINED CLOTH

1 Cut two identical circles, as fig. a, for fabric and lining.

2 Carefully clip and press under the seam allowance all round the edges of both main fabric and lining, making a smooth curve. You may want to allow a 2.5cm/1in seam allowance for the lining, so that it does not show in front of the fabric.

3 Put the lining on top of the fabric, with wrong sides and seams together. Lock the lining into the fabric at the seams (see p. 112, steps 4 and 5).

4 Slipstitch all round the edges of the lining and main fabric (fig. b).

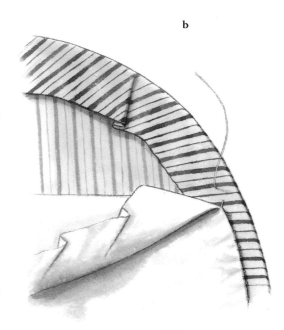

b

MAKING A CLOTH WITH A FABRIC BORDER

1 Calculate the lining as in *Estimating the fabric*; for the main fabric, deduct from the finished diameter twice the width required for the border, and add 4cm/1$\frac{1}{2}$in seam allowance. Cut two identical circles, as fig. a, for both the main fabric and the lining.

2 For the border, cut strips on the bias (see p. 201); they should be the width required plus 4cm/1$\frac{1}{2}$in seam allowance, and the length should be the same as the tablecloth circumference.

3 Machine stitch the bias-cut border strips end to end into a single long strip. With right sides together, machine stitch the long strip to the main fabric along the 2cm/$\frac{3}{4}$in seam allowance, following the curve carefully. Where the two ends of the long strip meet, turn under a 2cm/$\frac{3}{4}$in seam allowance on the bias and slipstitch closed (fig. c).

4 Either machine or hand stitch the main fabric to the lining along the seamline all around the circumference.

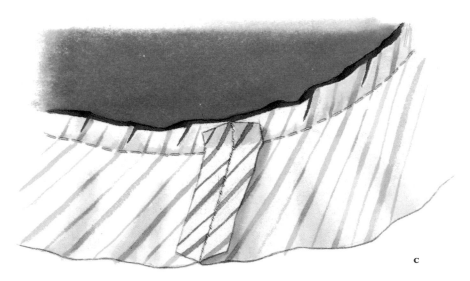

c

TECHNIQUES

I have gathered together in this short section the various practical skills that crop up time and again when making soft furnishings, and to which I have referred in specific instructions earlier in the book. I have taken for granted that anyone planning to make soft furnishings understands, at least, the rudiments of sewing. To some, the instructions on the following pages will be familiar but I hope that the short cuts I have included may, nevertheless, come in useful.

Those of you who have a knowledge of dressmaking will find that the usual criteria about setting up a workspace apply. Namely, that your sewing machine be set up in a well-lit position so that the light falls on your work; that you have space to set up a steam iron; that your machine has a sufficient range of stitch choices and accessories, including a zipper foot and gathering foot. You will also need a big table on which to lay your fabric while marking, measuring, cutting and handstitching. Being able to lay the fabric out flat and weighting it in position at the corners saves laborious pinning and tacking, and means that any handstitching can be done direct.

> ### BASIC EQUIPMENT
> - a steel measuring tape
> - a steel metre rule
> - a small plastic ruler
> - a pair of manageable, good quality cutting shears with large handles
> - small thread scissors
> - best-quality dressmaker's steel pins
> - any DIY equipment necessary for fixing poles or tracks to plaster or wood

FABRIC QUANTITIES

When calculating how much fabric you need for a particular item, take your time and work methodically, following the instructions given on the relevant pages for estimating total lengths and widths. Below, I simply outline a good way of calculating the number of fabric widths needed to make up a curtain or gathered blind; for details on joining the widths, turn to page 111.

CALCULATING WIDTHS

Before you can work out the number of fabric widths you need for a particular item, you must first find out the total fabric width required. A good general guideline to follow for curtains or gathered blinds is two and a half times the width of the curtain area (i.e. the length of the track or pole plus, in the case of tracks, any overlaps or returns), although this will vary according to the type of heading (see p. 108ff.) and weight of fabric used.

Once you have multiplied the finished width measurement by 2.5 to reach the total fabric width, you then divide by the width of fabric chosen (122cm/48in and 137cm/54in are fairly standard widths). Take, as an example, a finished width measurement of 234cm/93in. Multiply this by 2.5 to arrive at a total width of 585cm/234in and then divide by the width of the chosen fabric – in this case 122cm/48in – to give a figure of 4.79. As .79 is more than half a width, it is rounded up to the next full number, which means that, in total, five fabric widths are needed.

To find the total length of fabric required, multiply the working drop (see p. 206) by the number of fabric widths – in this case 5. Assuming a working drop of 264cm/105in, the total length of fabric needed will be 13.2m/43ft.

ALLOWING FOR PATTERN REPEATS

If you are calculating fabric widths for curtains or blinds in patterned fabric, make sure that you allow enough for pattern matching across the widths (fig. a). To calculate how much fabric you need, divide the working drop by the length of the pattern repeat,

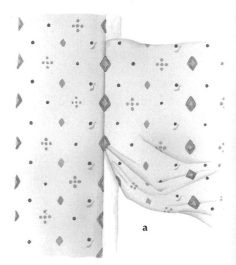

a

which can easily be measured if not already indicated by the fabric supplier. If the number you come up with is a fraction, round it up to the next full number and multiply this by the pattern repeat figure.

For example, assume that your curtains have a working drop of 313cm/125in and a pattern repeat of 91cm/36in. Dividing 313cm/125in by 91cm/36in gives you a figure of 3.4. This is rounded up to 4 and then multiplied by 91cm/36in to arrive at the full working drop: 364cm/144in.

CUTTING OUT

Cutting out comes second only in importance to accurate and thorough calculation of fabric quantities. The actual cutting process is simple and straightforward as long as you have a good pair of scissors and a relatively steady hand, but it is important to be aware of its irreversibility – if your measurements are inaccurate so that the fabric, hastily cut, is found to be insufficient, there is little that can be done. It is very distressing to discover you have cut all the fabric to the finished length but left no allowance for the hems. To avoid mishaps, it is always worthwhile spending time and effort at an earlier stage checking your calculations for accuracy.

CHECKING FOR FAULTS

Before cutting you should check the cloth carefully for faults, which are sometimes marked by a tag in the selvedge (fig. b). Stray threads or tiny dye spots can often be overlooked but where a thread has been pulled, a design badly printed or an area unevenly woven, the supplier should exchange the fabric. If this is impossible, make a note of the position of the fault and try to work round it.

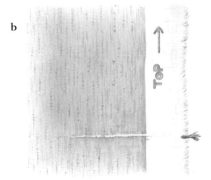

b

SELVEDGES

In order to give fabric a firm edge, extra threads of a stronger yarn are incorporated into the first few warp threads at either edge of the fabric to form the selvedges. With printed cloth, you may find information about the care of the fabric on the selvedge.

Once fabric has been cut, the selvedges should be removed. They are often more tightly woven than the rest of the fabric and can adversely affect the way the cloth lies.

If you need to cut fabric in half lengthways, fold selvedge to selvedge and cut along the fold.

BASIC RULES

It is essential that the fabric be cut straight and square (see p. 111). With loosely woven fabrics, a withdrawn weft thread can be used as a guideline (fig. c). On printed cloth, you will need to check whether or not the pattern is square to the selvedge. It may be slightly off, in which case you will have to accept a compromise and adjust the fabric as best you can.

Fabric lengths need to be joined from base to top so mark the fabric as you cut by snipping off a corner at the base of each length. In this way, you can be certain to join the lengths with any pile or shading running in the same direction.

CUTTING ALONG A THREAD

To ensure that loosely woven fabric is cut absolutely straight, pull a weft thread from the cloth to act as a guideline (fig. c).

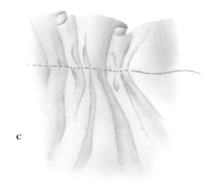

c

CUTTING A 'PERFECT' CURVE

If you are making any of the following items – swags, scallops, circular cloths or bolster ends – you will need to draw a curve onto the fabric before cutting. To do so, work out the radius of the circle from which you intend to draw the curve and cut a piece of string a bit longer than the radius measurement. Place one end of the string at a centre point on the wrong side of the fabric and use a drawing pin or weight to fix it. Attach a pencil to the other end of the string. Then keeping the string taut and the pencil upright, draw the curve onto the fabric (fig. d).

d

CUTTING ALONG THE BIAS

When cutting strips of fabric along the bias, make sure all edges are straight and then join the straight edge at an angle of 45° to the selvedge. The true bias lies along the diagonal fold that is formed. Cut along the fold keeping the fabric flat with your free hand.

STITCHES

I have chosen to illustrate only those hand stitches most commonly used in soft furnishings. In all cases, it is important to make the stitches a regular size and to keep the tension even so that the fabric is firmly secured. For a temporary tacking stitch, it is a good idea to use a contrasting coloured thread which will be visible for unpicking once the permanent stitching is in place.

TACKING STITCH

This is a temporary stitch, used to hold fabric in position while permanent stitching is being done, after which it is removed. It is also used to secure the first fold of a double base hem, and in this case it is not removed.

BUTTONHOLE STITCH

This is a strong, hardwearing stitch which is ideal for, say, securing rings to curtain fabric or hooks to fabric for hand-stitched curtain headings. Each stitch is finished with a small knot formed by looping the thread round the needle. A line of ten such stitches, closely spaced, provides a strong finish which would hold a curtain ring firmly in place.

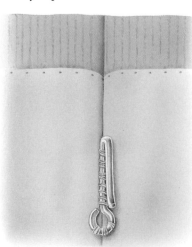

SLIPSTITCH

This stitch is used to hold a folded edge to flat fabric as for the hem of a curtain, and to hold two folded edges together as in a mitred corner (see opposite). It is worked from right to left and should be invisible when finished as only a few threads are picked up from the flat fabric at a time. The thread needs to be pulled through firmly but not too tightly or the fabric will pucker.

HERRINGBONE STITCH

This criss-cross stitch is used to secure single side hems as in curtains and Roman blinds. Working from left to right but with the needle pointing from right to left, a stitch is taken through the single layer of fabric, picking up only a couple of threads at a time. The needle is moved up and to the right and another stitch taken through the folded hem; the sequence is then repeated.

DAISY CHAIN STITCH

This stitch is used in the form of a chain to link lining to main fabric at the base of a curtain. The chain is worked by hand in the same way as the first row of stitching on any crocheted item. One end of the chain is then stitched to the hem of the lining and the other to the hem of the main fabric so that the two layers are linked.

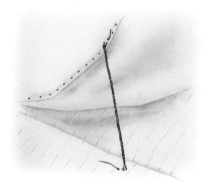

STAB STITCH

This stitch is used to secure several layers of fabric as in a curtain with a padded edge or to hold down the gathered folds of a decorative rosette (see below). It is a small stitch and should be invisible on the finished item.

HEMS

In order to achieve a flat, level hem, you must cut the fabric straight. As long as you have a straight cut edge, you can very simply fold over the required amount and press it into place with a steam iron, avoiding the extra work that pinning and tacking involves. If you wish the hem to be invisible on the top side of the fabric it should be finished by hand. Occasionally, if it is acceptable or even desirable that the stitching be seen, a machine-stitched hem can be used.

DOUBLE BASE HEM

As a general rule, all curtains are finished at the base edge with a double 10cm/4in hem, which neatly contains all raw edges and lies flat, as well as allowing you surplus fabric should you ever wish to lengthen the curtains. However, some unlined curtains may only be given a 5cm/2in double hem. The base hem on curtain lining is also finished with a double 5cm/2in hem. If you have insufficient fabric, a narrower hem can be used but it should still be double.

1 On the wrong side of the fabric, press up the full allowance along the base edge of the curtain – for a double 10cm/4in hem, this will be 20cm/8in. Open the hem out flat again (fig.a) and bring the bottom raw edge up to meet the pressed line. Press into position.

2 Fold the hem up along the first pressed line and slipstitch the upper folded edge to the main fabric (fig.b), mitring the corners at each end (see right).

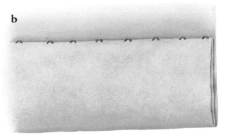

DOUBLE SIDE HEM

Double side hems are used to give a firm edge to the sides of items such as unlined curtains and Austrian blinds. A finished width of 1−2cm/½−¾in is usually enough for this type of hem. Make sure, however, that the edge of the fabric is cut straight before folding the hem over.

Start by folding the hem twice over on the wrong side of the fabric. Press into position and then begin to sew close to the inner folded edge, using a straight machine stitch or slipstitch. Continue to fold as you proceed down the side of the fabric.

SINGLE SIDE HEM

This type of hem is always used for items which are to be lined, or lined and interlined. You should aim for an allowance of at least 5cm/2in, although a narrower hem would do if you were short of fabric. For instance, if you were making Roman blinds to a finished width of 129cm/51in using a fabric width of 137cm/55in, the side hems could each be 4cm/1½in wide. To make the hem, simply fold over and press, mitre the corners (see right) and then secure with herringbone stitch (see opposite), using matching coloured thread.

MITRING CORNERS

This technique is used to form neat, flat corners, and is particularly useful for bulky fabrics. The advantage of this method is that the fabric is left intact so that, if required, the hems can be let down at a later stage. If making a mitred corner with a 10cm/4in double hem, press over the first 10cm/4in and then proceed as below.

1 Press over the required hem allowances – in this case, 5cm/2in for two single side hems – and open the fabric flat again. Turn over the corner of the fabric so that the diagonal folded line passes through the point where the two pressed lines meet (fig.c). If the fabric needs to be weighted, insert a weight under the folded corner (see fig.b, p. 112).

2 Turn in the hems along the pressed fold so that a neat diagonal seam is formed at the corner. Use slipstitch to secure the diagonal seam and any double hems. For single side hems, use herringbone stitch (fig.d).

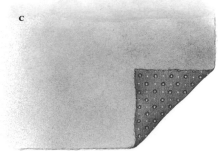

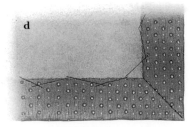

SEAMS

There are a wide variety of seams to choose from and making the right choice means taking into account a variety of factors, including the weight and thickness of the chosen fabric and the position of the seam on the item you are making. Always allow adequate fabric for the seam allowances, especially if the cloth is likely to fray, in which case oversewing may be advisable.

STRAIGHT STITCHED SEAM

This seam is used throughout soft furnishings to join widths or pieces of fabric. It is best to keep to a 2cm/$\frac{3}{4}$in seam allowance, although if you are joining bulky fabric or seaming cushion covers you may need a wider allowance, which can be trimmed after sewing.

1 With right sides together, machine stitch along the seam line (fig. a), making a few reverse stitches at the beginning and end of the seam to give a firm finish.

2 Using a steam iron, press the seam allowances open against the underside of the fabric (fig.b).

LAPPED SEAM

Interlining and interfacing are often made from bulky fabrics and are best joined with a lapped seam which gives a completely level finish. Since the seam will not be visible on the finished item, unfinished edges are acceptable.

1 With both pieces of fabric right side up, overlap one raw edge directly over the other one by 1−2cm/$\frac{1}{2}$−$\frac{3}{4}$in.

2 Machine stitch the two layers together using straight or zigzag stitch (fig. c). Trim the raw edges.

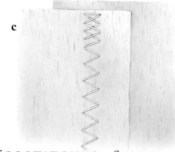

TOPSTITCHED SEAM

A simple way of making a decorative feature of a straight seam is to run a line of stitching along the right side of the fabric close to the original seam line. Topstitching can be done along one side of the seam or both, depending on the effect you are after.

1 Having stitched a straight seam, press the seam allowances open (see left, fig. b).

2 On the right side of the fabric, topstitch in a straight line close to the seam (fig. d).

FRENCH SEAM

This narrow double seam neatly contains all raw edges. It is used on unlined items, fine fabrics, and those which have a tendency to fray.

1 With wrong sides together, stitch a line 9mm/$\frac{3}{8}$in from the raw edge (fig. e). Trim close to the stitch line.

2 Press the seam back on itself so that the fabric is right sides together and then machine stitch 6mm/$\frac{1}{4}$in from the folded edge (fig. f). Press.

TURNING FABRIC TUBES INSIDE OUT

Making a tube of fabric can be surprisingly quick and easy if you follow the method outlined below.

1 Secure the end of a length of piping cord to the short edge of the strip of fabric and enclose it by stitching the long edges of the fabric strip, right sides together. Trim allowances and press the seam flat (see p.126, fig. d).

2 Pull the cord through the tube to turn right side out (see p.126, fig. e).

BINDING AN EDGE

Where an unlined Austrian or festoon blind is finished with a frill, the raw edge of the seam on the underside of the blind is neatly enclosed with a strip of bias-cut fabric (see p. 201) or a strip of bias binding.

1 Cut a strip of fabric along the bias or a piece of bias binding the length of the gathered frill plus 4cm/1½in for hems. For the width, allow 5–8cm/2–3¼in depending on the bulk of the fabric used.

2 Once the piping, if used, and frill have been applied (see pp. 125 and 88), lay the strip, right side down, against the underside of the frill so that raw edges are aligned.

3 Turn under a 2cm/¾in hem allowance on both short edges and,

g

h

leaving a 6mm/¼in seam allowance along the length of the binding strip, machine stitch into position, using a piping or zipper foot (fig. g). Remove from the machine.

4 Turn the blind over and bring the binding up over the raw edges so that they are neatly concealed. Fold under a 2cm/¾in seam allowance on the binding and secure with straight stitch the length of the folded edge (fig. h).

CLIPPING CURVES

Where a seam or hem allowance forms a curve, snipping the raw edge of the fabric close to the line of stitching allows the seam or hem to lie flat and reduces the strain on the fabric.

APPLYING ZIPS

These can be bought either cut to individual sizes and lengths or as one long roll of uncut teeth to which you apply individually bought zip tags. The advantage of the latter is that you can cut zips to any size you want and have only to neaten off the zip teeth above and below the tag.

LAPPED ZIP

In soft furnishings, zips are mostly used for fastening cushion covers and are best concealed by being inserted in the following way. The same method can be used for fastening the base of a duvet cover or the side of a bolster.

1 To make the opening into which the zip will be set, place the fabric right sides together and stitch an ordinary straight seam, leaving a gap into which the zip will fit.

2 With right sides together, place the right side of the zip to one side of the unstitched open section of the fabric so that the zip teeth extend over the opening by 2cm/¾in or so. Machine stitch close to the line of the seam allowance.

3 Open the zip and turn the item right side out. Open the seam out flat and position the zip underneath so that the folded edge of the seam

allowance completely covers all protruding zip teeth (fig. i).

4 On the right side, topstitch along the side of the zip, using a zipper foot. Then keeping the needle in the fabric, topstitch across the base of the zip to join the lines of stitching.

i

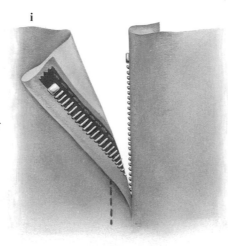

CENTRED ZIP

This is a simple, quick method of inserting a standard zip but it has one disadvantage – the zip can be seen on the finished item. For the zip to fit well, seam allowances on either side must be of equal width.

1 Stitch a straight seam, leaving a gap into which the zip will fit neatly. Press the seam allowances open along both the stitched and unstitched sections. On the right side of the fabric, roughly slipstitch the open section together so that the fabric stays in place while the zip is being inserted.

2 Centre the zip under the opening, right side to the fabric, and pin and tack in place. Then, on the right side of the fabric, topstitch the zip in place using a zipper foot. Finish off by stitching across the tape ends to join the lines of topstitching.

FABRIC CARE

Everyday wear and tear of furnishing fabrics is inevitable but can be greatly reduced by regular cleaning and fast action when it comes to removing stains of all types.

CLEANING FABRIC

On the selvedges of most fabrics, you will find cleaning instructions in the form of care symbols. If a fabric has not been pre-shrunk, take note of the shrinkage percentage and allow for this when estimating fabric. Any lined items will need to be dry-cleaned. For those fabrics which can be washed, follow the manufacturer's instructions as closely as possible.

STAIN REMOVAL

Man-made fibres do not absorb moisture as quickly as natural fibres and stains can generally be removed with blotting paper or a soft cloth, if applied at once. For more persistent stains, search out one of the various proprietary stain removers designed to work on specific fabrics or particular stains. These substances are often highly inflammable so follow the manufacturer's instructions carefully and use in well-ventilated areas. If you are unable to find a suitable cleaning agent, ask the advice of a reputable dry cleaner.

The short list that follows covers some simple, effective ways of removing some of the commoner staining liquids.

Grease and oil

Place a clean cloth or blotting paper under the stain and dab with petrol or a proprietary stain remover. Wash and rinse thoroughly.

Wine stains

Remove by general washing before the stain has had time to dry.

Biro and ink stains

Dab with turpentine or petrol, or blot with Toluene or a light paint remover, and then wash and rinse.

Paint and varnish

Dab with turpentine or petrol and then wash and rinse.

Coffee or tea stains

Apply boiling water before the stain has had time to dry, and wash and dry. White fabrics can be bleached with a mixture of hydrogen peroxide, ammonia and acetic acid.

Blood

Soak in cold water, or apply cold water if the fabric cannot be soaked. Wash with soap and cold water and rinse thoroughly. Wash normally.

A quick, effective way of removing tiny spots of blood is to use a piece of white cotton, moistened with saliva, to dab up the blood.

GLOSSARY OF TERMS

Architrave   A decorative timber band that frames a door, window or wall panel.

Batten   A flat, thin piece of timber that slots into the base hem of a roller or Roman blind so that the fabric hangs straight and rigid.

Buckram   Stiffened hessian fabric used to give a permanent shape to tie-bands and pelmets.

Cleat hook   A double-pronged hook around which the pulling cords of a blind can be securely wound.

Cornice   A decorative plaster moulding that runs around the wall of a room just below the ceiling.

Dado rail   A decorative timber or plaster moulding that runs around the walls of a room at approximately chair height.

Drop weight   A brass or wooden toggle which weights the pulling cords of a blind.

Hems   See p. 203.

Interlining   An additional layer of fabric which lies between the main curtain fabric and the lining, providing extra body and valuable insulation. It comes in several thicknesses. 'Domette' is used to interline lightweight fabrics, while 'bump' is suitable for more heavyweight fabrics. There is also a general purpose interlining made from a nylon and Sarill cotton mixture. 'Milium', a cotton sateen fabric with a metallized backing, provides insulation without much extra weight.

Mitring   See p. 203.

Return   The part of a curtain or blind heading that turns around the end of a track or lath.

Seams   See p. 204.

Selvedge   See p. 201.

Soffit   The ceiling of a recessed window.

Stencilling   The art of tracing patterns through holes in blocks of wood, cardboard or metal sheets.

Stitches   See p. 202.

Tarlatan   Stiffened organza used to give a crisp finish to French pleat headings.

Tie-band hook   A hook which is screwed into the wall and used to hold the rings at each end of a tie-band.

Timber dowel   A 9mm/$\frac{3}{8}$in timber rod which is inserted into the pockets of a Roman blind to form the structure by which the blind is raised in horizontal folds.

Warp   The lengthwise threads in woven fabric.

Weft   The crosswise threads in woven fabric.

Working drop (or **cut drop**)   The finished length of a curtain or blind plus allowances for the hem and turnover at the top.

GLOSSARY OF FABRICS

Black bolton twill   A cheap, plain fabric, made from cotton or wool, which is used for linings in upholstery.

Brocade   Traditionally a heavy, rich silk fabric decorated with gold or silver thread, this fabric is now also available in cotton or synthetic fibres. Extra threads are woven into the main fabric to create elaborate, raised designs.

Butter muslin or cheesecloth   A very light, soft cotton fabric, slightly more densely woven than muslin. It is also available heavily sized and stiffened.

Calico   A plain weave cotton of fairly poor quality, originally from India. Of coarser texture than muslin, it comes in various weights and has a creamy speckled colour when unbleached. The heavyweight form is particularly useful in soft furnishings.

Cambric   A plain weave cloth made from closely woven fine bleached cotton, with a smooth, bright finish.

Canvas   A coarse, heavy, closely woven fabric, made from cotton, linen or synthetic fibres. It is hard-wearing and used in upholstery.

Chinese cotton   A lightweight fine cotton used for shirting.

Chintz   Originally 'painted calicoes' imported from India, this fabric still retains its traditional floral pattern, but is now usually made from good quality, medium-weight cotton, which is closely woven, sized, starched and glazed. The starching and glazing are not usually permanent so it needs to be laundered with care.

Corduroy   A coarse corded fabric with a ribbed surface which is sheared to produce a velvet-like nap. Originally made of cotton, it is now also made from a mixture of cotton and synthetic fibres. It is strong, warm, durable and easy to clean.

Cotton   See p.14 for a general definition. Different types of cotton fabric are listed under their individual names in this glossary.

Cotton drill   A warp-faced coarse cotton, woven in different twill weaves.

Cotton sateen   A plain weave cotton which has a shiny finish.

Cotton satin   Originally a glossy silk fabric from China, it is now usually made from a very fine cotton.

Damask   Traditionally made of silk from Damascus, this fabric is now also made from cotton, linen or wool. With cotton, the richly figurative design is produced by the contrast of a sateen weft against a satin warp.

Egyptian cotton   A fine, silky cotton which is woven into a lustrous linen or muslin-like fabric.

Gingham   A fine yet firm cotton cloth of Indian origin with a striped warp and weft which creates a regular checked effect.

Hessian   A coarse-fibred jute cloth, plainly woven, used for sacking and in upholstery.

Italian blackout   A heavy black cotton lining fabric.

Lace   A delicate, open-work fabric of intricate patterned design usually made from linen, cotton, silk or metal threads.

Linen   See p. 14.

Moiré   See p. 24.

Muslin   A light, translucent, net-like fabric in plain weave, made of silk, worsted or cotton.

Organza   A stiff, slightly starchy textured sheer fabric which is made from a twisted silk warp yarn.

Poplin   A lightweight cotton with a slightly silky finish and a fine cross-ribbed pattern, formed by using a weft thread thicker than the warp.

PVC (polyvinyl chloride)   See p. 25.

Roclon blackout   A heavy rubberized fabric which completely blocks light and also acts as insulation.

Sailcloth   A strong canvas-like cotton fabric.

Scrim muslin   A rough loosely woven hessian-like fabric.

Sea Island cotton   A very fine variety of cotton, originally from the coast of Georgia and South Carolina. It is woven into a white, lustrous fabric, which somewhat resembles poplin.

Sheer   Any thin, fine or translucent fabric in white or off-white.

Shirting   A smooth, lustrous, plain woven fabric, usually made of poplin or fine cotton.

Silk   See p. 16 for a general definition. Different silk fabrics are listed under their individual names in this glossary.

Silk Ikat   An expensive fabric made from silk thread which is dip-dyed before weaving so that subtle patterns are created along the warp.

Silk noil   A waste product of spun silk which, mixed with cotton or wool, adds brilliance to the yarn and shows up as tiny balls on the fabric.

Tartan   A Scottish fabric, made of wool or worsted, which comes in a variety of elaborately checked designs, each associated with a particular Scottish clan.

Thai silk   An iridescent fabric which is often slubbed and dyed in vivid colours.

Ticking   A strong rather stiff fabric in twill weave with a warp stripe. Traditional mattress ticking is black and white striped, but other colour combinations are now available.

Tweed   A rough surfaced robust, woollen fabric in plain weave. It is often woven in two or more colours to obtain a checked or plaid effect.

Velvet   A closely woven pile fabric, usually made of cotton or synthetic fibre, with two warp threads – one for the pile and one for the ground.

SUPPLIERS' CREDITS

Addresses of mentioned suppliers are to be found on pp. 211–12. The letters next to each entry mean the following: *M* Manufacturer; *S* Supplier; *F* Fabric name.

Front cover *S* Osborne & Little; *F* Brume no. 316, édition Etamine, Paris.

10–11 1 *S* Osborne & Little, *F* Topkapi; 2 *S* Osborne & Little,

F Streamline; 3 *S* Jab International; 4 *S* Osborne & Little, *F* Kim; 5, 6 *S* H A Percheron; 7 *S* Osborne & Little, *F* Waterline; 8 *S* Marvic, *F* Misa Moiré Striped; 9 *S* Mary Fox Linton, *F* Linea; 10 *S* Marvic, *F* Avenue; 11 *S* Busby & Busby, *F* Faded Glory; 12 *S* Ian Sanderson; 13 *S* Busby & Busby, *F* Silkweave; 14 *S* Baumann; 15 *S* Ian Mankin; pole *S* Cope & Timmins.
14–15 1 *S* Peter Jones; 2 *S* Baumann; 3, 15 *S* MacCulloch & Wallis; 4, 5, 6,

7, 9, 10, 11, 12, 14, 16, 17 *S* Ian Mankin; 8 *S* Warner Fabrics; 13 *S* Ian Sanderson; 18 *S* MacCulloch & Wallis.
17 1, 2, 5, 6, 7 *S* Ian Mankin; 3 *S* Nice Irma's; 4 *S* MacCulloch & Wallis.
18–19 1, 10 *S* Mary Fox Linton, *M* Jim Thompson; 2 *S* Sahco-Hesslein, *F* Aida; 3 *S* Osborne & Little, *F* Topkapi; 4, 5 *S* Parkertex, *F* My Lady's Garden; 6, 9 *S* Marvic, *F* Misa Moiré Striped; 7 *S* H A Percheron, *F* Mitzli; 8 *S* Heal's.

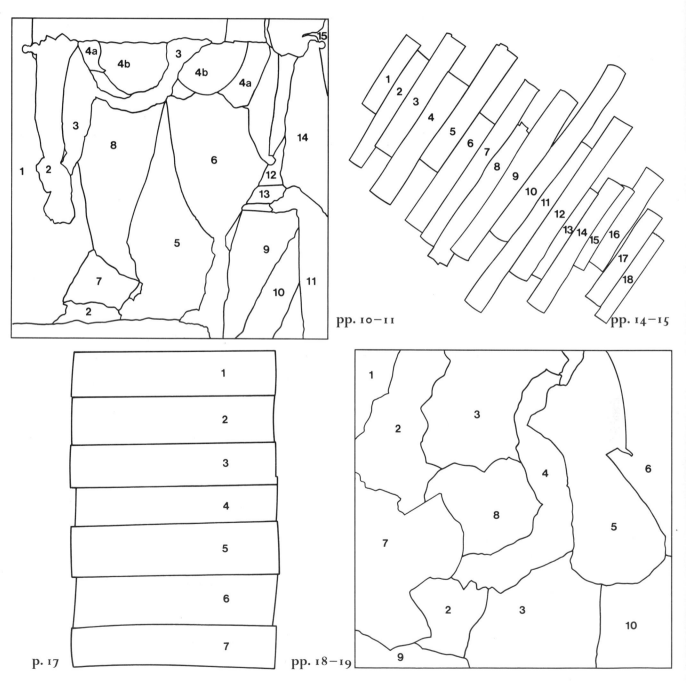

pp. 10–11

pp. 14–15

p. 17

pp. 18–19

20 bedcover *S* Antique & Ancient Textiles; pillows and drapes *S* Tribal Art & Antiquities.
21 all fabrics *S* Ian Mankin, *F* Park range.
22–3 1, 2, 3, 17, 18, 19 *M* H A Percheron, *S* Bisson Bruneel, *F* Chenille; 4 *S* Mary Fox Linton; 5 *S* Timney-Fowler; 6 *S* Christian Fischbacher, *M* Collier Campbell; 7 *S* Reputation, *F* Blue Zodiac; 8 *S* Timney-Fowler, *F* Broken Pillars

& Angel TF44; 9 *S* Reputation, *F* Fruit Punch; 10 *S* Timney-Fowler, *F* Strips TF26; 11 *S* Timney-Fowler, *F* Pillars TF28; 12 *S* Osborne & Little, *F* Kovanchina; 13, 14 *S* Celia Birtwell; 15 *M* Ian Sanderson, *S* J. Wellman; 16 *S* Reputation, *F* Small Square.
24 1 *S* Marvic; 2, 5, 6 *S* Practical Styling, *F* PVC; 3 *S* Christian Fischbacher, *M* Collier Campbell, *F* Foxtrot; 4 *S* F R Street, *F* waxed cambric; 7 *S* The Kite Store,

F rip-stop nylon.
29 1, 8, 10 *S* Arthur Sanderson & Sons; 2, 6, 12 *S* Osborne & Little, *F* Stippleglaze; 3 *S* H A Percheron, *M* Lauer, *F* Uni Transat (rayure negatif); 4, 9 *S* MacCulloch & Wallis; 5 *S* Heal's; 7 *S* Christian Fischbacher, *M* Collier Campbell, *F* Bedouin Stripe; 11 *S* F R Street.
32 1, 2, 4, 7 *S* Ian Mankin; 3, 9 *S* Arthur Sanderson & Sons; 5 *S* F R Street; 6, 8, 10 *S* Baumann, *F* Zigona.

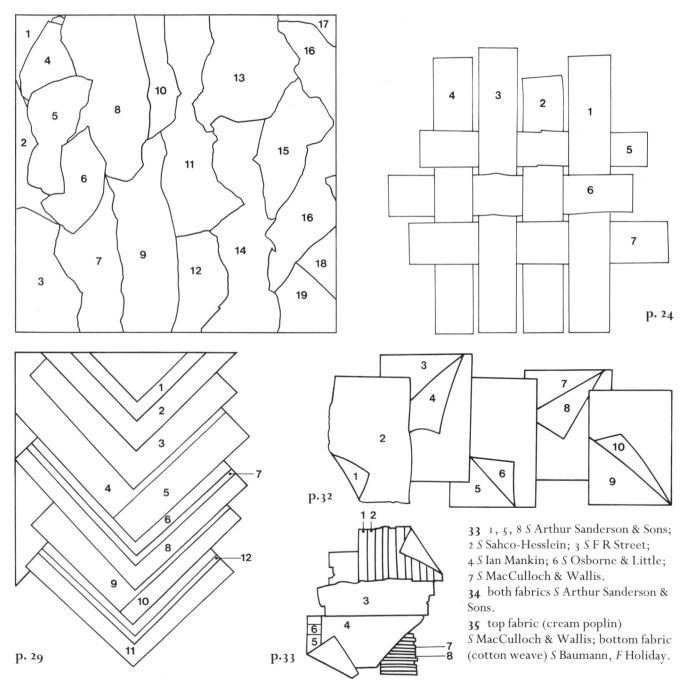

33 1, 5, 8 *S* Arthur Sanderson & Sons; 2 *S* Sahco-Hesslein; 3 *S* F R Street; 4 *S* Ian Mankin; 6 *S* Osborne & Little; 7 *S* MacCulloch & Wallis.
34 both fabrics *S* Arthur Sanderson & Sons.
35 top fabric (cream poplin) *S* MacCulloch & Wallis; bottom fabric (cotton weave) *S* Baumann, *F* Holiday.

74 1 S Ian Mankin; 2, 5 S F R Street; 3 S Osborne & Little, F Stippleglaze; 4 S Baumann, F Fuego; 6 S H A Percheron, M Lauer, F Uni Transat (rayure negatif).

83 top 1 S Christian Fischbacher, M Collier Campbell, F Harmony Stripe; 2 S Busby & Busby, F Faded Glory; 3 M H A Percheron; S Bisson Bruneel; 4 S Christian Fischbacher, M Collier Campbell, F Willow Weave; 5 S Osborne & Little, F Kim; 6 S Mary Fox Linton.

86 1 S Osborne & Little, F Ouni; 2 S H A Percheron, M Burger, F Toile Fête Naval; 3 S MacCulloch & Wallis; 4 S Nice Irma's; 5 M Johannes Wellmann, S Ian Sanderson.

88 1 S Marvic, F Sirocco; 2 S Hallis Hudson; 3, 5 S Reputation; 4 S Osborne & Little, F Stippleglaze; 6 S Arthur Sanderson & Sons; 7 S Christian Fischbacher, M Collier Campbell, F Foxtrot.

92 1 S H A Percheron; 2 S MacCulloch & Wallis; 3 S Mary Fox Linton; 4 S Mary Fox Linton, F Linea; 5 S Timney-Fowler, F Strips TF26.

100–1 1, 2, 3, 11, 12, 13 S Porter Nicholson; 4, 5, 6, 7, 8 S Hallis Hudson; 9, 10 S F R Street.

102–3 wooden poles S Cope & Timmins; café rods and brass brackets S Hallis Hudson; large brass pole S Kirsch.

146 Bed S Simon Horn Furniture.

162 1 S Materialisation; 2 S H A Percheron, M Lauer, F Uni Transat; 3 S Textiles FCD, F discontinued; 4 S Arthur Sanderson & Sons; 5 S Designers Guild.

165 1 S F R Street, 2 S Arthur Sanderson & Sons; 3 S Tissunique; 4 S Karl's.

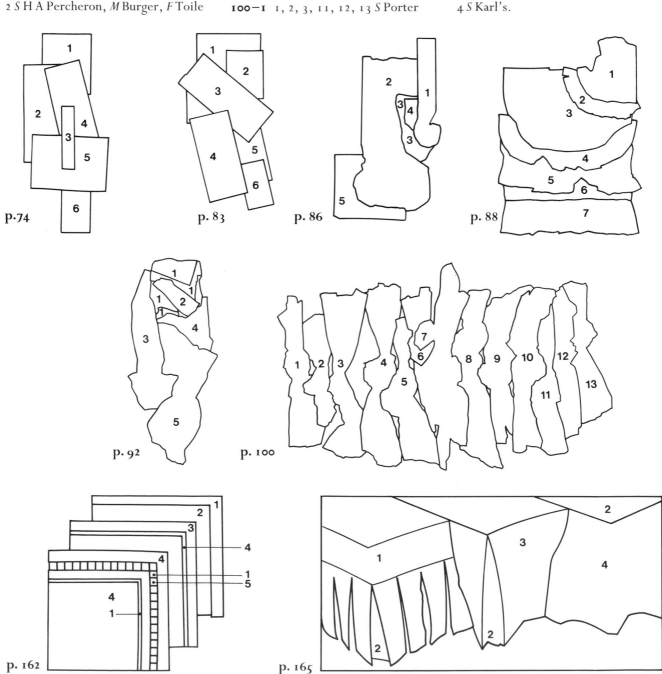

p.74   p. 83   p. 86   p. 88

p. 92   p. 100

p. 162   p. 165

USEFUL ADDRESSES

There are hundreds of companies producing fabrics and accessories. Some of them welcome enquiries from the general public, but others deal only with the trade. Firms only dealing with the trade are marked with an asterisk in the list below. Contact them to find out about your nearest retail outlet.

For fabrics
Antique & Ancient Textiles
3a Pembridge Square
London W2
01–242 8598

*G P & J Baker Ltd
17–18 Berners Street
London W1
01–636 8412

*Baumann Fabrics Ltd
41–42 Berners Street
London W1P 3AA
01–637 0253

Bentley & Spens
Studio 25
90 Lots Road
London SW10 0QD
01–352 5685
(hand-painted silks and cottons)

Celia Birtwell
71 Westbourne Park Road
London W2
01–221 0877

*Brooke Fairbairn & Co
The Railway Station
Newmarket
Suffolk CB8 9BA
0638 665766

*Busby & Busby Ltd
57 Salisbury Street
Blandford Forum
Dorset DT11 7PY
0258 55221

Colefax & Fowler Designs Ltd
39 Brook Street
London W1
01–493 2231

*Collier Campbell Ltd
41 Old Town
London SW4
01–720 7862

Designers Guild
271 & 277 Kings Road
London SW3 5EN

*Christian Fischbacher
40/44 Cupstone Street
London W1P 8AL
01–580 8937

*Fox & Floor
142 Royal College Street
London SW1 0TA
01–267 1467/8

*Mary Fox Linton Ltd
249 Fulham Road
London SW3 6HY
01–351 0273

Heal's
196 Tottenham Court Road
London W1
01–636 1666

*Hill & Knowles Ltd
133 Kew Road
Richmond, Surrey TW9 2PN
01–948 4010

*Jab International Furnishings Ltd
15 Cavendish Place
London W1
01–636 1343

The Kite Store
69 Neal Street
London WC2
01–836 1666

MacCulloch & Wallis Ltd
25 Dering Street
London W1
01–629 0311
(silk specialists)

Ian Mankin Ltd
109 Regents Park Road
London NW1
01–722 0997

*Marvic Textiles
12–14 Mortimer Street
London W1N 7DR
01–580 7951

Materialisation
35 Gosberton Road
London SW12
01–675 0534

McKinney Kidston,
1st floor, 184 Walton Street,
London SW3
01-225 0039
(antique curtains and accessories)

*Monkwell Furnishing Fabrics
Semple & Co Ltd
10–12 Wharfdale Road
Bournemouth
Dorset BH4 9BT
0202 762456

Nice Irma's Floating Carpet
46 Goodge Street
London W1
01–580 6921

Osborne & Little
304 King's Road
London SW3 5UH
01–352 1456/7/8

Paine & Co
49–51 Barnsbury Street
London N1 1TP
01–607 1176

*Pallu & Lake
The London Interior Designers Centre
1 Cringle Street
Nine Elms
London SW8 5BX
01–627 5566

*Parkertex
17–18 Berners Street
London W1
01–636 8412

*H A Percheron Ltd
97 – 99 Cleveland Street
London W1P 5PN
01 – 580 5156

Reputation
186 Kensington Park Road
London W11
01 – 221 7641/2

Russell & Chapple
23 Monmouth Street
London WC2
01 – 836 7521
(hardwearing canvas, calico etc)

*Sahco-Hesslein UK Ltd
58 – 59 Margaret Street
London W1N 7FG
01 – 636 3552

Arthur Sanderson & Sons
52 Berners Street
London W1P 3AD
01 – 636 7800

*Ian Sanderson (Textiles) Ltd
70 Cleveland Street
London W1P 5DF
01 – 580 9847

*Textiles FCD
16 Berners Street
London W1P 3DD
01 – 636 3461

Jim Thompson
via Mary Fox Linton (see above)

Timney-Fowler Prints
281 Portobello Road
London W10
01 – 968 5626

*Tissunique Ltd
9 Princes Street
London W1
01 – 491 3386

Tribal Art & Antiquities
191 Sussex Gardens
London W2
01 – 262 1775

*Warner & Sons Ltd
7 Noel Street
London W1
01 – 439 7012

For linings and interlinings
Hallis Hudson Ltd
Bushell Street Mill
Preston, Lancashire PR1 2SP
0772 24511
(also brassware and small accessories)

*Porter Nicolson
Portland House
Norlington Road
London E10
01 – 539 6654
(also upholstery fillings)

*F R Street Ltd
406 St John Street
London Ec1
01 – 837 7736

*Warren Fabrics Ltd
Stirling Works
Canning Road
London E15
01 – 519 1886
(also threads and small accessories)

For tracks and poles
Cope & Timmins Ltd
Angel Road Works
Angel Road
London N18 3AY
01 – 803 3333
(also fitting accessories)

Hunter & Hyland
201 – 5 Kingston Road
Leatherhead
Surrey KT22 7PB
0372 378511
(poles, tracks, and brassware made to
order)

For ropes, braids and trimmings
*Henry Newbery & Co Ltd
18 Newman Street
London W1
01 – 636 2053

*For unusual and ornamental poles and
brassware, braids and trimmings*
(Wemyss) Weavecraft Ltd
East Wemyss
Fife
Scotland KY1 4RZ
0592 712255

*For eyelets, cords, ropes and other small
accessories*
Arthur Beale (yachts chandlers)
194 Shaftesbury Avenue
London WC2
01 – 836 9034

For furniture
Karl's
6 Cheval Place
London SW7
01 – 225 2625
(some linens)

Simon Horn Furniture Ltd
117 – 121 Wandsworth Bridge Road
London SW6
01 – 731 1279

For feather pads
Featherdown
Unit 3
124 – 26 Brixton Hill
London SW2 1RS

FURTHER READING

Gale, E. *From Fibre to Fabrics* Unwin & Hyman, 1978

Noetzli, E. *Practical Drapery Cutting* Potterton Books, The Old Rectory, Sessay, North Yorkshire, 1986

Praz, M. *Illustrated History of Interior Decoration from Pompeii to Art Nouveau* Thames and Hudson, 1982

Thornton, P. *Authentic Decor: Domestic Interiors 1620 – 1920* Weidenfeld & Nicholson, 1984

Tidball, H. *Color and Dyeing* Pacific Grove, Cal., 1971

INDEX

Page numbers in *italic* refer to illustrations.

R

resist techniques 43–4, *39, 43*
rip-stop nylon 25, *24*
   joining 33–4
Roclon blackout 100
rods, curtain 103, *103*
roller blinds 69–70, 83–4, *68, 83, 85*
   construction 84
   fabrics *83*
Roman blinds 69–70, 71, 72, 74–82, *70, 75, 76, 77, 81, 82*
   borders 76, *76, 77*
   construction 77–82
   fabrics *74*
room dividers 183, *183, 185*
ruched blinds 54, 70–1, 86–95

S

satin weave 17
scalloped heading 120–21
screen printing 22
screens 183–84, *185*
seams 204–5
selvedges, cutting out 201
sheers 50, 123, *51, 123*
silk, description 16
slipstitch 202
slot headings 119, *116*
spattering paint 40–1
spinning 16
spraying paint 41
squab cushion cover 196
stabbing stitch 202
stencilling 42–3, *42*
stitched decoration 35
stitches 202
stripes 33–4, *10*
strips, joining 33–4
summer curtains 62–3
swags 59, 136, 138–40, *52, 53, 137, 140*

bedrooms 144, *149*
   binding 140
   fixing 140
   making 136–38

T

tablecloths 192, 198–99, *193, 198*
tacking stitch 202
tails 59, 136, 139, *52, 53, 137, 140*
   beds *149*
   binding 140
   fixing 140
   making 136, *139*
techniques 200–5
   binding edges 205
   calculating widths 200
   cutting out 201
   hems 203
   seams 204–5
   stitches 202
   zips 205
texture 14–17, *15*
   woven fabrics *18, 19, 20*
throwover bedcovers 162–63
throws, furnishings 187–88, *176, 177, 186*
tie and dye techniques 44
tie-bands 124, *124, 127*
   making 124–26
   padded 126
   plaited 126
   shaped 125
   straight 125
tracks 102, 104–5, *105*
   corded 104
   fixing 105
twill weave 16

U

unglazed fabrics 24
unlined curtains 113

V

valances 54, *133*
   bed 166–67
   fixing 132
   making 132

W

wall coverings 179–82, *178, 180, 181, 182*
wash and crinkle techniques 43–4
wax resist techniques 42–3, *43*
waxed cambric *24*
weave, types of 16
weighting
   curtains 107
   sheers *123*
windows 45–140
   blinds 68–95
   choosing a style 47–67
   curtains 96–140
   draping 54–9
   dressed *52*
   measuring 67
   pelmets 128–31, *128, 129*
   practical considerations 65–6
   proportions 65
   seasonal treatment 62–3
   sheers 50, *51*
   simple 48, *49*
   styles 65–6
   valances 128, 132, *133*
   see also curtains
winter curtains 62–3
wool, description 16
woven pattern 18–21, *19, 20*

Z

zips 205

PUBLISHERS' ACKNOWLEDGMENTS

Frances Lincoln Ltd would like to thank the many organizations and people who gave valuable advice and assistance in the production of this book, including: Richard Bird, Penny David, Carole McGlynn, Hilary More, Annabel Westman and Steven Wooster; Tig Sutton, Diana Leadbetter (Young Artists) and Sandra Pond for artwork; Michael Dunne and Jacqui Hurst for commissioned photographs; Radius for paste-up and key diagrams; Evergreen for colour reproduction; Barry Randall, Ralph Bell and everyone at Vantage for typesetting.

The publishers are grateful to all those who allowed their houses to be photographed: John Alexander, Patricia Boulter, Barbara Douglas, Paul Dyson, Anne and John Fraser, Toby Kalitowski, Shirley Mitchard, Gill Sheppard, Andrew Speak, Debbie and Mike Staniford, Althea Wilson and – especially – Christabel Brown.

PHOTOGRAPHIC CREDITS

Front cover Michael Dunne ©FLL
2 Camera Press/Bo Appeltofft
4 Jacqui Hurst ©FLL
5 all pictures Michael Dunne ©FLL
6–7 Michael Dunne ©FLL
10–11 Jacqui Hurst ©FLL
13 Julie Phipps
14–15 Jacqui Hurst ©FLL
17–19 Jacqui Hurst ©FLL
20 The World of Interiors/Bill Batten
21–4 Jacqui Hurst ©FLL
25 Michael Dunne ©FLL
26–7 Michael Dunne ©FLL
29 Jacqui Hurst ©FLL
30 Peter Woloszynski
31–5 all pictures Jacqui Hurst ©FLL
36–7 Michael Dunne ©FLL (designer Althea Wilson)
39 Michael Dunne ©FLL (designer Althea Wilson)
40–1 Jacqui Hurst ©FLL
42 Syndication International Ltd
43 Jacqui Hurst ©FLL
46–7 Michael Dunne ©FLL
48–9 The World of Interiors/John Vaughan
51 The World of Interiors/Roland Beaufre
52 Fritz von der Schulenburg
53 Michael Dunne ©FLL
54–5 Michael Dunne ©FLL
56 ARCAID/Lucinda Lambton (designers Amanda Fielding and Joey Mellens)
57 top Camera Press/Peo Eriksson
57 bottom The World of Interiors/Clive Frost
58–9 Michael Dunne ©FLL
60–1 Michael Dunne ©FLL
62–3 Syndication International Ltd

64 ARCAID/Richard Bryant (designer Charles Jencks)
68–9 Camera Press/Peo Eriksson
70 John Hall (designer Mark Hampton)
71 Michael Boys Syndication (designer Mimmi O'Connell)
72 Michael Dunne ©FLL
74 Jacqui Hurst ©FLL
75 Camera Press
76 Geoff Dann ©FLL
77 Michael Dunne ©FLL
81 Camera Press
82 Michael Dunne ©FLL
83 top Jacqui Hurst
83 bottom Michael Boys/Susan Griggs Agency Ltd
85 Fritz von der Schulenburg
86 Jacqui Hurst ©FLL
87 Michael Dunne ©FLL
88 Jacqui Hurst ©FLL
89 Michael Dunne ©FLL
92 Jacqui Hurst ©FLL
93 Elizabeth Whiting Assoc/Michael Dunne
96–7 Michael Dunne ©FLL
98 Michael Boys Syndication (designers Gabrielle and John Sutcliffe)
99 Michael Dunne ©FLL (designer Althea Wilson)
100–1 Jacqui Hurst ©FLL
102–3 Jacqui Hurst ©FLL
104–5 Jacqui Hurst ©FLL
108 Fritz von der Schulenburg
108–9 Ianthe Ruthven
116 top The World of Interiors/Tom Leighton
116 bottom Jan Baldwin/Good Housekeeping/The National Magazine Co
117 Camera Press/Peo Eriksson
123 Elizabeth Whiting Assoc/Ann Kelley
124 left Jacqui Hurst ©FLL

124 centre Michael Dunne ©FLL
124 right ARCAID/Lucinda Lambton
127 Fritz von der Schulenburg
129 Peter Woloszynski
133 The World of Interiors/Adam Inczedy-Gombos
134–35 Syndication International Ltd
137 Elizabeth Whiting Assoc/Di Lewis (designer Marion Jones)
140 Fritz von der Schulenburg
142–43 Michael Dunne ©FLL (designer Althea Wilson)
144 Carla de Benedetti
145 Ianthe Ruthven
146 Trevor Richards
147 Country Homes & Interiors/World Press Network/Simon Brown
148 The World of Interiors/Tom Leighton
149 The World of Interiors/Timothy Beddow
150 Michael Dunne ©FLL
152 The World of Interiors/Fritz von der Schulenburg
153 The World of Interiors/James Mortimer
154–55 Michael Dunne ©FLL
156 Michael Dunne ©FLL (designer Althea Wilson)
157 Michael Dunne ©FLL
158–59 Michael Dunne ©FLL
160 top Fritz von der Schulenburg (designer Mimmi O'Connell)
160 bottom Fritz von der Schulenburg
162 Jacqui Hurst ©FLL
165 Jacqui Hurst ©FLL
169 Michael Dunne ©FLL
170–71 Michael Dunne ©FLL
174–75 Fritz von der Schulenburg (designer Mimmi O'Connell)
176 Camera Press
177 Fritz von der Schulenburg (designer Mimmi O'Connell)
178–79 Country Homes & Interiors/World Press Network/Fritz von der Schulenburg
180 Syndication International Ltd
181 Carla de Benedetti
182 Fritz von der Schulenburg
183 Carla de Benedetti
185 top Michael Dunne ©FLL
185 bottom Carla de Benedetti
186–87 Fritz von der Schulenburg (designer Mimmi O'Connell)
188 Ingalill Snitt
189 Schöner Wohnen/Camera Press
190–91 Fritz von der Schulenburg (designer Mimmi O'Connell)
192 Elizabeth Whiting Assoc/Michael Dunne
193 Camera Press/Bo Appeltofft
195 Syndication International Ltd
198 Fritz von der Schulenburg (designer Mimmi O'Connell)